Beginning HTML5 & CSS3

FOR DUMMIES
A Wiley Brand

by Ed Tittel and Chris Minnick

FOR DUMMIES
A Wiley Brand

Beginning HTML5 & CSS3 For Dummies®

Published by
John Wiley & Sons, Inc.
111 River Street
Hoboken, NJ 07030-5774
www.wiley.com

For general information on our other products and services, please contact our Customer Care Department within the U.S. at 877-762-2974, outside the U.S. at 317-572-3993, or fax 317-572-4002. For technical support, please visit www.wiley.com/techsupport.

Wiley publishes in a variety of print and electronic formats and by print-on-demand. Some material included with standard print versions of this book may not be included in e-books or in print-on-demand. If this book refers to media such as a CD or DVD that is not included in the version you purchased, you may download this material at http://booksupport.wiley.com. For more information about Wiley products, visit www.wiley.com.

Library of Congress Control Number: 2013942775

ISBN 978-1-118-65720-1 (pbk); ISBN 978-1-118-69075-8 (ebk); ISBN 978-1-118-69070-3 (ebk)

Manufactured in the United States of America

10 9 8 7 6 5

Table of Contents

Introduction 1

About this Book 2
Foolish Assumptions... 3
Icons Used in This Book 4
Beyond the Book 4
Where to Go from Here.. 5

Part I: Getting Started with HTML and CSS on the Web... 7

Chapter 1: An Overview of HTML and CSS on the Web 9

How and Where Web Pages Come to Life Online 10
  HyperText 10
  Content versus presentation.. 14
  Web browsers 14
  Getting to know Internet protocols 16
Understanding HTML and Its Versions.................................. 17
  Different versions of HTML.. 17
  Creating HTML markup... 18
  Building HTML documents... 19
Understanding the Role of CSS 20
  Different versions here, too 20
  Creating CSS markup.. 21
Dissecting a Simple Markup Example 22
  Where's the HTML? 22
  Where's the CSS?.. 23
  A partnership of equals... 23

Chapter 2: Meeting the Structure and Components of HTML....... 25

Like Any Language: Syntax and Rules.................................. 25
  Color-coding the markup 26
  Breaking down the elements 27
Adding Attributes to Your HTML 29
Examining Entities in Markup 30
  Non-ASCII characters.. 30
  Character codes.. 31
  (Special) tag characters 32
Organizing Web Pages 32
  Organizing HTML text 34
  Complementing and enhancing text................................. 36

Chapter 3: Creating and Viewing a Web Page **37**

Before You Get Started 37
Creating a Page from Scratch... 39
Step 0: Gather your tools 39
Step 1: Planning a simple design....................................... 40
Step 2: Writing some HTML 41
Step 3: Saving your page 44
Step 4: Viewing your page 46
Editing an Existing Web Page... 47
Posting Your Page Online.. 49

Part II: Getting the Structure and Text Right *51*

Chapter 4: HTML Documents Need Good Structure. **53**

Establishing a Document Structure.. 53
HTML Document Organization Revisited 54
HTML DOCTYPE Starts Things Off 55
The <html> Element 56
Anatomy of the <head> 56
Meeting the <head> himself... 57
Handling metadata with <meta> 57
Redirecting users to another page 58
Naming your page with a <title> 61
The <body> Is a BIG Container 61

Chapter 5: Text and Lists. **63**

Formatting Text 63
Paragraphs.. 65
Headings.. 66
Controlling Text Blocks 68
Block quotes... 68
Preformatted text.. 69
Horizontal rules... 71
Organizing Information 73
Numbered lists 73
Bulleted lists... 75
Definition lists 77
Nesting lists 79

Chapter 6: Tip-Top Tables in HTML. **81**

How <table> Got a Bad Name in HTML................................... 81
What's in a Table? LOTS of Markup 82
Setting Up a Table Border 84

The Table Head (<thead>) and Its Elements..85
Managing Table Layouts...87
Making Good Table Bodies..89
        Shaping a solid table 89
Sitting at the Footer of the Table..92
Exploring and Explaining a Table...92
        Oh caption, my caption...93
        Is the header dead yet? 93
        Marching through the table body..94
        Finishing with the footer 94

Chapter 7: Working with Forms in HTML......................97
Exploring Types of Web Forms 97
        Search forms..98
        Data collection forms 99
Creating Forms..100
        Structure 101
        Input tags 102
        Input fields 103
        Form validation 113
Processing Data 115
        Processing forms on your pages..115
Designing User-Friendly Forms...117
Other Noteworthy Forms-Related Markup...118
Form Frameworks..120

Part III: Adding Links, Images, and Other Media 123

Chapter 8: Getting Hyper with Links in HTML....................125
Basic Links 101..125
        Exploring link options 127
        Avoiding common mistakes 129
Customizing Links 130
        Opening new windows 130
        Specifying locations in web pages..132
        Linking to non-HTML resources..134

Chapter 9: Working with Images in HTML.......................139
The Role of Images in a Web Page...139
Creating Web-Friendly Images 140
Adding an Image to a Web Page..142
        Image location 142
        Using the <img> element...143

Adding alternative and title text 143
Specifying image size..146
Image borders and alignment...149
Images That Link..149
Triggering links 149
Building image maps 150

Chapter 10: Managing Media and More in HTML 153

The Battle of the Media Formats 154
Meet the major audio formats..155
Meet the major video formats 156
Comparing Traditional and HTML5 Media Handling 157
Mastering HTML5 Media Markup 158
Making beautiful music with audio.......................................158
Moving media with video..159
Undergoing the conversion experience 162
Working with Web Page Controls..163
Displaying a meter bar 163
Tracking progress on activities 165
Tracking and reporting on time 166
Updating HTML5 controls...168

Part IV: Adopting CSS Style 169

Chapter 11: Advantages of Style Sheets 171

Advantages of Style Sheets..172
The four steps to style 173
Understanding the C in CSS..174
What CSS can do for a web page..174
Styling a Document with CSS 175
Using HTML5 Boilerplate 176
Normalize before you stylize..176
What you can do with CSS 180
Putting CSS in Its Place 182
Pixels, points, and dots — Oh my!..182
Understanding the viewport..183
Property measurement values 184
About the CSS3 Standard...186

Chapter 12: CSS Structure and Syntax 191

Exploring CSS Structure and Syntax 191
Selectors and declarations 194
The selectors...195
Inheriting styles 204
Understanding the Cascade 205

Chapter 13: Using Different Kinds of Style Sheets...............**207**

    Applying Inline Styles..208

    Getting to Know Internal Style Sheets 210

        Understanding the <style> element.................................210

        Figuring out internal style sheet scope..........................210

    Working with External Style Sheets 212

        CSS files 212

        Link element attributes...213

        Importing and when to use @import................................214

Part V: Enhancing Your Pages' Look and Feel *215*

Chapter 14: Managing Layout and Positioning..................**217**

    Managing Layout 217

        Tiny boxes 217

        Block versus inline elements..219

        Normal flow 222

    Managing Positioning...225

        About coordinates and offsets..226

        Relative positioning...226

        Absolute positioning 227

        Floating..228

    Using a Layout Generator 230

Chapter 15: Building with Boxes, Borders, and Buttons **233**

    Meeting the Box Model 233

    Putting the Box Model into Practice 235

        Specifying padding and margin widths...........................239

        Adding borders 243

        Aligning text..246

        Indenting text 247

        Creating buttons with CSS 247

Chapter 16: Using Colors and Backgrounds **251**

    Defining Color Values..251

        Color names...251

        Color numbers..253

    Defining Color Definitions...255

        Text..256

        Links 256

        Backgrounds...258

        Advanced backgrounds 259

Chapter 17: Web Typography **261**

    Finding Out about Fonts 261
        Font family 262
        Sizing 265
    Trying Out Text Treatments 268
        Embolden with bold 268
        Emphasizing with italic 269
        Changing capitalization 270
        Getting fancy with the text-decoration property 271
    Checking Out the Catchall Font Property 272
    Experimenting with Web Fonts 273
        Font file formats 273
        Finding fonts 274
        Linking fonts 274
        Using Google Fonts 275

Chapter 18: CSS Text and Shadow Effects **281**

    Creating Shadows 282
        text-shadow 282
        box-shadow 283
    Creating Inset Text 284
    Creating 3D Text 285
    Creating a Letterpress Effect 286
    Drop Shadows 287
    Text Rotation 289

Chapter 19: Multimedia and Animation with CSS **291**

    Using CSS with Multimedia 291
        Visual media styles 293
        Paged media styles 299
    Getting Animated 300
        Using the animation properties 302
        Creating animations with @keyframes 303
        Animating color 303

Part VI: The Part of Tens *305*

Chapter 20: Ten Keys to Mobile Web Design **307**

    Design for Different Mobile Devices 307
    Design for People 310
    Design for Small Screens 310
    Design for Low Bandwidth 311

Design for Touch 311
Design for Distracted Surfers...313
Test on Many Mobile Devices 313
Design for Simplicity 314
Set Up Mobile Web Addresses 314
Include a Link to the Desktop Site...315

Chapter 21: Ten HTML Do's and Don'ts **317**
Don't Lose Sight of Your Content...317
Do Structure Your Documents and Your Site............................318
Do Make the Most from the Least 318
Do Build Attractive Pages..319
Don't Lose Track of Those Tags 319
Do Avoid Browser Dependencies...320
Don't Make It Hard to Navigate Your Wild and Woolly Web 321
Don't Think Revolution, Think Evolution 322
Don't Get Stuck in the Two-Dimensional-Text Trap..................323
Don't Let Inertia Overcome You 323

Chapter 22: Ten Ways to Kill Web Bugs Dead **325**
Make a List and Check It — Twice..325
Master Text Mechanics..326
Lack of Live Links — a Lousy Legacy...327
When Old Links Must Linger 328
Make Your Content Mirror Your World......................................328
Look for Trouble in All the Right Places....................................328
Cover All the Bases with Peer Reviews 329
Use the Best Tools of the Testing Trade 330
Schedule Site Reviews...330
Foster User Feedback...331
If You Give to Them, They'll Give to You! 332

Chapter 23: Ten Cool HTML Tools and Technologies **333**
WYSIWYG HTML Editors 334
Dreamweaver...334
Other WYSIWYG editors 335
Helper HTML Editors 335
Aptana Studio...335
Other helper editors...336
Inexpensive Graphics Editors 337
Professional Graphics Editors 337
Adobe Photoshop..338
Adobe Fireworks...338

W3C Link Checker...339
Other Link Checkers...339
HTML Validators...340
FTP Clients..341
Miscellaneous Helpful Web Tools 341

Part VII: Appendixes...................................... *343*

Appendix A: Twitterati **345**

Appendix B: About the Dummies HTML Site....................**349**
About WordPress 349
The dashboard...349
Appearance and themes 350
Pages and posts 351
Widgets 351
Responsive Design...352
HTML5 Cafe 352
The home page 352
About Us...354
The Menu 354
Contact Us..354
HTML5 Boilerplate...355

Index *357*

Introduction

*A*nyone can create or edit web pages. Crafting such pages doesn't require an especially high IQ or an advanced degree. Creating or editing web pages simply requires a desire to learn and enough gumption to see the process through to its natural end — a page visible on the web.

In this book, we reveal the ins and outs of the markup languages that are the web's lifeblood — the HyperText Markup Language (HTML) used to capture text, graphics, and other content, and the Cascading Style Sheets (CSS) language used to make web pages look good wherever they appear. Because HTML and CSS are basic building blocks for creating web pages, knowing how to use them adds you to the fold of web authors and content developers.

If you've tried to build your own web pages but found it too daunting, it's okay to relax now. If you can dial a telephone or find your keys in the morning, you too can create web pages. No kidding!

This book keeps the technobabble to a minimum and sticks with plain English whenever possible. Besides plain talk about hypertext, HTML, and the web, we include lots of examples, plus tag-by-tag instructions to help you build web pages with minimal fuss and bother. We also provide examples about what to do with your web pages after you've built them, so you can publish them online. We explain the differences between various flavors of HTML (HTML4, HTML5, and even something called XHTML) so you can pick the style that works best for you. Spoiler alert: We think you should choose HTML5, but that choice is entirely up to you.

This book has its own companion website with HTML and CSS examples from all of its chapters in usable form. In addition to the book content, we share web-only content and live pointers to all of the widgets, websites, and other cool stuff to which we refer, so you can use the techniques we show you to embellish your own web pages and amaze your friends. Please visit `www.dummieshtml.com/html5cafe` and start browsing from there. (Appendix B in this book covers all of that material in more detail.)

About this Book

Think of this book as a friendly, approachable guide to taking up HTML and CSS and building readable, attractive web pages. These things aren't hard to pick up, but they pack lots of details. Topics covered in this book include the following:

- ✔ Understanding web page structure and organization
- ✔ Uploading and publishing web pages for the whole world to see
- ✔ Checking and validating your web pages
- ✔ Diving deep into markup with HTML5 and CSS3

You too can build web pages without years of arduous training, advanced aesthetic abilities, or ritual ablutions in ice-cold streams. If you can tell a friend how to prepare your favorite mac-'n'-cheese, you can build a useful web document. The purpose of this book isn't to turn you into a rocket scientist (or for that matter, to turn rocket science into HTML). Its purpose is to show you the structural and technical elements needed for good-looking, readable web pages and to give you the confidence to build some!

This book explains how to use HTML and CSS to get your pages up and running on the World Wide Web. We tell you what's involved in structuring and building effective web documents that can bring your ideas and information to the online world — if that's what you want to do — and maybe even have some high-tech fun communicating them to others.

To make this book easier to read, keep in mind the following things about working with the markup:

- ✔ As a convention for this book, all HTML and CSS markup appears in monospaced type like this:

  ```
  <head><title>What's in a Title?</title></head>
  ```

- ✔ When you type HTML markup, CSS, or other related stuff, copy the information exactly as you see it, including the angle brackets (< and >) because they're part of the magic that makes HTML and CSS work.

- ✔ The margins on a book page don't have the same room as do the vast reaches of cyberspace. Therefore, long lines of HTML and CSS markup, or designations for web sites (called *URLs,* or *Uniform Resource Locators*), may break across multiple lines. Remember, your computer sees such lines as a *single line of HTML or CSS,* or as a single URL — so if you type all of that text, be sure to put it all on one line. Don't insert any hard returns (or press the Enter key) if you see the line wrap. We show you that everything is supposed to be *all on one line* by breaking at a punctuation character or space and then indenting any overage, like so:

```
www.infocadabra.transylvania.co/nexlus /plexus/lexus/
        praxis/okay/this-is-all make-believe-but-real-
        ones-get LONG.html
```

✔ HTML4 doesn't care whether you type tag text in uppercase, lowercase, or both (except for character entities, also known as character codes). HTML5 and CSS, however, want tag text in lowercase only. Thus, to make your work look as much like ours as possible, enter all HTML and CSS tag text, and all other markup, *in lowercase only.*

✔ Our code listings may be color-coded, where specific colors signify different kinds of markup. We explain this in Chapter 2 in the section about color-coding. (Note: All illustrations use pretty colors, too!)

One more thing: Readers may notice that we refer to the web, websites, and so forth in this book, even though we also call it the World Wide Web. We've decided to follow common usage, which no longer treats "web" as a proper name. Finally, the wheels of progress have turned long enough to wear off the top of the initial capital "W" in web!

Foolish Assumptions

Some say that making assumptions makes a fool out of both the person who makes them and the person who falls subject to them. (And just who are *they* anyway? We *assume* we know but . . . never mind.)

You don't need to be a wizard in the arcane arts of programming, nor do you require a PhD in computer science. You don't even need a detailed sense of what's going on in the innards of your computer to deal with the material in this book.

Even so, practicality demands that we make a few assumptions about you, our gentle reader: You can turn your computer on and off, you know how to use a mouse and a keyboard, and you want to build your own web pages for fun, profit, or some reason entirely of your own. We also assume you have a working Internet connection and a web browser.

If you can write a sentence and know the difference between a heading and a paragraph, you can build and publish your own documents on the web. The rest consists of details — and we help you with those.

Icons Used in This Book

Here's a list of the icons we use in this book to flag text and information that's especially noteworthy.

This icon signals technical details that are informative or interesting but aren't absolutely essential for writing or understanding HTML and CSS.

This icon flags useful information that makes HTML markup or other important stuff even less complicated than you feared it might be.

This icon points to stuff you shouldn't skip — don't overlook these reminders. (The sanity or web page you save could be your own.)

Watch out when you see this icon. It warns you against things you shouldn't attempt. Consequences can be severe if you ignore these admonitions.

This icon points you to resources available online. Most notably, we steer you to `www.dummieshtml.com/html5cafe` when we discuss example files you can find there.

Beyond the Book

This section describes where readers can find the book's companion content. Some of it is available at `www.dummies.com`, and some of it — including all the markup examples in the book — is available at `www.dummieshtml.com/html5cafe`:

- **Cheat Sheet:** Visit `www.dummies.com/cheatsheet/beginning html5css3` to see a quick compendium of HTML and CSS markup, plus some handy-dandy color charts.

- **Extras:** We've posted articles that extend the content covered in the book, with one extra short article for Parts II through IV of this book. Parts II and III deal with HTML, and Parts III and IV with CSS. The URL for this material is `www.dummies.com/extras/beginninghtml5css3`.

- **Updates:** Each _For Dummies_ technical book explains where readers can find updates in case the book changes substantially. This is where any updates or corrections that we make to the book's content and coverage will appear, along with any errata we find and fix. The URL for this stuff is also www.dummies.com/extras/beginninghtml5css3.

For example, our book is chock-full of HTML5 and CSS 3 markup, and the specifications for both HTML5 and CSS3 are still in development, so changes are bound to occur in the months and years ahead.

✏ **Companion files:** Our book site offers per-chapter downloads with the source HTML and/or CSS files for each chapter, and a one-shot-gets-everything download for the whole book, all at www.dummieshtml/html5cafe. See Appendix B for details about the Dummies HTML website.

Where to Go from Here

This is where you hit the road. Where you start doesn't matter. Don't worry — you can handle it. We know you're ready to have the time of your life. Enjoy!

Part I

Getting Started with HTML and CSS on the Web

getting started
with
HTML5
and CSS3

In this part . . .

- Taking in HTML from 10,000 feet (an overview)
- Understanding the role that Cascading Style Sheets (CSS) play on the web
- Digging into HTML-speak: markup, elements, tags, entities, and more
- Getting your web pages organized
- Creating and viewing your very first web page
- Moving pages from your PC to a web server online

An Overview of HTML and CSS on the Web

In This Chapter

▷ Bringing web pages to life

▷ Understanding the role that HTML plays on web pages

▷ Appreciating what CSS does to give web pages style

▷ Exploring and analyzing simple markup examples

*W*elcome to the wonderful world of the web, HTML, and CSS. With just a little knowledge, some practice, and something to say, you can create your own little virtual acre of cyberspace or improve on existing work.

We use the term HTML throughout this book. Using this term lets us refer to the HyperText Markup Language in general, including both HTML4 and HTML5, plus XHTML), all in one go. Although HTML4 and HTML5 are different (and XHTML differs from both of them, too), they're all enough alike for this reference to make sense.

This book is your down-and-dirty guide to understanding web documents, sprucing up existing web pages, and crafting complex and exciting pages that use intricate designs, multimedia, and scripting.

The best way to start working with HTML is to jump right in, so that's what this chapter does: It explains the basics of how HTML and CSS work behind the scenes inside web pages, and it introduces you to their underlying building blocks. When you're done with this chapter, you'll know how HTML and CSS work so you can start creating or editing web pages right away — albeit very, very simple ones.

How and Where Web Pages Come to Life Online

Web pages can accommodate many kinds of content, such as text, graphics, forms, audio and video files, streaming media, and even interactive games.

Browse the web for only a moment or two, and you see a smorgasbord of information and content displayed in many ways. Every website is different, but all have one thing in common: HyperText Markup Language (also known as HTML). You also run into Cascading Style Sheets (CSS) regularly.

Regardless of what information a web page contains, every page is created using some form of HTML. HTML is the mortar that holds web pages together: graphics, text, and other information are the bricks. CSS tells web pages how they should look (and to some extent, behave) when on display.

HTML files that produce web pages are simple text files, whether those files contain HTML4, HTML5, or even XHTML. Same thing goes for CSS. Reliance on simple text files, or documents, explains why the web works as well as it does. Text is a universal way of representing data for computers. Any text file you create on a Windows PC — including any HTML or CSS file — works equally well on a Mac, Linux/Unix, or any other operating system.

But web pages aren't *merely* text documents. Web pages are made using special, attention-starved, sugar-loaded text called HTML or CSS. Each web page uses its own specific sets of instructions and directives that you include (along with your content) inside text files to specify what's on the page and how that page should look and behave. Stick with us to uncover everything you need to know about HTML and CSS!

HyperText

Special instructions in HTML permit lines of text to point to (that is, *link*) something else in cyberspace. Such pointers are called *hyperlinks*. Hyperlinks are the glue that holds the World Wide Web together. In your web browser, hyperlinks usually appear in blue and are underlined. When you click a hyperlink, it takes you somewhere else.

Hypertext or not, a web page is a text file, which means you can create and edit a web page in any application that creates plain text (such as Notepad or TextEdit). Some software tools offer fancy options (covered in Chapter 23) to help you create web pages, but they generate the same text files you can create using a plain-text editor. We recommend you start with a simple, free web page editor named Aptana Studio. Visit www.aptana.com, where you can download the program. (You can also find instructions for Windows, Mac OS, and Linux.)

Steer clear of word processors such as WordPad or Microsoft Word when creating HTML. These tools introduce all kinds of extra markup to web pages that you don't want gunking up your work. If you don't believe us, try creating a web page inside Word and then look at all the stuff it adds inside some other editor. You won't believe your eyes!

The World Wide Web comes by its name honestly. It's literally a web of online pages hosted on web servers around the world, connected in trillions of ways by hyperlinks that tie individual pages together. Without such links, the web would be just a bunch of isolated, stand-alone documents. Boo hoo!

Much of the web's value comes from its ability to link pages and other resources (such as images, downloadable files, and media of all kinds) on a single website, or across many websites. For example, USA.gov (www.usa. gov) is a *gateway* website — its primary function is to provide access to other websites. If you aren't sure which government agency handles first-time loans for homebuyers, or you want to take a tour of the Capitol, visit the site shown in Figure 1-1 for information.

Figure 1-1: USA.gov uses hyperlinks to help visitors locate government information.

Web browsers were created specifically for the purpose of reading HTML markup and displaying the resulting web pages such markup describes. Markup lives in a text file (along with your content) to give orders to a browser. For example, look at the web page shown in Figure 1-2. You can see how the page is made up by examining its underlying HTML; its underlying CSS governs its formatting, layout, and appearance.

This page includes a graphic, a title that describes the page (HTML5 Cafe: Home), a brief welcome, navigation text, and not much else.

Here, different components of the page use different formatting:

- The title for the page appears in its browser tab.
- A brief and simple text navigation bar (HOME | ABOUT US | MENU | CONTACT US) appears at the top border.
- The welcome statement is a text heading in large-format type, followed by a brief description of what's there.
- A coffee cup image appears next, followed by our favorite morning slogan (powered by coffee).

Figure 1-2: This page incorporates multiple parts and numerous bits of HTML and CSS.

The browser knows to display these components of the page in specific ways thanks to the somewhat simplified HTML markup for this page we present in Listing 1-1. Eventually we get around to all the real stuff that's on the actual web page, but for the moment, we present a stick-figure equivalent.

Listing 1-1: The HTML5 Cafe Home Page

```html
<!DOCTYPE html>
    <head>
        <meta charset="utf-8">
        <title>HTML5 Cafe: Home</title>
        <meta name="description" content="sample site for 9781118657201">
        <meta name="viewport" content="width=device-width">
        <link rel="stylesheet" href="css/normalize.css">
        <link rel="stylesheet" href="css/main.css">
    </head>
    <body>
        <div id="container">
          <nav id="topnav">
            <a href="index.html">HOME</a> |
            <a href="about.html">ABOUT US</a> |
            <a href="menu.html">MENU</a> |
            <a href="contact.html">CONTACT US</a>
          </nav>
        <div id="content">
          <h1>Welcome to HTML5 Cafe!</h1>
          <p>Here you will find all sorts of delicious HTML5 and CSS3 treats.
             This is the sample site for <a href=
             "http://www.amazon.com/Beginning-HTML5-CSS3-Dummies-
             Computer/dp/1118657209">Beginning HTML5 and CSS3 for Dummies</a>,
             by <a href="http://www.edtittel.com">Ed Tittel</a> and
             <a href="http://www.chrisminnick.com">Chris Minnick</a>. To view
             all of the code samples from the book, visit the
             <a href="menu.html">Menu</a>.
          </p>
          <figure id="home-image">
            <img src="img/pitr_Coffee_cup_icon.png"
            width="400" height="400" alt="delicious coffee">
            <figcaption class="warning">powered by coffee.</figcaption>
          </figure>
        </div>
        <footer>
         copyright &copy; dummieshtml.com
        </footer>
      </div>
    </body>
</html>
```

Nearly all text enclosed between angle brackets (less-than and greater-than signs, or < >) is an HTML *tag* (often called *markup*). For example, the *p* within brackets (<p></p> tags) identifies text inside paragraphs. The markup between <head> and </head> at the beginning of the document defines data that describes the entire document, including the character set it uses (charset="uft-8"), the title that appears on the browser tab, description and display information, and links to some standard style sheets to manage the look and feel. The markup between <body> and </body> contains everything you can actually see on the page (and some values that control how big the included coffee cup image appears). That's really all there is to it. You embed the markup in a text file, along with text for readers to see, to instruct the browser how to display your web page.

Tags and the content between (and inside) them are also called *elements*. Angle brackets < > enclose HTML markup; curly braces { } enclose CSS markup. (You haven't seen those yet, but they show up in the next chapter.)

Content versus presentation

Simply put, *content* is stuff you can see on a web page. When developers talk about "web page content," they often mean text information that appears on a web page. But images are content, too, as is any of the various types of multimedia that you find on many web pages nowadays, such as music, videos, animations, slide shows, and all kinds of other stuff. In general, HTML handles and packages content on web pages.

Equally simply, presentation is what stuff on a web page looks like when you see it. When web developers talk about "presentation," they're referring to a multitude of characteristics. These include a plethora of typography controls for text (font family, font weight, font size, font color, and much more) but also precise positioning controls that can determine exactly where elements will appear as they're displayed. CSS includes hundreds of presentation controls, which define how web content looks and behaves when it's displayed somewhere, or printed, or even spoken (for those people making use of text-to-speech rendering facilities).

Web browsers

The user's primary tool in the web puzzle is called a *web browser*. Web browsers are programs that read HTML and CSS instructions and then use those instructions to make web page content appear on a screen.

Always write your HTML with the idea that people will view the content using a web browser. Just remember that there's more than one kind of browser out there, and each one comes in several versions.

Usually, web browsers request and display web pages that come from a web server on the Internet. But you can also display HTML pages you've saved on your own device before making them available on an Internet web server. When you develop your own HTML documents (web pages), you view those pages (called *local* pages) in your browser. You can use local pages to get a good idea of what people will see after those pages go live on the Internet.

Each web browser interprets HTML in its own way (though HTML5 is designed to improve this situation). Thus, the same HTML may not look exactly alike from one browser to the next. When you work with basic HTML, variations will be minor, but as you add other elements (such as scripting and multimedia), rendering markup can get hairy. Again, HTML5 is supposed to fix many such problems, but HTML5 isn't completely finished yet as we write this book, so it's still too early to tell whether that promise in theory will be kept in practice.

Chapter 3 explains how to use a web browser to view a local copy of your very first web page, in case you don't already know how to do this.

Some people use text-only web browsers such as Lynx because either:

- They're visually impaired and can't use a graphical display.
- They like a lean, fast web browser that displays only text.

A bevy of browsers

The web may be viewed through browsers of many types, each in its own versions, and each with its own feature sets. Some of the most popular web browsers include Microsoft Internet Explorer, Mozilla Firefox, Apple Safari, and Google Chrome. Other browsers, such as Lynx and Opera, are also widely used. As an HTML developer, you must think beyond your own browser experience and preferences. That's because every user has his or her own personal browser preferences and settings, and they are by no means all alike — not even close!

Each browser renders HTML a bit differently. Every browser handles JavaScript, multimedia, style sheets, and other add-ins differently, too. Throw in different operating systems, and a mix of smartphones and tablets, plus notebook and desktop PCs, and things get really interesting.

Usually differences between browsers are minor. But sometimes a combination of HTML, text, and media can bring a specific browser to its knees. When you work with HTML, test your pages on as many different browsers as you can. Install at least four browsers on your system for testing. We recommend the latest versions of Internet Explorer, Safari, Chrome, and Firefox.

If you want information about more browsers, Yahoo! maintains a fairly complete list (over 60 items altogether):

```
http://dir.yahoo.com/computers_
    and_internet/software/
    internet/world_wide_web/
    browsers
```

Getting to know Internet protocols

Under the hood, the Internet works because of extraordinarily durable and capable sets of rules and formats for networked communication. These things are called protocols, and they define the ways in which computers can talk to each other across the Internet.

In fact the web is made up of billions of resources, each of them linkable. A resource's exact location is the key to linking to it. Without an exact address (a *Uniform Resource Locator,* or URL), you can't use the address bar in a web browser to visit a web page directly.

URLs are the standard addressing system for web resources. Each resource (web page, site, or individual file) has a unique URL. URLs work a lot like your postal address. Figure 1-3 identifies the components of a URL.

Figure 1-3: The components of a URL help it define an exact location for a file on the web.

The devil is in the protocol details

A collection of related protocols is often called a *protocol suite.* For the Internet, that protocol suite is TCP/IP taken from the abbreviation for the names of two of its most important protocols — namely the Transmission Control Protocol (TCP) and the Internet Protocol (IP). Together, in fact, both TCP and IP transport web communications safely across the Internet. They also support the HyperText Transfer Protocol, also known as HTTP, which is what moves web pages and ancillary materials (images, graphics, media, and so forth) around the Internet.

HTTP isn't the only protocol at work on the Internet riding atop TCP and IP. The Simple Mail Transfer Protocol (SMTP) and the Post Office Protocol (POP) make e-mail possible, and the File Transfer Protocol (FTP) allows you to upload, download, move, copy, and delete files and folders across the Internet. The good news is that web browsers and web servers do all the HTTP work for you, so you need only put your pages on a server or type a URL into a browser.

To see how HTTP works, check out David Gourley and Brian Totty's chapter on HTTP Messages, available through Google Books. Go to http://books.google.com, search for *"understanding http transactions,"* double-click *HTTP: The Definitive Guide* in the results, and browse around inside this excellent reference.

Each URL component helps to define the location of a web page or resource:

- ✓ **Protocol:** Specifies the protocol the browser should use to request the resource. This is usually HTTP but could be HTTPS (Secure HTTP), FTP, or something else.

- ✓ **Domain:** Points to the General website, such as `www.usa.gov`, where the resource resides. A domain may host a few files (like a personal website) or thousands of files (like a large government or corporate site, such as `www.usa.gov` or `www.ibm.com`).

- ✓ **Path:** Names the sequence of folders through which to navigate to get to a specific file or resource.

   For example, to get to a file in the `services` folder that resides in the `system` folder, use the `/system/services/` path.

- ✓ **Filename:** Specifies which file in a directory path the browser is to access.

Although the URL shown in Figure 1-3 is not publicly accessible, it points to a domain and defines a path that leads to a specific resource named `file.html`:

```
http://www.domain.com/mainfolder/subfolder/file.html
```

Chapter 8 provides the complete details on how to use HTML and URLs to add hyperlinks to your web pages, and Chapter 3 shows how to obtain a URL for your website after you're ready to move it to a web server.

Understanding HTML and Its Versions

You already know that HTML's primary job is to label and accommodate content on web pages. But HTML comes in various versions, each of which handles content, but each of which is slightly different from the other. The basic rules and components stay more or less the same, but some important details differ. The following sections explore those versions and explain what makes them different.

Different versions of HTML

HTML stands for HyperText Markup Language, markup developed in the late 1980s and early 1990s to describe web pages. HTML is now enshrined in numerous standard descriptions called *specifications* from the World Wide Web Consortium (W3C) and the Web HyperText Application Technology Working Group (WHATWG). Work on HTML specifications for versions 1–4 ended in 1999.

When you add an X in front of HTML, you get XHTML, a reworked version of HTML based on the *eXtensible Markup Language* (XML). XML was designed to work and behave well with computers, software, and the Internet.

The original versions (1–4, that is) of HTML included some irregularities that could cause heartburn for software that reads HTML documents. XHTML was designed to use an extremely regular and predictable syntax that's easier for software to handle. XHTML was supposed to replace HTML, but increasing technical complexity in later versions caused it to fall by the wayside. (XHTML 2.0 was so complicated, it was neither widely adopted nor used very much at all.)

In 2004, the WHATWG began work on what is called a "Living Standard" for what is called HTML5 today. It's been in process for a long time now, and the standard is finally nearing completion as we write this book. Some areas of HTML5 are still under development or subject to unresolved controversy. We steer clear of them in this book so that we can provide you with a solid foundation for your web pages for the foreseeable future.

HTML5 already appears to be succeeding where XHTML did not. Even though the standard is still under construction, HTML5 is widely adopted and used on the web today. In fact, the HTML5 specification is in what's called "Candidate Recommendation" form as of December 2012. That's one step before final Recommendation status is reached; most experts expect that final version to be approved and ratified in late 2013 or early 2014.

This book concentrates on the safe parts of HTML5, which use the same kind of regular and straightforward syntax that XHTML offered, but is much simpler to understand and use. Earlier books we've written show how to create both HTML and XHTML; in this book, we stick to HTML5, period.

Creating HTML markup

HTML is a straightforward language for describing web page contents. Its components are easy to use and come in three basic types:

- **Elements:** Identify different parts of an HTML document using tags.
- **Attributes:** Provide additional information about a particular instance of an element.
- **Entities:** Non-ASCII text characters, such as the copyright symbol (©) and accented letters (É). Entities come from the Standard Generic Markup Language (SGML) used to define early HTML versions.

This chapter covers basic form and syntax for elements, attributes, and entities. Parts II through V of this book show how elements and attributes do the following:

- Describe various kinds of text (such as paragraphs, articles, or tables).
- Create effects on a web page (such as changing fonts or colors, or creating buttons with rounded corners and beveled edges).
- Add images and links to a page.

We provide links to some tables of basic entities on our companion website, or you can consult the complete Unicode Character Code Charts at www. unicode.org/charts, where you can find codes for nearly every known human language, and a huge collection of abstract shapes and symbols. Find this information by browsing around at this site:

```
www.dummieshtml.com/html5cafe
```

Building HTML documents

Building an HTML document requires assembling a sequence of elements. Some of that sequence is prescribed, which means certain elements always appear in a specific order. Other aspects of the sequence are optional, which gives you the ability to pick and choose the elements for a particular page that are best-suited to accommodate and deliver your content.

Hopefully, this helps to explain why building HTML documents often proceeds from predefined skeletons called *templates*. Because everybody knows in advance what the prescribed HTML elements are and in what order they must appear, there's no reason why work on a web page can't start with such a skeleton — which is more or less content-free when you start work on it anyway. Templates make it a little quicker and easier for you to flesh out your web page (and to make sure you don't forget any of its obligatory elements).

Human error on web pages is inevitable, so web browsers are designed to do their best to compensate for errors and omissions in those pages. But even though HTML5 is simple and straightforward, it comes with certain basic requirements that must be met for a web page to display properly. We get into those requirements in Chapter 2 and Parts II and III of this book. For now, please accept that there are good reasons for following HTML's rules of the road, the best of which is that if you do, your pages should work (and look good) in almost any web browser.

Basically, building a web page consists of inserting a sequence of HTML elements into a document, along with text and pointers to resources, to give the page some content. This means adding elements (and sometimes providing them with attributes and values), writing text, preparing images or media, and so forth. When all the pieces are put together, you can check your work to make sure that the page says what you want, does what you want, and looks the way you want.

Understanding the Role of CSS

Cascading Style Sheets (CSS) manage web page presentation, and govern how pages look and behave when on display to users (or being printed to paper or listened to in a text-to-speech converter). CSS is another markup language that mixes special symbols and keywords to define rules for handling specific HTML elements (and even, specific instances of HTML elements, when "special handling" is needed). CSS is best understood as a tool to manage formatting, layout, and behavior on web pages.

CSS offers an incredible array of presentation controls, including positioning and layout of document elements, identification and assignment of colors for text and backgrounds, and selection and manipulation of specific typefaces, called *fonts,* for textual information. CSS provides methods so that a single page of markup can be presented in different styles for different forms of rendering, so that a document can be tweaked and tuned for delivery on a screen, a printed page, by voice, or even on a Braille-based tactile device.

When an author builds a web page, he or she can define a style sheet for that document. Nevertheless, the reader's web browser can override its definitions with a different style sheet if the reader so chooses. CSS defines a priority scheme, called the *cascade,* that defines which style rule should be applied to individual HTML elements in a document. Such priorities or weights are calculated to apply to style rules so that results are predictable and repeatable.

Different versions here, too . . .

Like HTML, CSS has been around for a while. Today, three finalized versions of CSS have been defined:

- **Version 1, also called CSS Level 1,** was published by the W3C in December, 1996. This version defines all basic CSS capabilities, including font properties such as typeface and emphasis, color for text and backgrounds, text attributes for spacing between letters, words, and lines of text, alignment values for text, images, and tables, margins, borders, padding and positioning of elements, and unique identifiers and generic classifications for groups of attributes.

✓ **Version 2 (CSS Level 2),** published in May 1998, adds absolute, relative, and fixed positioning for elements, and a z-index to position multiple layers on a document, along with media types, aural (sound) styles, bidirectional text, and new font properties such as drop shadows.

Version 2.1 (CSS Level 2 Revision 1, also known as CSS2.1) repaired errors in CSS2. It went through many versions and revisions itself, first reaching Candidate Recommendation status in February 2004. It wasn't finally published as a Recommendation until June 2011.

✓ **Version 3 (CSS Level 3)** is broken into a collection of items called modules, each of which extends features defined in CSS2. At present, 50 CSS modules have issued from the W3C's CSS Working Group, but only four have attained Recommendation status — namely, Media Queries, Namespaces, Selectors Level 3, and Color. Others are relatively stable and have reached Candidate Recommendation status, including the Backgrounds and Borders module, as well as Multi-Column Layout. The rest are still in various stages of completion.

CSS4 follows the module approach introduced with CSS 3 so there is no single, monolithic CSS4 specification. Only a few Level 4 modules are currently in development, because so few Level 3 modules have been completed. (Image Values, Backgrounds and Borders, and Selectors are the best-known Level 4 modules being worked on at present.)

Most modern web browsers, such as Internet Explorer versions 9 and 10, Chrome versions 20 and later, Firefox version 17 or later, and so forth, fully support CSS2.1. Support for CSS3 varies by module, where all of the Recommendation status items are typically supported, but with varying degrees of support for other modules. CSS4 enjoys little or no support from these same browsers (except for experimental or beta implementation).

As with HTML5, we provide information only about widely adopted and used CSS markup in this book. We assume you want to build workable and predictable web pages and sites. That's why we steer clear of specifications and modules that aren't well understood and widely implemented here.

Creating CSS markup

Interestingly, any HTML document can include style information written using CSS markup. Nevertheless, most web developers isolate CSS markup in separate style sheet documents and use links to those independent external style sheets in their web pages (HTML documents). This technique helps keep content separate from presentation, encourages reuse of style sheets, and makes it easy to update presentation for multiple pages by editing the style sheets they reference rather than having to incorporate changes into a whole raft of web pages. Another important advantage to this approach is that it encourages use of standard style sheets — like the ones you see referenced in Listing 1-1 in this very chapter, in fact — where local customization comes from reference to local style sheets.

Building a style sheet requires some knowledge of the HTML elements that will appear on your web pages, and it requires you to define properties and values to manage how those elements will look and where they should be positioned on those pages. CSS offers incredible control over presentation, which in turn requires extensive testing and tweaking to get things just right. Furthermore, CSS permits classes or unique identifiers to be used, so you can associate a set of style rules with a single type or even a single instance of an HTML element on your pages. Thus, you can define basic style rules for entire HTML elements and then override them with specific rules for things such as page headers, page footers, certain types of paragraphs, and even individual instances of HTML elements. This provides incredible power over layout, look, and feel on web pages.

Dissecting a Simple Markup Example

Flip back to take another look at Listing 1-1. Careful examination of this short listing shows quite a bit of HTML, but only indirect references to CSS.

Where's the HTML?

The HTML elements you see in Listing 1-1 are as follows, in their order of appearance:

- ✓ The `<html>` tag starts the web page, and `</html>` ends it.
- ✓ The markup between `<head>` and `</head>` defines general information for the entire web page.
- ✓ The text inside the `<title></title>` element provides the page title.
- ✓ The `<meta>` element provides information about page content and display layout.
- ✓ A `<link>` element establishes a link to an external resource; in this case, to two different CSS style sheets.

- The markup between `<body>` and `</body>` supplies actual page content.

- The `<div></div>` element defines two different content divisions on the page, one for navigation, the other for page content.

- The navigation `<nav></nav>` element defines a navigation bar.

- The anchor `<a></a>` element defines hypertext links.

- The heading1 `<h1></h1>` element defines a level-1 heading.

- The paragraph `<p></p>` element defines a paragraph of text.

- A figure `<figure></figure>` element defines a graphic with a caption.

- The image `<img>` element links to a graphic for display, with horizontal and vertical dimensions and alternative text in case the image doesn't appear.

- A figure caption `<figcaption></figcaption>` element labels the figure caption.

- A document footer `<footer></footer>` element defines text for the bottom of the page.

Put all these elements together, add attribute values and text, and you have the web page shown in Figure 1-2.

Where's the CSS?

There is no CSS per se in Listing 1-1. Rather, you find links to two external style sheets, one named `main.css` and the other `normalize.css`. As it happens, these two style sheets are the results of considerable work from the HTML5 community to create standard HTML styling that looks the same (or at least, very close) across multiple browsers. This project is called HTML5 Boilerplate, and it describes itself as "a professional front-end template for building fast, robust, and adaptable web apps or sites." Check it out at `http://html5boilerplate.com`; you can also find a nice showcase of cool examples based on this template at `http://h5bp.net`.

A partnership of equals

It's tempting to treat CSS as an afterthought to HTML or somehow secondary to HTML. You must have content before you can have presentation, right? Although that's true, you can't deliver content without presentation, either, and a good presentation is just as important to the success and usability of a web page as is the content that it handles in a web browser.

That's why it's important to understand both HTML and CSS. You use HTML to control what goes into a web page, and you use CSS to control where and how it appears; what it looks (or sounds, or even feels) like; and how it behaves. Both HTML and CSS are essential to a well-crafted web page, so you should devote equal attention and energy to understanding both HTML and CSS, neither one to the detriment of the other.

'Nuff said!

2

Meeting the Structure and Components of HTML

In This Chapter

▷ Understanding syntax and rules in markup languages

▷ Examining entities in markup

▷ Organizing web pages

▷ Exploring a web page

*W*orking with a markup language such as HTML requires that you understand the conventions used to insert markup into a text file and make sense of the sometimes-cryptic strings of text you may see as a result. But as you dig into the details, it all starts to make a certain kind of sense — a sense you should seek to develop and cultivate if you want to build or edit markup on web pages. Stick with us here, please, as we talk you through some important details involved in reading and understanding HTML.

Like Any Language: Syntax and Rules

HTML is called a markup language for a very good reason: It grabs ordinary, normal text and inserts various strings into that text to define, organize, and manage the flow and sequence of content on web pages. The inserted strings define the markup, which web browsers — or other special programs known as *user agents* — pore over and use (along with CSS, of course) to guide their display of the content included.

Like any language, HTML is subject to a specific syntax, which defines the order in which markup must or can appear in a web page. There are also lots of interesting rules about what kinds of markup is legal in certain places but illegal in others. This may seem like a difficult concept, but these restrictions in HTML illustrate what this means and why it makes very good sense:

✓ The `<caption>` element is for providing a caption for a table. Thus it can appear only inside `<table>` markup. If you want to provide a caption for a figure, you must use the `<figcaption>` element instead. You need to employ the right markup for the right uses in HTML.

✓ HTML recognizes various kinds of lists, which can organize text items with numbers or bullets, as the markup directs. List items employ the `<li></li>` tags to identify individual items in such lists. That's why those particular tags are legal only if they occur within some kind of list element, such as `<ul></ul>` (an unordered, or bulleted list) or `<ol></ol>` (an ordered, or numbered list).

Chapter 5 covers lists in great detail. That chapter tells you about the markup to create various lists in web pages using HTML.

✓ HTML supports all kinds of fields and input controls for online forms. As with tables, forms-related elements can appear only inside a pair of `<form></form>` tags. There are lots of forms-related elements and attributes that can appear only in such a context. These include numerous input types, various kinds of text boxes, button controls, and more. All of them are legal only in a form, so they must occur between `<form>` and `</form>` on a web page if they are to work.

Chapter 7 covers forms in great detail. That chapter explains the markup to create all kinds of forms on web pages using HTML.

Understanding HTML largely boils down to grasping how to create the markup it uses (that's the syntax) and understanding the order (or context) in which individual markup elements may appear. Those are the rules for creating valid or legal HTML. Much of this book is devoted to one or both of these topics. The same observations are true for CSS also, by the way, except that the syntax and the rules for its expression are different because CSS is a different markup language from HTML.

Color-coding the markup

As we present HTML and CSS information in our code examples in this book, we use color-coding to help you distinguish what's what by way of markup. Here is a color key that you should keep in mind as you peruse our various code listings elsewhere in the book:

Purple	Denotes HTML markup elements (single tags and tag pairs), plus the DOCTYPE declaration.
Medium Blue	CSS selectors (names of CSS properties) in boldface.
Dark Blue	HTML attribute values are in normal-weight text.
Light Blue	CSS property/selector values and character entity strings.
Green	Markup comments in HTML and CSS.
Brown	HTML attribute names, CSS class and ID names and references.

We colorize markup only in code listings and code blocks because it affects readability too much when code appears in body copy — that is, within ordinary paragraphs of text like this one. In paragraphs like this, we simply use a different, monospaced font — as you've already seen in our discussions of `<form>` and `<table>` markup (and other HTML elements) in the preceding section.

One more thing: If you use an HTML editor, such as Aptana Studio, HTML-Kit, Dreamweaver, KompoZer, or whatever, you find these tools also use text color to help you identify different kinds of markup. Alas, none of them do this in the exact same way, so the color scheme we present here in this book will be different depending on the HTML editor you use.

Breaking down the elements

Elements are the building blocks for HTML. You use them to describe each piece of text on your web page. Elements are made up of tags and the content within (or between) those tags. In HTML, there are two main kinds of elements:

- Elements with content made up of a tag pair and whatever text sits between the opening and closing tags in the pair
- Elements that insert something into the page, using a single tag

Tag pairs in HTML

Elements that describe content use a *tag pair* to mark the beginning and end, with everything inbetween representing the element content. Tag pairs begin with an opening tag, followed by some content, and end with a closing tag, like this: `<title>Titles Are Easy, Content Is Hard</title>`.

Content — such as articles, asides, paragraphs, headings, tables, and lists — always uses tag pairs, where

- The opening tag (`<tag>`) tells the browser, "The element begins here."
- The closing tag (`</tag>`) tells the browser, "The element ends here."

Actual content is the stuff between the opening and closing tags. Here's a paragraph snippet from Ed's bio at `www.edtittel.com/about/about-ed.html`:

```
<p>Ed Tittel has worked over 30 years in the computing
industry. He's worked as a software developer and
development manager, a networking consultant, a trainer
and course developer, and a technical evangelist . . . </p>
```

Single tags

Elements that insert something into a page are called *empty* elements (because they enclose no content) and use a single tag, like this: `<single-tag>`. Images and line breaks insert something into an HTML file and use a single tag (empty element) — namely, `<img . . .>` and `<br>`, respectively.

In HTML5, empty elements don't require special treatment. In an earlier version known as XHTML (based on the XML markup language), empty elements are required to end with a slash just before the closing angle bracket, so what we wrote as `<single-tag>` on the previous page in HTML5 (and HTML4, for that matter) would be written as `<single-tag/>`. For backward compatibility with HTML4, this would often be written as `<single-tag />` because that space preceding the slash enabled older browsers to recognize the element properly even if they didn't parse the markup as XHTML. You may encounter the extra space and the closing slash in pages you look at, so don't let it bother you. These contortions no longer apply in HTML5.

For example, the `<img>` element references an image. When the browser displays the page, it replaces the `<img>` element with the file that it points to. (An attribute does the pointing, as is shown in the next section.)

However appealing the concept may seem, you can't make up your own HTML elements. Legal elements for HTML belong to a very specific set — if you use elements that don't belong to that set, the browser simply ignores them. The elements you can use are defined in the various HTML specifications. (The version of the HTML5 specification that was current as we were writing this book can be found at `www.w3.org/TR/html51`.)

Nesting markup

Some HTML page structures can contain nested elements. Think of them as *suitcases* that fit neatly inside one another. For example, a bulleted list uses two kinds of elements:

- The `<ul>` element specifies that the list is unordered (bulleted).
- The `<li>` element marks each item in the list. (The li stands for "list item.")

When you combine elements using this approach, you must close all inside list item elements before you close the unordered list element, like this:

```
<ul>
  <li>Item 1</li>
  <li>Item 2</li>
</ul>
```

Adding Attributes to Your HTML

Attributes introduce variety or specificity into how an element describes content or how that element works or behaves. Attributes let you use elements differently depending on the circumstances. For example, the `<img>` element uses the `src` attribute to specify a location for an image you want to display:

```
<img src="images/header.png" alt="header graphic"
     width="800" height="160" title="banner graphic">
```

In this bit of HTML, the `<img>` element is a general flag to the browser that you want to include an image. The attributes handle all the fine details:

- The `src` attribute provides the specifics for the image you want to use — `header.png` in this case.

- The `width` and `height` attributes provide information about how to display that image on the page.

- The `alt` attribute provides a text alternative to the image, which is useful because a text-only browser can display the text, or a text-to-speech reader can say it aloud for the visually impaired.

- The `title` attribute creates a pop-up text message that appears over the image when a user moves the mouse inside its borders.

Chapter 9 describes the `<img>` element and its attributes in glorious detail.

If you want to define attributes for any HTML element, they must appear inside the opening tag for that element, or inside the only tag for an empty element. They belong after the element name but before the closing angle bracket in that tag, like this:

```
<tag attribute1="value" attribute2="value">
```

HTML5 syntax rules decree that attribute values must always appear inside quotation marks, but you can include attributes and their values in any order you like within the opening tag or a single tag for an empty element.

Every HTML element has a collection of attributes that may be used with it, but you can't mix and match attributes and elements however you please. Some attributes can take any text as a value because that value might be anything, such as the location of an image or a page to which you'd like to link. Other attributes impose a specific list of `values` they can take, such as your options for aligning text in a table cell (`left`, `right`, `center`, and so on).

The various HTML specifications define exactly which attributes you can use with any given element, and which values (if explicitly defined) each attribute can take.

Each chapter in Parts II and III covers the attributes you can use with each HTML element mentioned therein. Also, please see our online content for complete lists of deprecated HTML (and XHTML) tags and attributes. (**Note:** In HTML-speak, *deprecated* means that a tag or attribute should no longer be used, as it may become obsolete soon and will no longer be legal markup.)

Examining Entities in Markup

Text makes the web possible, but it's subject to limitations. *Entities,* also known as *character entities,* define codes to display special characters in your web pages.

Non-ASCII characters

Basic American Standard Code for Information Interchange (ASCII) text defines a fairly small number of characters (127 in the basic 7-bit codes; 255 in the 8-bit extended codes). It doesn't include some special characters, such as trademark symbols, fractions, and accented characters.

For example, if we translate a paragraph of text from Ed's bio into German, the result includes three *u* characters with umlauts (ü), depicted in Figure 2-1.

Figure 2-1: ASCII text can't represent all text characters, so HTML uses entities, too.

ASCII text doesn't include an umlauted *u*, so HTML uses entities to represent such characters. The browser replaces the entity reference with the character it stands for. Each entity begins with an ampersand (&) and ends with a semicolon (;). Entities originate from a markup language called SGML and appear in a light blue font in Aptana Studio. In Listing 2-1, look in the paragraph of text to find all three instances of the ü entity for each umlauted *u* therein.

Listing 2-1:   Adding an Umlaut

```
<!DOCTYPE html>
<html>
<head>
<meta http-equiv="Content-Type" content="text/html; charset=UTF-8" />
<style type="text/css">
  body {
    font-family: sans-serif;
    font-size: large;
    }
  cite {
    font-family: serif;
    font-style: italic;
    }
</style>
<title>Ed auf Deutsch</title>
</head>
<body>
<p>Ed Tittel hat seinen technischen Schriften im Jahre 1986 angefangen, als er
f&uuml;r einen Macintosh monatlichen Zeitschrift Artikeln schrieb. In drei mehr
Jahren, hat er auch f&uuml;r anderen Journalen wie <cite>LAN Times</cite>,
<cite>Network World</cite>, und <cite>LAN Magazine</cite> merhrere Artikeln
beigetragen. Er fertigte seinen ersten Buch im Jarhe 1991, und beim Ende des
Jahres 1994 hat er auf ein Dutzend B&uuml;cher gearbeitet.</p>
</body>
</html>
```

Character codes

Encodings for the ISO Latin-1 character set are supplied by default in all modern web browsers. (Search for *"ISO Latin-1 character set"* to find a complete table of values.) Thus, the character entities in that set may be used directly in HTML markup without going through any special contortions. However, using other encodings requires inclusion of special markup to tell the browser to interpret Unicode character codes. (Unicode is an international standard — ISO standard 10645, in fact — that embraces enough codes to handle most human alphabets, plus plenty of symbols and non-alphabetic characters, too.) This special markup takes this form:

```
<meta charset="UTF-8">
```

Because the charset value reads UTF-8, you can reference all common Unicode values. (UTF-8 stands for Unicode Transformation Format 8-bit, an encoding format that represents all Unicode characters. Search for *"Unicode UTF-8 character table"* to skim over its one-million-plus character codes.)

Although today's browsers support UTF-8 more or less universally, expect to see support for UTF-16 character codes sometime soon. UTF-16 character codes let browsers deal more effectively with non-Roman alphabets such as Arabic, katakana (Japanese ideographs), and Hangul (Korean ideographs), which some browsers struggle to render correctly and completely today.

(Special) tag characters

HTML-savvy software assumes that certain HTML characters, such as the left and right angle brackets (less-than and greater-than signs in math notation) are meant to be hidden and not displayed on your finished web pages. If you actually want to display these characters on your pages, you must make your wishes clear to the browser. The following entities enable display of characters that are normally part of hidden HTML markup:

- **left angle bracket (<):** `&lt;`

- **right angle bracket (>):** `&gt;`

- **ampersand (&):** `&amp;`

If you need these symbols to appear, include their entities in your markup like this:

```
<p>The paragraph element identifies some text as a Paragraph: </p>
<p>&lt;p&gt;This is a paragraph&lt;/p&gt;</p>
```

Figure 2-2 shows how these entities appear inside a browser window.

Figure 2-2: Character entities enable display of special characters in a browser window.

Organizing Web Pages

HTML documents — also known as *web pages* — always follow a regular, predictable structure. There's also one special type of markup element, called a *comment,* that lets content developers (that's you) insert remarks that won't be displayed in any web browser, but will be readable to anyone who looks at the HTML markup itself. You can do this for any web page you visit by choosing View⇨Source in Internet Explorer or choosing equivalent operations in Chrome (Tools⇨View Source), Firefox (Tools⇨Web Developer⇨Page Source), and so forth.

In HTML, two special sequences of markup characters enclose a comment:

- Begin a comment with the string < ! - -
- End a comment with the string - - >

HTML elements are organized into a structure, where

- Some elements may occur only inside other specific elements.
- Certain elements must appear within any well-structured HTML document, err, web page.

In Listing 2-2, we use HTML comments to document basic HTML document structure.

Listing 2-2: Documenting Basic HTML Structure

```
<!DOCTYPE html>
<html>  <!-- This tag should always occur at or near the beginning of any
            well-formed HTML document -->
<head>  <!-- The head element supplies information to label the whole HTML
            document -->
<title>Welcome to Ed Tittel.com</title> <!-- The text in the title element
            appears in the title bar of the browser window when the page
            is viewed -->
</head> <!-- closes the head element -->

<body>  <!-- The content that appears on any Web page appears or is
            invoked from inside the body element -->
        <!-- Skip a bunch of copy here . . . -->
<!-- Subtitle text -->
  <h1>Contact:</h1>
  <!-- List -->
    <ul>
      <li><b>Email:</b> etittel at yahoo dot com</li>
      <li><b>Address:</b> 2443 Arbor Drive, Round Rock, TX 78681-2160</li>
      <li><b>Phone:</b> 512-252-7497 (No solicitors, please)</li>
      <li>List of publications available in: <a href="docs/v_et.doc"
          target="_blank">MS Word</a></li>
      <li>Resume available in: <a href="docs/Resu-et13.doc" target="_blank">
          MS Word</a></li>
    </ul></body>  <!-- End of the body section -->
</html>  <!-- End of the HTML document -->
```

The preceding document is broken into two major divisions: a <head> and a <body>. Within each of those divisions, certain kinds of elements appear. Many combinations are possible: That's what you see throughout this book!

The file for the preceding example is named `02Listing01.html` and appears under the menu at the HTML5 Cafe (our complete collection of examples and markup files found in this book, along with live links to any URLs you encounter, organized by chapter number):

```
www.dummies.html\html5cafe\menu.html
```

Files associated with figures are named *cc*figure*nn*.html, where *cc* is the two-digit chapter number, and *nn* is the two-digit figure number.

Organizing HTML text

Beyond their mandatory division into `head` and `body` sections, text in the body of an HTML document may be organized in any number of ways.

Document heads

Inside the `<head>` section, you may (and probably should) define all kinds of labels and information, including a title. Such definitions help you describe the document that follows, including the character sets it uses, metadata for search engines and page descriptions, and instructions to the web server that delivers your page, default style sheets, page refresh behavior, and lots more. (**Note:** Metadata literally means "data about data" — in this case, it means information about the web page that follows.) To find out more about the HTML `<meta>` element, please visit these sites:

```
www.w3schools.com/tags/tag_meta.asp
www.quackit.com/html_5/tags/html_meta_tag.cfm
www.w3.org/TR/2011/WD-html5-author-20110705/the-meta-
          element.html
```

The `<body>` section is where real content lives in HTML documents and where the vast majority of HTML elements and markup appears. In the following sections, we cover typical elements in an HTML `<body>`.

Document headings

Headings in HTML are usually denoted using elements `<h1>` through `<h6>`. These are different from an HTML document `<head>` because they establish running heads within document content in the `<body>`.

Text containers

The paragraph (`<p>`) element in HTML is probably the best known text container, but HTML supports all kinds of other text containers, too. Other such elements include the following (in alphabetical order):

✔ `<article>`: Represents an article, a piece of standalone content.

✔ `<aside>`: Represents content related to surround content that could stand alone. (We use sidebars in *For Dummies* books for this kind of thing.)

✔ `<nav>`: Declares the navigation section in an HTML document. This element is usually reserved for tabs, buttons, or links to access major site components.

✔ `<header>`: Presents standard content or information at the top of a web page (banner, navigation aids, shared text, and so forth).

✔ `<footer>`: Presents standard content or information at the bottom of a web page (copyright notices, minor navigation, feedback solicitation, and so on).

HTML also includes all kinds of ways to emphasize or identify text inside paragraphs or other text containers; Parts II and III of this book introduce the important ones.

Lists

HTML supports easy definition of numerous kinds of lists, including bulleted (unordered) lists, numbered (ordered) lists, and even lists of definitions (which include terms and descriptions). You can nest lists within lists to create as many levels of hierarchy as you might need. (Nesting your lists is particularly useful when outlining a complex subject or modeling a table of contents with numerous heading levels.) Chapter 5 covers lists in more detail.

Tables

In addition to a variety of listing mechanisms, HTML includes markup for defining tables. Tables were really popular in the 1990s for managing complex page layouts; today they're used primarily for tables of information, as they should be. Structure is part of how markup works, so within the definitions for an HTML table, you can

✔ Distinguish between column heads, table data, and table footers or comments.

✔ Manage how rows and columns are defined, with controls that let you span rows or columns for grouping and organization.

Cascading Style Sheets (CSS) markup

CSS markup may occur in separate style sheet documents, in a block of text inside an HTML document `<head>`, in a `style` attribute for an individual HTML element within the document body, or in some combination of all three forms. CSS provides detailed control over font selection, use of color for text and backgrounds, positioning of text and other elements on a page, and (as the old Ronco ad intones) much, much more!

You can dig into CSS in more detail in Parts IV and V of this book, but we cover bits and pieces of CSS throughout the book as appropriate for the subject matter at hand. You can build a website without using CSS (using CSS requires more work), but it's the right tool for precise control over look and layout. Highly recommended!

Complementing and enhancing text

Text-only web pages get boring fast. A spot of color, a few links, and some nice-looking images can do a lot to add visual interest to your pages and to help you retain your viewers' interest and attention. That's why we devote considerable attention to this subject matter in various parts of this book.

Inserting images in HTML documents

Adding an image to any HTML document is easy. Careful and well-planned use of images adds greatly to web pages. Chapter 9 explains how to grab images from text files and shows you how to include them in your web pages. It also explains how to use complex markup to position and flow text around graphics or images. Along the way, you discover how to select and use interesting, compelling images to add allure and information to your content.

Links and navigation tools

Web page structure should help visitors find their way around collections of pages, look for items of interest, and get where they want to go quickly and easily. Links provide the mechanism to bring people and your web pages together, so Chapter 8 shows how to do the following:

- Reference external items or resources
- Jump from one page to the next
- Jump around inside a page
- Add structure and organization to your pages

The importance of structure and organization increases in direct relation to the amount of information you want to present to visitors. The more you've got to say or show, the more structure and organization count.

Navigation tools (which establish standard mechanisms and tools for moving around inside a website) provide ways to create and present your web page (and site) structure to visitors so they can use organized menus of choices.

When you add it all up, your result should be a well-organized set of information and images that is easy to understand, use, and navigate.

3

Creating and Viewing a Web Page

In This Chapter

▹ Planning what you practice and assembling the ingredients

▹ Working through the edit-save-test cycle

▹ Viewing your very first web page

reating your own web page may seem scary, but it's definitely fun, too. Experience shows that the best way to get started is to jump in with both feet. You might splash around a bit at first, but you can keep your head above water if you try.

This chapter walks you through the steps involved in creating a web page. We don't stop to explain every last bit of markup you use — we save that for other chapters. Instead, we want to make you comfortable working with markup and content to create and view a suitably simple web page.

Before You Get Started

Creating HTML documents differs from creating word processor documents using an application such as Microsoft Word. The difference comes from having to use two applications with HTML document creation:

✔ Your text or HTML editor, where you create the web pages

✔ Your web browser, where you view the results

Even though many HTML editors, such as Dreamweaver and HTML-Kit, provide a browser preview, it's still important to preview your web pages inside actual web browsers (such as Internet Explorer, Chrome, Firefox, and Safari) so you can see them as your end users do. Editing inside one program and then switching to another to look at your work might feel odd, but you'll be switching between the editor and the browser like a pro in no time.

Because not all web browsers are created equal (or identical), web pages may look different depending on the browser you use. Get in the habit and regular practice of previewing web pages in multiple browsers so that you see what your end users see when they open that page. We used Chrome to make all the screenshots in this book, by the way.

To get started on your first web page, you need two types of software:

- ✔ **The latest version of Aptana Studio:** Studio 3 is the current version as we write this book. Go to www.aptana.com to get your copy.

    We discuss these tools in more detail in Chapter 23, but here's a thumbnail sketch: Aptana Studio is a web project tool that works on Windows, Mac OS, and Linux PCs.

- ✔ **A web browser:** Internet Explorer, Chrome, Firefox, and Safari are the most popular web browsers, so make sure to test your pages in each of them if possible.

We use the free web Aptana Studio development toolkit in this book, and here's why:

- ✔ **Working with markup:** Although an advanced HTML editor, such as Expression Web or Dreamweaver, often hides your HTML from you, Aptana lets you interact directly with the markup. For your first page, you want to see your HTML in all of its (limited) glory.

    When you become familiar with XHTML and CSS markup, syntax, and structure, you can really start to make Aptana Studio sing. It's a good tool and provides great HTML5 and web page template support, handles CSS3 nicely, and offers good PHP, Ruby, and Rails support.

- ✔ **Keeping the code clean:** Word processors decked out with bells and whistles (such as Microsoft Word) often insert extra information behind the scenes (for example, formatting instructions to display or print files). You can't see or change that information while you're editing, but it messes with your HTML. With Aptana, you don't have to worry about those bells and whistles making noise in the background.

Creating a Page from Scratch

Using HTML to create a web page from scratch takes four basic steps, plus a little advance preparation (programmers like to start counting from zero, so we assign "Step number 0" to the necessary preparation activities):

0. **Gather your tools.**
1. **Plan your page design.**
2. **Combine HTML and text in a text editor to make that design a reality.**
3. **Save your page.**
4. **View your page in a web browser.**

Break out your text editor, fire up your web browser, and roll up your sleeves.

Step 0: Gather your tools

As you collect your tools, be sure to collect your wits about you, too. If you haven't already downloaded and installed Aptana Studio, please do so. The download is about 146MB (size varies slightly by the OS you use), so it might take a while to transfer, depending on the speed of your Internet connection. After you've downloaded the file, launch it on your PC. (It self-installs on all three operating systems.)

Next, if you want your code listings in Aptana studio on your screen to look like ours do in the book, you need to visit the HTML5 Cafe and download our special Aptana theme. You can find it listed as Book Theme on this menu:

```
www.dummieshtml.com/html5cafe/menu.html
```

After you get the theme (it's only 17KB, so it should download in a flash), choose Window⇨Preferences⇨Aptana Studio⇨Themes. Finally, click the Import button, select the downloaded theme, and then click Apply. Figure 3-1 shows what this looks like in Windows; other OSs look something like this but not exactly the same.

Figure 3-1: After you import the Beginning HTML5 and CSS3 FD theme, your Aptana preferences should look like this.

Step 1: Planning a simple design

We've discovered that a few minutes spent planning an approach to the page at the outset makes creation faster and easier. You don't have to create a complicated diagram or an elaborate layout in this step. Just jot down some ideas for what you want on the page and how you want it arranged.

You don't even have to be at your desk to plan a simple design. Take a note-pad and pencil outside and design in the sun, or scribble on a napkin while you're having lunch. Remember, this is supposed to be fun!

Our example is a take on the traditional "Hello World!" exercise used in nearly every programming language: The first thing you practice when programming a new language is how to make "Hello World!" appear onscreen. In our example, we create a short letter to the world instead, so the page is more substantial with additional text. Figure 3-2 shows a basic design for this page.

Figure 3-2: Taking a few minutes to sketch your page design makes writing HTML easier.

The design for the page includes four components:

- ✔ A serviceable title: Hello World!
- ✔ A few paragraphs explaining how HTML can help you communicate with the whole world
- ✔ A closing: Sincerely
- ✔ A signature

You may want to choose a basic color scheme for your page, to start. For our example, we chose a teal background and white text with the title as noted.

When you know what kind of information you want on the page, you can move on to Step 2 — writing the markup.

Step 2: Writing some HTML

You have a couple of options when you're ready to create your HTML. In the end, you'll probably use some combination of the two:

  ✔ If you already have some text that you just want to describe with HTML, save that text as a plain text file and add HTML markup around it.

  ✔ Start creating markup and add the content while you go.

Our example starts with some text created in a simple text editor such as Notepad (PC) or TextEdit (Mac). Save your content as a text file. (Leave your text editor open — you're going to return to it in a minute.) Next, fire up Aptana and choose File➪New➪Web Project. In the New Web Project window, click Next, name your project BegHTML5&CSS3, browse to put the project in an easy-to-remember location (we used a folder named Aptwork where we keep all our Aptana projects), and then click Finish.

Next, choose File➪New➪File, pick your project folder in the Parent Folder frame, and name your file `html-letter.html` in the File Name text box. Now you can cut and paste the contents of your plain-text file into Aptana and add markup around the text. When you're done, you should see what's shown in Figure 3-3.

```
To Everybody on the World-Wide Web:

We sincerely believe that basic HTML knowledge is essential to
designing, building, and maintaining readable and workable Web
pages. Our goal in this book is to explain what HTML, XHTML, and
CSS are and how they work, and then to show you exactly how to
use them to best advantage.

Along the way, we will examine the principles and best practices
that govern Web page design and construction, and help you
understand how to make your content accessible to the broadest
possible audience.

By the time you work your way through this book's contents, you
should feel comfortable with creating and managing your own Web
site. You should also understand what it takes to identify your
audience, communicate with that audience, and keep your content
fresh and interesting to keep them coming back for more.

Sincerely,
Chris Minnick and Ed Tittel, your humble authors
```

Figure 3-3: Here's the plain text for our page, completely sans markup in Aptana.

The following code shows you what you must add to this prose to turn it into a fully functional HTML file. As you type HTML tags in Aptana, the program creates complete tag pairs as soon as it recognizes what you're typing. You'll have to cut the closing tags from where they appear and then paste them where you want them to go, as shown in the following listing.

Listing 3-1:   The Complete HTML Page for the "Hello World!" Letter

```html
<!DOCTYPE html>
<html>
  <head>
    <title>Hello World!</title>
    <meta charset= "UTF-8" />
  </head>
  <body style="color: white;
        background-color: teal;
        font-size: 12pt;
        font-family: sans-serif;">

    <h1>To Everybody on the World-Wide Web:</h1>

    <p>We sincerely believe that basic HTML knowledge is essential to
       designing, building, and maintaining readable and workable Web
       pages. Our goal in this book is to explain what HTML and CSS
       are and how they work, and then to show you exactly how to
       use them to best advantage.</p>

    <p>Along the way, we will examine the principles and best practices
       that govern Web page design and construction, and help you
       understand how to make your content accessible to the broadest
       possible audience.</p>

    <p>By the time you work your way through this book's contents, you
       should feel comfortable with creating and managing your own Web
       site. You should also understand what it takes to identify your
       audience, communicate with that audience, and keep your content
       fresh and interesting to keep them coming back for more.</p>

    <p>Sincerely,</p>
    <p>Chris Minnick and Ed Tittel, your humble authors</p>

  </body>
</html>
```

The HTML markup includes a collection of markup elements and attributes
that describe the letter's contents:

- ✔ The `<html>` element defines the document as an HTML document.

- ✔ The `<head>` element creates a header section for the document.

- ✔ The `<title>` element defines a document title that is displayed in the
     browser's title bar.

     The `<title>` element is *inside* the `<head>` element.

✔ The <body> element holds the text that appears in the browser window.

The markup that follows the style attribute inside the <body> element is CSS, otherwise known as the Cascading Style Sheets markup language. This particular bit of CSS says we want white text on a teal background, where the text is larger than usual, and in a sans-serif font. (You find out all about styles and attributes in Chapters 11 and 12.)

✔ The <h1> element marks "To Everybody . . ." as a first-level heading.

✔ The <p> elements identify each paragraph of the document.

Don't worry about the ins and outs of how these HTML elements work. They're covered in detail beginning with Chapter 4. Also, a web page includes graphics, scripts, and other elements that we deliberately avoid in this contrived and simple example to keep things, well, simple! We cover all these things in profuse detail later in the book, though.

After you create an HTML page (or the first chunk of it that you want to review), you must save it before you can see your work in a browser.

Step 3: Saving your page

You use an editor to create HTML documents and a web browser to view them. Before you can let your browser loose on your HTML page, you must save that page. When you're just building a page, you should save a copy of it to your local hard drive and view it locally with your browser. To save a file in Aptana, click the Save icon on the toolbar at the top-left corner of the window. (The icon looks like a small, blue floppy disk, for readers old enough to know what that means.)

Choosing a location and name for your file

When you save your file to a hard drive, keep the following in mind:

✔ **You need to be able to find it again.** Create a project folder on your hard drive especially for your web pages. Call it something that makes sense to you and be sure to put it somewhere easy to find. We put ours on a project drive, in a project named BegHTML5&CSS34D. Choose File➪New➪Web Project, click the Next button, and then select the Default Project (No Template) option to set this up. Create a project name that makes sense to you, such as LearningHTML.

✔ **The name should make sense to you so you can identify file contents without actually opening the file.** Don't put spaces in filenames. Some operating systems — most notably Unix and Linux, the most popular web-hosting operating systems around — don't like spaces in filenames;

use an underscore (_) or a hyphen (-) instead. Avoiding other punctuation in filenames and keeping them short is also good.

✏ **The name should work well in a web browser.** Create a short descriptive name for the page that tells you what it's for or about. We used `html-letter.html` for this example because it identifies the content nicely. You may also use names to identify structure and content, such as `pt1-toc.html` for a table of contents for part 1 of a complex page sequence, and perhaps `pt1-pg1.html`, `pt1-pg2.html`, and so forth for subsequent pages in that same sequence.

In our example, we saved our file in a project called BegHTML5&CSS3FD and named it (drum roll, please) `html-letter.html`, as shown in Figure 3-4.

Figure 3-4: Use a handy location and logical project and filenames for your web pages.

Using .htm or .html

You can actually choose from one of two suffixes for your pages: `.html` or `.htm`. (Our example filename, `html-letter.html`, uses the `.html` suffix.)

The shorter `.htm` is a relic from the 8.3 DOS days when filenames could only include eight characters plus a three-character suffix that described the file's type. Today, operating systems can support filenames and suffixes that are longer than three letters, so we suggest you stick with `.html`.

Web servers and web browsers handle both `.htm` and `.html` equally well.

Stick with one filename approach. The `.html` and `.htm` files are treated the same by browsers and servers, but because they're different suffixes they represent different filenames; therefore, `html-letter.html` is different from `html-letter.htm`. This matters a lot when you create hyperlinks (covered in Chapter 8).

Step 4: Viewing your page

After you save a copy of your web page, you're ready to view it in a web browser. Follow these steps to view your web page in Internet Explorer. (The steps may be different if you're using a different browser.):

1. **If you haven't opened your browser, do that now.**

2. **Choose File➪Open in Internet Explorer. If you're using Chrome, press Ctrl+O (in Windows) or ⌘+O (on the Mac).**

3. **In the Open dialog box that appears, click the Browse button.**

4. **In the new dialog box that appears, navigate your file system until you find your HTML file and then select it so it appears in the File Name area.**

   Figure 3-5 shows a highlighted HTML file ready to be opened.

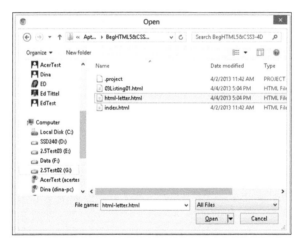

Figure 3-5: Using Chrome to navigate to your web pages.

5. **Click the Open button.**

   You're brought to the Open dialog box. (**Note:** If you're connected to the Internet, some versions of Internet Explorer warn you that for security reasons they must open a new browser window for your local file; this is perfectly okay.)

6. **Click OK.**

   The page appears in your web browser in all its glory, as shown in Figure 3-6.

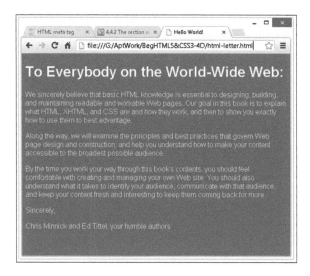

Figure 3-6: Viewing a local file in Chrome.

You aren't actually viewing this file on the web just yet; you're just viewing a *copy* of it saved on your local hard drive. So don't give anyone the URL for this file — but do feel free to edit the HTML source file and view any changes you make.

An even faster way to view a web page locally in a browser is to drag and drop the HTML file into an open browser window. You can do this from File Explorer, Finder, or any program that gives you file-level access.

Editing an Existing Web Page

Chances are good that you'll want to change one thing (at least) about your page after you view it in a web browser for the first time. After all, you can't really see how the page looks when you're creating the markup. You might decide that a first-level heading is too big or that you really *want* purple text on a green background (horrible idea, actually).

To make changes to the web page you've created in Aptana and are viewing in a browser, repeat these steps until you're happy with the final appearance:

1. **Leave the browser window with the HTML page display open and go back to Aptana.**

2. **If the HTML page isn't open in Aptana, open it.**

   You should have the same file open in both the browser and the text editor, as shown in Figure 3-7.

Figure 3-7: Viewing an HTML file in your editor and web browser at the same time.

3. **Make your changes to the HTML and its content in the text editor.**

4. **Save those changes.**

   This is an important step. If you don't save your changes, you won't see them in the web browser.

5. **Move back to the web browser and click the Refresh button.**

If you keep an HTML file open in both an editor and a browser while you work, checking changes is a breeze. You can quickly save a change in the editor, flip to the browser and refresh, flip back to the editor to make more changes, save, then flip back to the browser and refresh again, and so on.

In our example letter, we decided — after our initial draft of the HTML page — that we should add a date to the letter. Figure 3-8 shows the change we made to the HTML to add the date, and the result appears in the browser.

This approach to editing an HTML page applies only to pages saved *on your local hard drive.* If you want to edit a page that you've stored on a web server, you have to save a copy of the page to your hard drive, edit it, verify your changes, and then upload the file again to the server, as discussed in the following section.

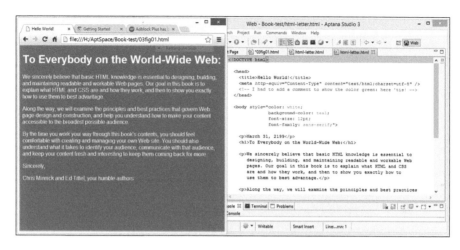

Figure 3-8: A change in the HTML displays in a browser after a quick save and refresh.

Posting Your Page Online

When you're happy with your web page, it's time to put it online. Here's a lightning-fast overview of that process:

1. **Find a web hosting provider to proffer your web pages.**

   Your web host might be a company web server or a server that you pay an Internet service provider (ISP) to use. If you don't have a host yet, double-check with your Internet ISP to find out whether you get web-server access along with your service package. Regardless of where you find space, get details from the provider on where to move your site's files and what URL to use.

2. **Use an FTP client or a web browser to make a connection to your web server.**

   Use the username and password, as specified in the information from your hosting provider, to transfer files to your web server.

3. **Copy the HTML file from your hard drive to the web server.**

4. **Use your web browser to view the file via the Internet.**

For example, to host our letter online at www.dummieshtml.com, we used the FileZilla FTP client to access the site and provided a login name and password, which we set up on our server. A collection of folders and files appeared.

We copied the file to the server with a simple drag-and-drop operation inside FileZilla.

The URL for this page is `www.dummieshtml.com/html5cafe/ch03/html-letter.html`, and that page is now served from the Internet instead of from a local file system, as shown in Figure 3-9.

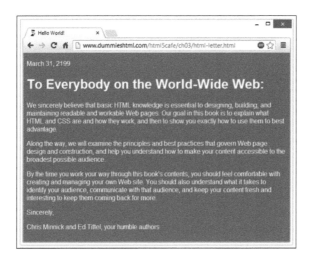

Figure 3-9: A file on a web server is available to anyone with an Internet connection.

Part II
Getting the Structure and Text Right

To find out more about HTML5 markup elements and attributes, visit www.dummies.com/extras/beginninghtml5css3. You can also visit our book site at www.dummieshtml.com.

In this part . . .

- ⌐ Digging into HTML document structure
- ⌐ Building better bodies to go with great heads
- ⌐ Appreciating block-level versus inline text elements
- ⌐ Building better lists with bullets, numbers, or definitions
- ⌐ Teasing out tables in HTML markup — using lots of options!
- ⌐ Soliciting user input or feedback by using HTML forms

4

HTML Documents Need Good Structure

In This Chapter

▷ Creating basic HTML document structure

▷ Defining an HTML document header

▷ Creating a full-bodied HTML document

*T*he framework for a simple HTML document consists of a head and body. The *head* provides information about the document to the browser (and sometimes also to the web server), and the *body* contains content that appears in the browser window. The first step in creating any HTML document is to define its framework.

This chapter covers all major elements needed to craft basic structure for an HTML document — including its head and body. We also show you how to tell a browser which version of HTML you're using. Although version information isn't strictly necessary for users, browsers use it to make sure they display document content correctly.

Establishing a Document Structure

Although no two HTML pages are alike — each employs a unique combination of content and elements to define a page — every properly constructed HTML page follows the same basic document structure:

   ✔ A statement that identifies the document as an HTML document

   ✔ A document header

   ✔ A document body

Each time you create an HTML document, you start with these elements. Then you fill in your content and markup to create an individual page.

Although a basic document structure is a requirement for every HTML document, creating it over and over again can get monotonous. Most HTML-editing tools set up basic document element structure automatically whenever you create a new document. Or you can check out the HTML5 Boilerplate project (`http://html5boilerplate.com`) for a complete site-building template — but first, you should probably work through this book so you'll understand better what you'll find there.

HTML Document Organization Revisited

An HTML document consists of a collection of markup elements — some required, many optional — where you can always find at least three elements:

- The `<html></html>` opening and closing tags follow the DOCTYPE declaration and contain everything else inside the HTML document.

- The `<head></head>` opening and closing tags follow the opening `<html>` tag. They contain definitions, labels, and information about the HTML document body that follows.

Only certain markup elements are legal inside an HTML document head (which is another way of saying "may appear between the `<head>` and `</head>` tags"). The legal elements include base, link, meta, script, style, and title. (Collectively, these are known as HTMLHeadElements in the language of the HTML5 specification.)

- The `<body></body>` opening and closing tags follow the closing `</head>` tag. They include the content and related markup for the HTML document. This is where 99 percent of the stuff that actually appears inside a web browser lives.

Any HTML markup element can appear in an HTML document body *unless* that element is the DOCTYPE, a major organizational container (namely, `<html>`, `<head>`, or `<body>`), or an element allowed only in a document head.

You could create an HTML document with no content in the `<body>`, but why would you want to? It would display only a title and no other information. We actually do just that later in this chapter, so you can observe this exercise in futility without having to try it for yourself.

Likewise, you could build a complex body with only minimal markup in the `<head>` section (the `<title>` element is required, all other head-only elements are optional), but users and search engines that find your page might miss out on important info. That's why a properly structured HTML document includes a well-constructed `<head>` along with an equally well-crafted `<body>`. For HTML documents, a body needs a head, and a head needs a body.

Going back in time gets complicated

If you choose to create an HTML 4.01 or an XHTML 1.0 document by using previous versions of markup languages, you must choose from three possible DOCTYPE declarations for each of the following flavors:

- **HTML 4.01 Transitional:** This is the most inclusive version of HTML 4.01, and it incorporates all HTML structural elements as well as all presentation elements:

  ```
  <!DOCTYPE HTML PUBLIC "-//W3C//DTD HTML 4.01 Transitional//EN"
          "http://www.w3.org/TR/html4/loose.dtd">
  ```
- **HTML 4.01 Strict:** This streamlined version of HTML excludes all presentation-related elements in favor of style sheets as the means to drive page display:

  ```
  <!DOCTYPE HTML PUBLIC "-//W3C//DTD HTML 4.01//EN" "http://www.
          w3.org/TR/html4/strict.dtd">
  ```
- **HTML 4.01 Frameset:** This version begins with HTML 4.01 Transitional and adds all the elements that make frames possible (frames are no longer recommended, though):

  ```
  <!DOCTYPE HTML PUBLIC "-//W3C//DTD HTML 4.01 Frameset//EN"
          "http://www.w3.org/TR/html4/frameset.dtd">
  ```
- **XHTML 1.0 Transitional:** This is the most inclusive version, as with HTML 4.01 Transitional:

  ```
  <!DOCTYPE html PUBLIC "-//W3C//DTD XHTML 1.0 Transitional//EN"
          "http://www.w3.org/TR/xhtml1/DTD/xhtml1-transitional.dtd">
  ```
- **XHTML 1.0 Strict:** This version drops presentation markup, as in HTML 4.01 Strict:

  ```
  <!DOCTYPE html PUBLIC "-//W3C//DTD XHTML 1.0 Strict//EN" "http://
          www.w3.org/TR/xhtml1/DTD/xhtml1-strict.dtd">
  ```
- **XHTML 1.0 Frameset:** This version adds the elements that make frames possible, as with HTML 4.01 Frameset, but see also the nearby warning about framesets (they're no longer recommended).

  ```
  <!DOCTYPE html PUBLIC "-//W3C//DTD XHTML 1.0 Frameset//EN"
          "http://www.w3.org/TR/xhtml1/DTD/xhtml1-frameset.dtd">
  ```

HTML DOCTYPE Starts Things Off

First up in any HTML document sits a Document Type Declaration (DTD), or DOCTYPE declaration. This line of markup specifies which version of HTML (or XHTML) you're using and also lets browsers know how to interpret what follows. We use the HTML5 specification in this chapter because that's what we want our readers to use. As an added bonus, it's dead simple — much more so than earlier HTML (and XHTML) versions, in fact.

HTML5 uses a minimal Document Type Declaration at the very outset of HTML documents. Here's what it looks like:

```
<!DOCTYPE html>
```

No kidding: That's all you need. That's as simple as HTML gets.

Using HTML framesets or XHTML framesets is no longer considered a best practice. It exposes pages to security problems and makes markup much trickier to test and debug. That's why we skip frame markup in this book!

All the HTML DTDs are documented in detail at www.w3.org/TR/html401/ sgml/dtd.html; the XHTML DTDs are documented at www.w3.org/TR/ xhtml1/dtds.html.

The best possible course of action for you is to get with the HTML5 program and breeze past all that old-fashioned HTML 4.01 and XHTML 1.0 stuff.

The <html> Element

After you specify the HTML DOCTYPE, you must add an <html> element to contain all other HTML markup and document content in your page:

```
<!DOCTYPE html>

<html>


</html>
```

The opening <html> element says "Hey! HTML document starts here." The closing </html> element says, "Okay, this is the end of the document. Game over!"

Anatomy of the <head>

HTML document structure is hierarchical, so an entire document includes a head section. Thus, immediately following the opening <html> element is where you define the head section, starting with an opening <head> element and ending with a closing </head> element.

Meeting the <head> himself

The *head* is one of two main components in any HTML document; the *body* is the other main component. The head, or *header,* provides basic information about the document, including its title and *metadata* (information about information), such as keywords, character encoding, author information, and a description. If you want to use an external style sheet within a page, information about that style sheet also goes into the header. Please do likewise — that is, add information to the head — if you want to establish a base for URLs referenced in a document, or call a script.

Chapter 11 provides a complete overview of creating Cascading Style Sheets (CSS) and shows how to include them in HTML documents.

The <head> element, which defines the page header, immediately follows the <html> opening element:

```
<!DOCTYPE html>

<html>
  <head>
  </head>
</html>
```

Handling metadata with <meta>

Literally, *metadata* means data or information about data. Thus, the meta element is used to provide information about the HTML document inside which it appears. All <meta> elements always appear inside the HTML <head>, and may be used to define the character encoding — that is, the bit level codes used to represent character data — inside an HTML document. They can also define keywords for search engines, describe document content, identify the document's author, define a document refresh interval (the interval at which a page automatically reloads itself), and more.

Listing 4-1 shows all of these things for a hypothetical HTML document.

Listing 4-1: An HTML Document

```
<!DOCTYPE html>

<html>
  <head>
    <meta charset="UTF-8"> <!-- defines default HTML character codes -->
    <meta name="keywords" content="HTML, CSS, meta tag examples">
    <meta name="author" content="Ed Tittel"> <!-- identifies author -->
```

```
      <meta name="description" content="meta element discussion -->
      <meta http-equiv="refresh" content="1800"> <!-- refresh every 30 mins -->
      <title>Lots of head markup, no body</title>
   </head>
   <body></body>
</html>
```

A `<meta>` element that identifies a `charset` is required for a web page to validate at `validator.w3.org`. (as is a `<title>` element, covered in the next section). Don't leave them out! For more information about the HTML `<meta>` element, for which there are umpty-ump cases and examples, please consult one or more of the following:

- HTML5: Edition for Web Authors (The meta Element)

  `www.w3.org/TR/2011/WD-html5-author-20110705/the-meta-element.html`

- HTML <meta> Tag (W3Schools)

  `www.w3schools.com/tags/tag_meta.asp`

- <meta> (Mozilla Developer Network)

  `https://developer.mozilla.org/en-US/docs/HTML/Element/meta`

If you take the time to enter the HTML markup from Listing 4-1, you see a web page with the title "Lots of head markup, no body" but nothing else to show for itself. If you can't see the full title in the browser tab, hover the mouse cursor over the title, and the whole thing appears in a small text box. If you'd rather skip the text entry work, check out the screenshot in Figure 4-1.

Figure 4-1: A page with no content shows title text in the header but nothing else.

Redirecting users to another page

You can use metadata in your header to send messages to web browsers about how they should display (or otherwise handle) your web pages. Web builders commonly use the `<meta>` element this way to redirect page visitors from one page to another automatically. For example, if you've ever come across a page that reads This page has moved. Please wait 10 seconds to be automatically sent to the new location. (or something similar), you've seen this trick at work.

To use the <meta> element to send messages to the browser, here are the general steps you need to follow:

1. **Use the http-equiv attribute in place of the name attribute.**

2. **Choose from a predefined list of values that represent instructions for the browser.**

   These values use instructions that you can send to a browser in the HTTP header, but changing the HTTP header for a document is harder than embedding the instructions into the web page itself.

To instruct a browser to redirect users from one page to another, here's what you need to do in particular:

1. **Use the <meta> element with http-equiv="refresh".**

2. **Adjust the value of the content attribute to specify how many seconds before the refresh happens and what URL you want to access.**

For example, the <meta> element line in the following markup creates a refresh that jumps to www.w3.org after 15 seconds:

```
<!DOCTYPE html>

<html>
  <head>
    <title>All About Markup</title>
    <meta charset="UTF-8">
    <meta http-equiv="refresh" content="15; url=http://www.w3.org/">
  </head>

  <body>
    <p>This page is still in development. Until we are done, please visit
       the <a href="http://www.w3.org">W3C Website</a> for the definitive
       collection of markup-related resources.
    </p>

    <p>Please wait 10 seconds to be automatically redirected to the W3C.</p>
  </body>
</html>
```

Use metadata with caution when redirecting a web page. When some search engines see metadata redirects in use, they may assume the site is trying to create spam. This could result in your website or page being *delisted,* or removed from a search engine's listings. When you become a pro at using

metadata to redirect, you can step up to the next level and try redirecting using HTTP status code 301 to force a server-based redirect from an
`*.htaccess` file located in the root directory on your web server. Although
server-based 301 redirects are outside the scope of this book, a simple
Google search can lead you to a number of good resources, such as the 301
Redirects page at

```
http://support.google.com/webmasters/bin/answer.
          py?hl=en&answer=93633
```

Older web browsers may not know what to do with `<meta>` elements that
use the `http-equiv` element to redirect a page. Be sure to include some
text and a link on the page so a visitor can link manually to your new target
page if your `<meta>` element fails to work. We discuss linking, which uses the
anchor (`<a>`) element, in Chapter 8.

If a user's browser doesn't know what to do with your redirect, the user
simply clicks a link, like the one shown in Figure 4-2, on the page to go to the
new page.

Figure 4-2: When you use a <meta> element to redirect a
page, include a link in case the redirect fails.

You can use the `http-equiv` attribute with the `<meta>` element for a variety
of purposes, such as setting an expiration date for a page. To find out more
about what your `http-equiv` options are (and how to use them), check out
the Dictionary of HTML META Tags at

```
http://vancouver-webpages.com/META/metatags.detail.html
```

Naming your page with a <title>

Every HTML page needs a descriptive title to tell visitors what the page is about. This text appears in the title bar at the very top of the browser window, as shown previously in Figure 4-1. A page title should be concise yet informative. (For example, *My Home Page* isn't as informative as *Ed's Web Design Services.*)

Define a page title by using the <title> element inside the <head> element:

```
<!DOCTYPE html>

<html>
  <head>
    <meta charset="UTF-8" >
    <title>Ed's Design Services</title>
  </head>
</html>
```

Search engines use <title> content to list web pages in response to queries. A page title may be the first thing a web surfer reads about a page, especially if she finds it via a search engine. In fact, a search engine will probably list your page title among many others on a results page, which gives you only one chance to grab a surfer's attention and convince her to choose your page. A well-crafted title can do just that.

The title is also used for bookmarks/favorites and in a browser's history, so keep your titles short and sweet.

The <body> Is a BIG Container

After you set up a page header, create a title, and define some metadata, you're ready to create HTML markup and content that will show up in a browser window. The body element holds your document content.

If you want to see something in your browser window, put it in the <body> element, like this:

```
<!DOCTYPE html>

<html>
  <head>
    <meta charset="UTF-8">
    <title>Ed's Web Design Services</title>
    <meta name="keywords"
```

```
              content="Web consulting, page design, site construction">
    <meta name="description" content="About Ed's skills and services">
  </head>


<body  style="color: white;
      background-color: teal;
      font-size: 1.2;
      font-family: sans-serif">
    <h1>Ed's Web Design Services</h1>
    <p>Ed has helped many Texas clients, large and small, to design and
       publish their company and professional web sites. He specializes in
       cutting-edge web designs, dynamic multimedia, and companion print-
       design solutions to suit all business needs.</p>

    <p>For more information, e-mail
       <a href="mailto:ed@edtittel.com">Ed Tittel</a></p>
  </body>
</html>
```

Figure 4-3 shows how a browser displays this complete HTML page:

✔ The content of the `<title>` element is in the window's title bar.

✔ The `<meta>` elements don't affect the page appearance at all.

✔ Only the text contained between the `<h1>` and `<p>` elements (in the `body` element) actually appears in the browser window.

Figure 4-3: Only content in the <body> element appears in the browser window.

5

Text and Lists

In This Chapter

▷ Working with basic blocks of text

▷ Manipulating text blocks

▷ Creating bulleted, numbered, and definition lists

*H*TML documents include text, images, multimedia files, links, and other bits of content that you mold into a web page by using markup elements and attributes. You use blocks of text to create such things as headings, paragraphs, and lists. The first step in creating a solid HTML document is laying a firm foundation to establish the document's structure.

Formatting Text

Here's an ultratechnical definition of a *block of text:* some chunk of content that fills one or more lines inside an HTML element.

In fact, any HTML page is a collection of blocks of text:

✔ Every bit of content on your page must be part of some block element.

✔ Block elements usually end with a line break when rendered in a web browser.

✔ Every block element sits inside the `<body>` element on your page. In fact, `<body>` is the ultimate block!

Inline elements versus text blocks

The difference between inline elements and a block of text is important. HTML elements in this chapter describe blocks of text. An *inline element* is a word or string of words *inside* a block element (for example, text-emphasis elements, such as `<em>` or `<strong>`). Inline elements must be nested within a block element; otherwise, your HTML document isn't syntactically correct.

Inline elements, such as linking and formatting elements, are designed to link from (or change the appearance of) a few words or lines of content found inside those blocks.

HTML recognizes several kinds of text blocks that you can use in your document, including (but not limited to) the items shown in Table 5-1.

Table 5-1	A Majority of HTML5 Block-Level Elements		
Element	*Description*	*Element*	*Description*
`article`	Article content	`header`	Section or page header
`aside`	Aside content	`h1–h6`	Heading levels 1–6
`blockquote`	Block quotation	`hr`*	Horizontal rule
`body`	Page body	`p`	Paragraph
`br`[1]	Line break	`pre`	Preformatted text
`div`	Division in web page	`section`	Section in web page
`figure`	Groups image and caption	`table,` and so on[2]	HTML tables
`footer`	Section or page footer	`ul, ol, dl`	Lists by type

[1] *Denotes an empty element (single tag only, no pair).*

[2] *All table elements fall into this cell, but we don't have room for them here. See Chapter 6 for details.*

For more about HTML block elements, see "HTML5 Block Level Elements: Complete List" at

```
www.tutorialchip.com/tutorials/html5-block-level-
            elements-complete-list
```

Paragraphs

Paragraphs appear more often than any other text block in web pages.

HTML browsers don't recognize hard returns that you enter when you create your page inside an editor. You must use a `<p>` tag to tell the browser to package all text up to the next closing `</p>` tag as a paragraph.

Formatting

To create a paragraph, follow these steps:

1. **Add `<p>` in the body of the document.**

2. **Type the content of the paragraph.**

3. **Add `</p>` to close that paragraph.**

Here's what it looks like:

```
<!DOCTYPE html>
<html>
  <head>
    <meta charset="UTF-8">
    <title>All About Blocks</title>
  </head>

  <body>
    <p>This is a paragraph. It's a very simple structure that you will use
        time and again in your web pages.</p>
    <p>This is another paragraph. What could be simpler to create?</p>
  </body>
</html>
```

This HTML page includes two paragraphs, each marked with a separate `<p>` element. Most web browsers add a line break and a full line of white space after every paragraph on your page, as shown in Figure 5-1.

Figure 5-1: Web browsers delineate paragraphs with line breaks.

Sloppy HTML coders don't use the closing `</p>` tag when they create paragraphs. Although some browsers permit this dubious practice without yelling, omitting the closing tag isn't good practice because it

- Isn't correct syntax.
- Causes problems with style sheets.
- Can cause a page to appear inconsistently from one browser to another.

You can control paragraph formatting (color, style, size, and alignment) with Cascading Style Sheets (CSS), covered in Chapters 11 through 19.

Headings

Headings break a document into sections. This book uses headings and sub-headings to divide each chapter into sections, and you can do the same with your web page. Headings

- Create an organizational structure.
- Break up the text flow on the page.
- Provide visual cues as to how pieces of content are grouped.

HTML includes six elements for different heading levels in documents:

- `<h1>` is the most prominent heading (Heading 1)
- `<h6>` is the least prominent heading (Heading 6)

Follow numerical order from lowest to highest as you use HTML heading levels. That is, don't use a second-level heading until you use a first-level heading, don't use a third-level heading until you use a second, and so on. If this doesn't make sense to you, think about how the six heading styles work in Microsoft Word and you'll have it. Should you want to change how headings look, Chapters 11 and 12 show you how to use style sheets for that purpose.

Formatting

To create a heading, follow these steps:

1. **Add <hn> in the body of your document.**

2. **Type the content for the heading.**

3. **Add </hn>.**

When used in this context, *n* means the number of the heading level you want to create. For example, to create a first-level heading, you would substitute the number 1 for *n* and would add <h1> to your page, for a second-level heading, add <h2>, and so forth.

Browser displays

Every browser has a different way of displaying heading levels, as you see in the next two sections.

Graphical browsers

Most graphical browsers use a distinctive size and typeface for headings:

- First-level headings (<h1>) are the largest (usually two or three font sizes larger than the default text size for paragraphs).

- All headings use boldface type by default, and paragraph text uses plain (nonbold) type by default.

- Sixth-level headings (<h6>) are the smallest and may be two or three font sizes *smaller* than the default paragraph text.

The following snippet of HTML markup shows all six headings at work:

```
<!DOCTYPE html>
<html>
  <head>
    <meta charset="UTF-8">
    <title>All About Blocks: Headings 1-6</title>
  </head>

  <body>
    <h1>First-level heading</h1>
    <h2>Second-level heading</h2>
    <h3>Third-level heading</h3>
    <h4>Fourth-level heading</h4>
    <h5>Fifth-level heading</h5>
    <h6>Sixth-level heading</h6>
  </body>
</html>
```

Figure 5-2 shows the headings in the HTML page as rendered in a browser.

Use CSS to control how headings look, including color, size, spacing, and alignment.

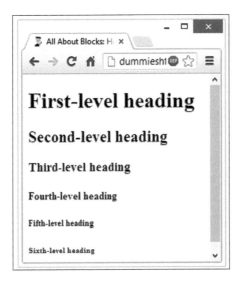

Figure 5-2: Web browsers display headings from level one to level six.

By default, most browsers use Times Roman fonts for headings. The font size decreases as the heading level increases. (Default sizes for first- through sixth-level headings are, respectively, 24, 18, 14, 12, 10, and 8 point font.) You can override any of this formatting by using CSS.

Text browsers

Text-only browsers use heading conventions that are different from those of graphical browsers because text-only browsers use a single character size and font to display all content. Some good text-only browsers to consider include Lynx, ELinks, Cygwin, and MIRA.

Controlling Text Blocks

Blocks of text build the foundation of your page. You can break those blocks into smaller pieces to better guide readers through your content.

Block quotes

A *block quote* is a quotation, or an excerpt from a copyrighted source, that you set apart on a page. Use the `<blockquote>` element to enclose quotations:

```
<!DOCTYPE html>
<html>
  <head>
    <meta charset="UTF-8">
    <title>Famous Quotations</title>
  </head>

  <body>
    <h1>An Inspiring Quote</h1>
    <p>When I need a little inspiration to remind me of why I spend my days
       in the classroom, I just remember what Lee Iococca said:</p>
    <blockquote>
      In a completely rational society, the best of us would be teachers
      and the rest of us would have to settle for something else.
    </blockquote>
  </body>
</html>
```

Most web browsers display block quote content with a slight left indent, as shown in Figure 5-3.

Figure 5-3: Web browsers typically indent a block quote to separate it from paragraphs.

Preformatted text

Ordinarily, HTML ignores white space inside documents. That's why a browser won't display any of a block element's

- Hard returns.
- Line breaks.
- Large white spaces.

The following markup includes various hard returns, line breaks, and lots of spaces. Figure 5-4 shows that the web browser ignores all of this.

```
<p>This is a paragraph

   with a lot of white space

       thrown in for fun (and as a test of course).</p>
```

Figure 5-4: Web browsers routinely ignore white space.

The preformatted text element (<pre>) instructs browsers to keep all white space intact while it displays your content. (See the following sample.) Use the <pre> element in place of the <p> element to make the browser apply all your white space, as shown in Figure 5-5.

```
<!DOCTYPE html>
<html>
  <head>
    <meta charset="UTF-8">
    <title>White Space</title>
  </head>

  <body>
    <pre>This is a paragraph

                   with a lot of white space

                       thrown in for fun (and as a test of course).
    </pre>
  </body>
</html>
```

Figure 5-5: Use preformatted text to force browsers to recognize white space.

You may want the browser to display white spaces in an HTML page where proper spacing is important, such as for

- ✔ Code samples
- ✔ Columnar data, numbers, or other format-sensitive text
- ✔ Text tables

You could nest `<pre>` elements inside `<blockquote>` elements to carefully control how lines of quoted text appear on the page. Or better yet, forget about these tags and use CSS to position text blocks inside `<div>` elements.

Horizontal rules

Using a horizontal rule element (hr) lets you include solid straight lines called *rules* on your page.

The browser creates the rule based on the hr element, so users don't wait for a graphic to download. A horizontal rule is a good option to

- ✔ Break a page into logical sections.
- ✔ Separate headers and footers from the rest of the page.

Formatting

When you include an `<hr>` element on your page, as in the following HTML, the browser replaces it with a line, as shown in Figure 5-6.

```
<!DOCTYPE html>
<html>
  <head>
    <meta charset="UTF-8">
    <title>Horizontal Rules</title>
  </head>

  <body>
    <p>This is a paragraph followed by a horizontal rule.</p>

    <hr>

    <p>This is a paragraph preceded by a horizontal rule.</p>
  </body>
</html>
```

A horizontal rule always sits on a line by itself; you can't add the `<hr>` element in the middle of a paragraph (or other block element) and expect the rule to appear in the middle of the block.

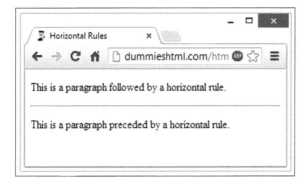

Figure 5-6: Use the <hr> element to add horizontal lines to your page.

The following bit of HTML creates a horizontal rule that takes up 45 percent of the page width, is 4 pixels (px) high, is aligned to the center, and has shading turned off:

```
<p>This is a paragraph followed by a horizontal rule.</p>

<hr width="45%" size="4" align="center" noshade="noshade">

<p>This is a paragraph preceded by a horizontal rule.</p>
```

Figure 5-7 shows how adding attributes in the preceding example alters how a rule appears. (*Note:* These attributes are deprecated, and best replaced with CSS equivalents as described in Chapters 11 through 19. Deprecated attributes are covered online, and the preceding HTML is not valid.)

Figure 5-7: Don't use deprecated <hr> attributes; use CSS instead.

Organizing Information

Lists are powerful tools to group similar elements, and lists give visitors to your site an easy way to zoom in on groups of information. Just about anything fits in a list, from sets of instructions to collections of links.

Lists use a combination of elements — at least two components:

- A markup element that says, "Hey browser! The following items go in a list."
- Markup elements that say, "Hey browser! This is an item in the list."

HTML supports three types of lists:

- Numbered lists
- Bulleted lists
- Definition lists

Numbered lists

A *numbered list* consists of at least two items, each prefaced by a number. Use a numbered list when the order or priority of items is important.

You use two kinds of elements for a numbered list:

- The ordered list element (`<ol>`) specifies a numbered list.
- List item elements (`<li>`) mark each item in the list.

Formatting

A numbered list with three items requires elements and content in the following order:

1. `<ol>`
2. `<li>`
3. Content for the first list item
4. `</li>`
5. `<li>`
6. Content for the second list item
7. `</li>`

8. `<li>`

9. Content for the third list item

10. `</li>`

11. `</ol>`

The following markup defines a three-item numbered list:

```
<!DOCTYPE html>
<html>
  <head>
    <meta charset="UTF-8">
    <title>Numbered Lists</title>
  </head>

  <body>
    <h1>Things to do today</h1>
    <ol>
      <li>Feed cat</li>
      <li>Wash car</li>
      <li>Grocery shopping</li>
    </ol>
  </body>
</html>
```

Figure 5-8 shows how a browser renders this markup. You don't have to specify a number for each item in a list; the browser identifies list items from the markup and adds numbers, including a period after each one by default.

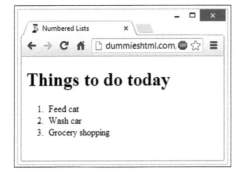

Figure 5-8: Use <ol> and <li> tags to create a numbered list.

If you swap the first two items in the list, they're still numbered in order when the page appears, as shown in Figure 5-9.

```
<ol>
  <li>Wash car</li>
  <li>Feed cat</li>
  <li>Grocery shopping</li>
</ol>
```

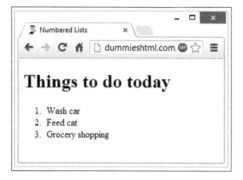

Figure 5-9: Web browsers set numbers for your list by their order of appearance.

Bulleted lists

A *bulleted list* contains one or more items each prefaced by a *bullet* (often a big dot; this book uses check marks as bullets). Use this kind of list if the items' order isn't necessary for understanding the information it presents.

Formatting

A bulleted list requires the following:

- The unordered list element (`<ul>`) specifies a bulleted list.

- A list item element (`<li>`) marks each item in the list.

- The closing tag for the unordered list element (`</ul>`) indicates that the list has come to its end.

An *unordered list* (another name for bulleted list) with three items requires elements and content in the following order:

1. `<ul>`

2. `<li>`

3. Content for the first list item

4. `</li>`

5. `<li>`

6. Content for the second list item

7. `</li>`

8. `<li>`

9. Content for the third list item

10. `</li>`

11. `</ul>`

The following markup formats a three-item list as a bulleted list:

```
<!DOCTYPE html>
<html>
  <head>
    <meta charset="UTF-8">
    <title>Bulleted Lists</title>
  </head>

  <body>
    <h1>Things to do today</h1>
    <ul>
      <li>Feed cat</li>
      <li>Wash car</li>
      <li>Grocery shopping</li>
    </ul>
  </body>
</html>
```

Figure 5-10 shows how a browser renders this with bullets.

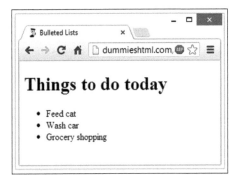

Figure 5-10: An unordered list uses bullets instead of numbers to mark items.

Use CSS to exert more control over the formatting of your lists, including the ability to use your own graphics as bullet symbols.

Definition lists

Definition lists group terms and definitions into a single list and require three elements to complete the list:

- ✔ <dl>: Holds the list definitions (dl = definition list)
- ✔ <dt>: Defines a term in the list (dt = definition term)
- ✔ <dd>: Defines a definition for a term (dd = definition list definition)

You can have as many terms (defined by <dt>) in a list (<dl>) as you need. Each term can have one or more definitions (defined by <dd>).

Creating a definition list with two items requires tags and content in the following order:

1. <dl>
2. <dt>
3. First term name
4. </dt>
5. <dd>
6. Content for the definition of the first item
7. </dd>
8. <dt>
9. Second term name
10. </dt>
11. <dd>
12. Content for the definition of the second item
13. </dd>
14. </dl>

The following definition list includes three terms, one of which has two definitions:

```
<!DOCTYPE html>
<html>
  <head>
    <meta charset="UTF-8" />
    <title>Definition Lists</title>
  </head>

  <body>
    <h1>Markup Language Definitions</h1>
    <dl>
      <dt>SGML</dt>
        <dd>The Standard Generalized Markup Language</dd>
      <dt>HTML</dt>
        <dd>The Hypertext Markup Language</dd>
        <dd>The markup language you use to create web pages.</dd>
      <dt>XML</dt>
        <dd>The Extensible Markup Language</dd>
    </dl>
  </body>
</html>
```

Figure 5-11 shows how a browser displays this HTML.

Figure 5-11: Definition lists group terms and their related definitions into one list.

If you think items in a list are too close together, you can use CSS styles to carefully control all aspects of list appearance, as shown in Chapters 14 and 17.

Note that definition lists often display differently inside different browsers, and they aren't always handled the same by search engines or text-to-speech translators. About.com has a nice discussion of definition lists at

```
http://webdesign.about.com/od/htmltags/a/aa112006.htm
```

Alas, this means that definition lists may not be the best choice of formatting for lists you create (even lists of definitions). For a more detailed discussion, see the excellent coverage of this topic at

```
www.maxdesign.com.au/articles/definition
```

Nesting lists

You can create subcategories by *nesting* lists within lists. Some common uses for nested lists include the following:

- Site maps and other navigation tools
- Tables of content for online books and papers
- Outlines

You can combine any of the three kinds of lists to create *nested lists,* such as a multilevel table of contents or an outline that mixes numbered headings with bulleted list items as the lowest outline level.

The following example starts with a numbered list that defines a list of things to do for the day and uses three bulleted lists to break down those items further into specific tasks:

```
<!DOCTYPE html>
<html>
  <head>
    <meta charset="UTF-8">
    <title>Nested Lists</title>
  </head>
  <body>
    <h1>Things to do today</h1>
    <ol>
      <li>Feed cat
        <ul>
          <li>Rinse bowl</li>
          <li>Open cat food</li>
          <li>Mix dry and wet food in bowl</li>
          <li>Deliver on a silver platter to Pixel</li>
        </ul></li>
      <li>Wash car
        <ul>
          <li>Vacuum interior</li>
          <li>Wash exterior</li>
          <li>Wax exterior</li>
        </ul></li>
```

```
        <li>Grocery shopping
          <ul>
            <li>Plan meals</li>
            <li>Clean out fridge</li>
            <li>Make list</li>
            <li>Go to store</li>
          </ul></li>
      </ol>
    </body>
</html>
```

All nested lists follow the same markup pattern:

- Each list item in the top-level ordered list is followed by a complete second-level list.

- The second-level lists sit inside the top-level list, not in the list items.

Figure 5-12 shows how a browser reflects this nesting in its display.

Figure 5-12: Nested lists combine lists for multilevel organization of information.

While you build nested lists, watch opening and closing tags carefully. "Close first what you opened last" is an important axiom. If you don't open and close tags properly, lists might not use consistent indents or numbers, or text might be indented incorrectly because a list somewhere was never properly closed.

6

Tip-Top Tables in HTML

In This Chapter

▷ Understanding table capabilities and benefits

▷ Getting to know the pieces and parts of table markup

▷ Mapping out a table design

▷ Building simple tables

▷ Graduating to complex tables

▷ Making the most of best table practices and techniques

*I*n HTML, tables make it easy to lay out data, text, and even images in a grid. Tables help make it easy to present numerical data (which naturally appears in tabular form in spreadsheets and other similar applications). But tables also make it easy and convenient to present all kinds of information that naturally falls into rows and columns, and to help maximize space when introducing lots of terms or other items that would waste too much white space if run up against the left or right margins on a page.

How <table> Got a Bad Name in HTML

Before we dig into the pile of markup you can use to contain and create tables in an HTML document, we must first discuss and dismiss a massive wrong turn that HTML markup took from the mid-1990s up through 2002. This was the period before CSS really made itself a force to be reckoned with in managing web page presentation, with its pinpoint controls over how elements are placed and positioned in a web browser.

Essentially, tables became a go-to design tool for web page layout because they were relatively easy to understand, specify, and use. Designers employed tables to manage what pages looked like and where individual elements would appear. This technique proved especially useful for creating multicolumn page layouts — a technique still beloved by many web page designers even today. But because CSS can handle such things more directly and easily, there's no reason to use tables for that purpose any more.

However, the "table era" in web page design left a bad taste in the mouths of many web page designers. Since then, too many of them have decided to forgo tables altogether simply because they were put to inappropriate uses at a time when CSS couldn't pick up the slack.

Today, we think it's time to redeem tables and to put them back to work where it makes sense to use them. When you have lots of numbers, or numerous fields of text information that fall naturally into rows and columns tables can be useful and informative. What's more, they provide the most compact and intelligible way to present such information on a web page, so you should use them for that purpose.

What's in a Table? LOTS of Markup

The primary markup container for tables in HTML is the table element. That is, you use the opening `<table>` tag to denote the start of a table, and you add the closing `</table>` tag to end it. Also, the basic building blocks for table data in HTML are the table row (`<tr>`) and table data (`<td>`) elements, when a table consists of as many rows as there are `<tr>` elements (plus any header or footer rows) and as many columns as the maximum number of `<td>` elements in any given table row.

Between these opening and closing tags, you can find the following elements in this very interesting and prescribed (in other words, mandatory) order:

- **Zero or one `<caption>` elements** to define a caption for a table (if there's one such element, or no caption for the table if it is absent). If it is used, a `<caption>` element must follow immediately after the opening `<table>` tag.

- **Zero or one column group (`<colgroup>`) elements** to define column groupings for the table (if there's one such element, or no column groupings if the element is absent). It must appear after any `<caption>` element, if one is present, and before any of the following table elements.

- **Zero or one table heading (`<thead>`) elements** to define the heading section for a table (if there's one such element, or no table heading section if the element is absent). Often, a first table heading row spans the entire width of the table to identify the whole thing, and the first heading row is followed by a second row of individual headings for each column in the table.

- **Zero or more table body (`<tbody>`) elements** to identify actual content for the table. A table may have multiple `<tbody>` elements, so it's unusual in HTML in that a table can have only one head but multiple bodies!

✔ **Zero or one table footer (`<tfoot>`)** to provide information for the bottom of a table. Browsers can use `<thead>`, `<tbody>`, and `<tfoot>` to decide what to scroll (the table body, usually) and what to leave always present on the screen. The table footer is a special case when it comes to where in the sequence of table markup it can appear. It can always appear last in the sequence (as it does in this list), but it can also appear right after any of these elements that are present (in this order): `<caption>`, `<colgroup>`, and `<thead>`. However, it would appear before `<tbody>` and `<tr>` elements. In this special case, `<tfoot>` cannot also appear at the end of the table. Not allowed!

✔ **If there is no `<tbody>` element present** (which would ordinarily define the table body in a table with a defined table header and possibly also a footer section), the table row (`<tr>`) element defines rows for the data that the table actually presents. Inside each table row are as many table data (`<td>`) elements as there are cells in that row.

Because HTML table syntax and markup order can be tricky and complicated, it's even more worthwhile than usual to run all of your table markup through the W3C validator (`http://validator.w3.org`) to make sure it's correct.

The structure of an HTML table is easier to understand if we represent it by using basic container markup only, with some hopefully illuminating comments, like so:

```
<!DOCTYPE html>
<html>
  <head>
    <meta charset="UTF-8">
    <title>Basic Table Markup Structure and Sequence</title>
  </head>
  <body>
    <table border="1">
      <caption>Table 6-1: HTML Markup Structure and Sequence</caption>
      <thead><tr><th>Element</th><th>Description</th></tr></thead>
      <!-- inside all table containers, you still use table rows -->
      <!-- this includes thead, tbody, and tfoot as shown here   -->
      <!-- Use th for bold headings in both header and footer     -->
      <tbody>
        <tr><td>table</td><td>overall table container</td></tr>
        <tr><td>caption</td><td>table caption text</td></tr>
        <tr><td>tbody</td><td>table body container</td></tr>
        <tr><td>tfoot</td><td>table footer container</td></tr>
      </tbody>
      <tfoot><tr><td>Element</td><td>Description</td></tr></tfoot>
    </table>
  </body>
</html>
```

Figure 6-1 shows how a browser displays this table. (We added the `border="1"` entry to the `table` element to draw an outline around the edge of each table cell, which makes the table stand out a little better.)

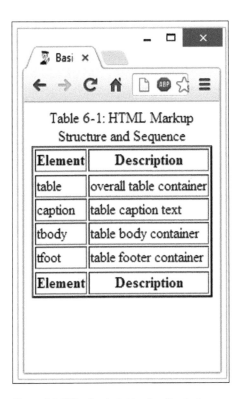

Figure 6-1: This simple table also illustrates typical HTML table structure.

Setting Up a Table Border

As shown in the HTML document rendered earlier in Figure 6-1, you can apply the `border` attribute to the table element like this:

```
<table border="1">
```

This is an interesting beast in that you must define the border as having the value one (`"1"`) for it to validate properly. Even so, our various test browsers showed us a border around the table as long as any value was supplied for the `border` attribute. To turn off the border, we had to remove the `border="`*`value`*`"` text entirely from the markup. Earlier versions of HTML used the value to define the width of the border around the table. That's no longer the case for HTML5, where it's strictly a toggle (turns on border if present, no border if absent). You must use CSS to control table border thickness, shading, color, and all the other great properties it allows you to manage.

The Table Head (<thead>) and Its Elements

In the preceding section, we discuss numerous elements associated with the head of an HTML table, itself a table element called `<thead>`. Those table elements are summarized in . . . wait for it . . . Table 6-1! (Alas, to build this puppy, we had to use Word's far-less-transparent table-handling features rather than the glorious and crystal clear HTML markup we prefer.)

Table 6-1	HTML Table Head Markup
Element	*Description/Notes*
caption	Encloses a caption for the table (appears above the table content).
colgroup	Specifies properties for a group of columns within a table. (Use the col element within a colgroup element to apply properties on a per-column basis.)
col	Specifies per-column properties within a column group.
thead	Defines the overall container for table header content.
tr	Identifies each row of content inside a table header.
th or td	Use th for bold, centered column heads; use td for plain, left-justified heads.

A complex table heading might have multiple rows of headings above the columns and do interesting things with column properties. Here's some slightly more advanced markup to give you an idea of what this can mean. Here we take the markup rendered in Figure 6-1 and snaz up the table headings and column handling. Figure 6-2 shows the results.

```
<!DOCTYPE html>
<html>
  <head>
    <meta charset="UTF-8">
    <title>Basic Table Markup Structure and Sequence</title>
  </head>
```

```
<body>
  <table border="1">
    <caption>Table 6-1: HTML Markup Structure and Sequence</caption>
    <colgroup>
       <col style="background-color: orange; font-size: 120%;">
       <col style="background-color: gray; color: white;"
    </colgroup>
    <thead>
       <tr> <th colspan="2">Table Markup Explained</th></tr>
       <tr><th>Element</th><th>Description</th></tr>
    </thead>
    <!-- inside all table containers, you still use table rows -->
    <!-- this includes thead, tbody, and tfoot as shown here   -->
    <!-- Use th for bold headings in both header and footer     -->
    <tbody>
       <tr><td>table</td><td>overall table container</td></tr>
       <tr><td>caption</td><td>table caption text</td></tr>
       <tr><td>tbody</td><td>table body container</td></tr>
       <tr><td>tfoot</td><td>table footer container</td></tr>
    </tbody>
    <tfoot><tr><th>Element</th><th>Description</th></tr></tfoot>
  </table>
  </body>
</html>
```

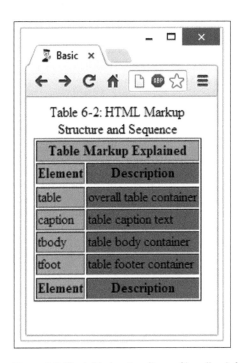

Figure 6-2: The table has two lines of heading information,
and the colors for table columns spice it up.

Managing Table Layouts

If you look at things the right way, all the interesting capability and complexity in HTML tables builds from three basic elements:

- ✔ **Borders:** Every basic table has exactly four edges that compose a rectangle.

- ✔ **Cells:** These are the individual areas for data, information, images, or whatever, inside the borders of a table.

- ✔ **Cell span:** Within the four-walled structure of a table, you can add or delete cell walls (as shown with the cells on the right side of the table in Figure 6-3). When you delete cell walls, you make a cell *span* multiple rows or columns — and that's exactly what makes tables so flexible in accommodating different and interesting cell arrangements.

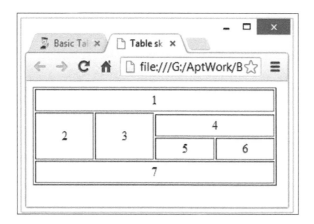

Figure 6-3: It's not quite a Chinese puzzle box layout, but it is visually interesting.

Cell spanning and cell width work differently. When you span cells, you change cell space by combining or merging cells. This step removes cell walls, so to speak. When you adjust the dimensions of a cell, usually using CSS `width` and `height` controls, you can specify how much space they will occupy. In Figure 6-3, we show how you can create an interesting layout simply by spanning the cells in the top and bottom rows (labeled 1 and 7), with two left cells (cells 2 and 3) that span two rows, and three right cells (cell 4 spanning two columns, and cells 5 and 6 side by side).

Leaving aside details on how to control overall table width and individual cell heights and widths, here's what the basic HTML for such a table looks like:

```
<!DOCTYPE html>
<html>
  <head>
    <meta charset="UTF-8">
    <title>Table sketch</title>
  </head>
  <body>
    <table border="1">
      <tr><td colspan="4"> 1 </td></tr>
      <tr><td rowspan="3" > 2 </td>
          <td rowspan="3" > 3 </td></tr>
      <tr><td colspan="2"> 4 </td></tr>
      <tr><td> 5 </td><td> 6 </td></tr>
      <tr><td colspan="4"> 7 </td></tr>
    </table>
  </body>
</html>
```

Tables can become complex. You need to plan them carefully. You can find the HTML file for the preceding figure on the book's website at:

`www.dummieshtml.com/html5cafe/ch06/06fig03.html`

Careful examination of this file shows that we included numbers for each of the boxes in that table, numbered 1 through 7, to demonstrate how the table lays out. As you're developing your own table structures, we encourage you to take a similar approach so you can see and understand exactly what you're doing. Try labeling the individual boxes with incrementing numbers so you can see how the organization plays itself out on a web page.

You don't need to populate your table with real content or mess around much with the sizing approach that the file contains in its CSS style sections. (Using CSS style is covered in Chapters 11 through 19 of this book.) Count the total number of cells across in your table (four in the example case presented in the preceding section), add one to that number, and then multiply the result by four em-widths to get the table width (20em in the example). Use 4em as the cell width in the table data (`<td>`) element style information, and you're good to go. If you keep the overall table width in sync with the number of cells across, you can't go wrong!

After you've worked out all the kinks with the arrangement of the individual cells, you can start tweaking the style attributes to your heart's content to make the table as readable and attractive as possible. First, though, you'll want to get the arrangement right. After that, everything else is window dressing.

Making Good Table Bodies

If you want to get a really good idea about the representational power of HTML tables, you could do a lot worse than to check out the monthly *Employment Situation Summary* that the United States Bureau of Labor Statistics cranks out near the beginning of each month to report on the previous month's employment (and unemployment) statistics. You can find archived versions of these reports at:

```
www.bls.gov/schedule/archives/empsit_nr.htm
```

For the discussion that follows, we used the report archived for March 2013 as the data source. You can find that report at:

```
www.bls.gov/news.release/archives/empsit_04052013.htm
```

It was published on April 5, 2013, in case you're wondering about the numbers at the end of the HTML filename you see. To open that page, you can type the URL if you like, or visit the Chapter 6 section of our HTML5 Cafe to access a live link. If you call that page up in your web browser and scroll down a bit, you see a whole slew of tables, including Summary Tables A and B, and then a bit farther down inside this mammoth document are Tables A-1 through A-15, and B-1 through B-9. That's a lot of tables!

By all means, please dig into the source markup for these tables. (You can access them by clicking the tool icon at the far top-right corner in Chrome, then clicking Tools, and then clicking View Source. In Internet Explorer, simply click the View menu and choose Source. Similar methods apply to Firefox, Safari, Opera, and so forth.) The source markup is a great source of information and inspiration for how to make good use of HTML table markup, as well as how CSS helps you control the positioning, formatting, look, and feel of such tables. It takes some time to puzzle through these examples (they're BIG), but they will repay your efforts with insight and understanding. Try it: It's a great way to hone your skills.

Shaping a solid table

For this table-construction exercise, you're going to draw some data from the hard-working economists and statisticians at the U.S. Bureau of Labor Statistics. Go to `www.bls.gov/news.release/archives/empsit_04052013.htm` and scroll down to Table B-9: Indexes of Aggregate Weekly Hours and Payroll, shown in Figure 6-4. The figure no-doubt shows teeny-tiny type, but it should nonetheless give you some idea of what you're looking for online.

ESTABLISHMENT DATA
Table B-9. Indexes of aggregate weekly hours and payrolls for production and nonsupervisory employees on private nonfarm payrolls by industry sector, seasonally adjusted(1)
[2002=100]

Industry	Index of aggregate weekly hours(2)					Index of aggregate weekly payrolls(3)				
	Mar. 2012	Jan. 2013	Feb. 2013(a)	Mar. 2013(a)	Percent change from: Feb. 2013 - Mar. 2013(a)	Mar. 2012	Jan. 2013	Feb. 2013(a)	Mar. 2013(a)	Percent change from: Feb. 2013 - Mar. 2013(a)
Total private	103.5	104.7	105.5	105.6	0.1	136.0	139.7	141.2	141.3	0.1
Goods-producing	83.6	84.1	84.8	84.8	0.0	106.9	108.6	109.8	109.9	0.1
Mining and logging	161.5	150.2	156.3	155.5	-0.5	240.3	229.1	238.4	237.4	-0.4
Construction	84.1	85.5	86.6	87.3	0.8	108.5	111.8	113.3	114.3	0.9
Manufacturing	80.2	80.5	81.0	80.6	-0.5	99.8	100.9	101.8	101.4	-0.4
Durable goods	81.2	81.5	82.1	82.0	-0.1	102.0	102.8	103.6	103.6	0.0
Nondurable goods	78.6	78.8	78.9	78.7	-0.3	95.8	97.2	98.2	97.7	-0.5
Private service-providing	109.1	110.6	111.1	111.6	0.5	145.2	149.6	150.8	151.3	0.3
Trade, transportation, and utilities	101.5	102.3	102.9	103.1	0.2	125.7	128.2	129.3	129.4	0.1
Wholesale trade	103.2	105.2	105.7	105.4	-0.3	134.6	138.4	139.5	139.4	-0.1
Retail trade	99.2	98.3	98.8	99.2	0.4	117.3	117.4	117.9	118.6	0.6
Transportation and warehousing	107.7	111.3	111.9	113.1	1.1	133.9	137.9	139.0	139.8	0.6
Utilities	91.2	93.9	97.2	96.9	-0.3	118.5	126.3	130.6	130.1	-0.4
Information	88.8	88.4	88.8	89.0	0.2	117.9	121.5	122.0	122.0	0.0
Financial activities	102.7	103.9	104.2	104.2	0.0	142.1	150.0	151.3	151.7	0.3
Professional and business services	115.7	118.8	120.1	120.5	0.3	159.9	166.6	168.5	169.3	0.5
Education and health services	124.0	125.3	125.9	125.7	-0.2	171.3	175.3	176.7	176.0	-0.4
Leisure and hospitality	110.6	112.6	112.9	113.6	0.6	145.8	149.0	150.2	151.0	0.5
Other services	98.0	98.2	98.8	98.2	-0.6	125.0	127.3	128.6	127.3	-1.0

Footnotes
[1] Data relate to production employees in mining and logging and manufacturing, construction employees in construction, and nonsupervisory employees in the service-providing industries. These groups account for approximately four-fifths of the total employment on private nonfarm payrolls.
[2] The indexes of aggregate weekly hours are calculated by dividing the current month's estimates of aggregate hours by the corresponding 2002 annual average aggregate hours. Aggregate hours estimates are the product of estimates of average weekly hours and employment.
[3] The indexes of aggregate weekly payrolls are calculated by dividing the current month's estimates of aggregate weekly payrolls by the corresponding 2002 annual average aggregate weekly payrolls. Aggregate payrolls estimates are the product of estimates of average hourly earnings, average weekly hours, and employment.
[a] Preliminary

Figure 6-4: As tables in the Employment Situation Summary go, B-9 is simple and compact.

As you examine Table B-9, here's what you see:

1. The caption at the top is a sort of rust color and begins with ESTABLISHMENT DATA Table B-9: Indexes of Aggregate. . . . This kind of information is just what the caption element is intended to capture and deliver.

2. Below the caption is a set of table headings — a table header, in other words — with a light gray background and various column headings. At the left is a list of industries. Then the table has two sets of columns (labeled Index of Aggregate Weekly Hours and Index of Aggregate Weekly Payrolls), each with four columns of dates and a Percent Change column from February to March 2013.

3. The table body starts with text that reads Total Private and continues down 19 rows until it gets to Other Services, with rows in column 1 (Industry) alternating between a white and a light blue background color. After that, the two sets of columns spell out data for aggregate weekly hours and weekly payrolls, respectively, with five individual columns in each set: March 2012, January through March 2013, and a percent change from the previous month (February 2013) to the present month (March 2013).

4. The table footer includes three footnotes numbered 1 through 3. The special marker, (p), indicates preliminary (that is, not final) data.

Guess what? You already know how to mark up all of this data! We don't spell out all the details completely, though you're welcome to play around with this information to recreate the table if you like. We can tell you how to build such a table by the numbers, as it were:

1. The table caption can be captured inside a `caption` element. You can use the line break (`<br>`) element to break the line after ESTABLISHMENT DATA and before the actual detailed caption that begins Table B-9: Indexes of Aggregate. . . . Use the line break element again to break the line before stating the scale indicator "[2002=100]."

2. All of the headings should be contained inside a `<thead>` element. You use the table heading (`<th>`) element for each heading cell, so it will be centered and in boldface inside each such cell. The Industry cell should take a `rowspan="2"` attribute so it fills the entire height of the header area at left, and the Index of . . . cells should each take a `colspan="5"` attribute so each one covers the four date and percent change columns for its category. All three of those items will appear in the first table heading row, each in its own table heading (`<th>`) cell. The remaining ten items appear in the second table heading row in their order of appearance in the table. Each of those ten items also appears in its own table heading (`<th>`) cell. Setting widths for the Industry and various date and percentage columns in the CSS for the header sets widths for the entire rest of the table.

3. In the table body, one row corresponds to each line of data from the online source, starting with the industry name at left and then continuing with the numerical values for dates and percentages in each of the two groups at the right. This task involves 11 table data (`<td>`) elements for each row shown in that table. Very simple, very mechanical, very easy.

4. The table footer entries all appear in a footer section, which should take a `colspan="11"` attribute to flow across the entire width of the table. The Footnotes legend can appear inside a single table row (`<tr>`) and table data (`<td>`) cell, the latter set to boldface. (Don't use `<th>`, or the footnote text will be centered.) Each remaining footnote appears inside a single table row and table data cell as indicated in the table.

By using these techniques, you can create a solid, attractive table for presenting numerical and textual data. If you take your time and think your way through what you want your users to see, you can build a preliminary structure in HTML. Then you can start arranging cells and tweaking them until you get them just right. You and Goldilocks — what a team!

Sitting at the Footer of the Table

As the table example from the preceding section shows, you can do all kinds of interesting things with the footer. Here are some ideas for information that you might want to include, should your data require interpretation, explanation, or additional information:

- Use footnotes with numeric or letter keys to provide information about specific entries. Where such entries recur, one common footnote entry works well to label such information. For instance, in the table from Figure 6-4, the (p) for preliminary occurs in multiple column headings, but has just one footnote.

- If your table features icons, specific graphical elements, or special characters as labels, you can use the footer to provide a legend or a key for such things. You can set up a simple two-column layout with the icon or whatever on the left and its explanation or value on the right.

- When you reproduce tabular data from an online or published source, you can use a footer entry to provide proper attribution to the source, along with a link to the original (which many owners of copyrighted material require you to include).

- When your tables repeat over time — as with the U.S. Bureau of Labor Statistics reports — you can include notes in the footer to explain what's new, what's been removed, or what's changed as the content and layout adapt to fluid events and situations.

- Where data cell values result from specific calculations or corrections, you can use footer information to document the calculations that apply, or the corrections used to produce the data shown.

We could go on forever in this vein, but we have to imagine you have the idea by this point and can go on to spin out more ideas and applications for table footers. Go ahead: Knock yourself out. We approve!

Exploring and Explaining a Table

We have uploaded the HTML markup for Table B-9 to the HTML5 Cafe website. You can find it at:

`www.dummieshtml.com/html5cafe/ch06/TableB-9.html`

If you look through this markup, you can see that we did an almost-perfect job of predicting how the table was architected. In fact, the only item we got wrong deals with the table footer — of which there isn't one. Instead, the U.S. Bureau of Labor Statistics page designers elected to include straightforward text paragraphs for the footnote head, and each of the footnotes that follow, before closing out the table markup. This keeps the text inside the table frame without obligating column management for text data that's intended to span the entire width of the table anyway.

Oh caption, my caption

The caption uses a line break element to separate the all-caps ESTABLISHMENT DATA from the actual table name (Table B-9: Indexes of Aggregate Weekly Hours . . .). But the separation of the scale information ([2002=100]) depends on use of a pair of span elements in the thead section, which forces a line break when transitioning from the main caption text to this supplementary label.

If you examine the table header source code in the file, you also find that they use inter-document links (explained in Chapter 8) to make it easy to jump directly to footnotes as they appear in the table. (Savvy users employ a Back button or backspace key to return to whence they jumped, too.) These are all nice touches worth emulating.

Is the header dead yet?

With all apologies to Glenn Frey for this section title, there's nothing to complain about in how the U.S. Bureau of Labor Statistics designers put this table head together in the table shown earlier in Figure 6-4. They used the `rowspan` and `colspan` attributes in the first table row to get the layout as it appears, and the column headings in the second row march out in sequence just as they should.

As you look at the source code, notice how the designer lays out each row in the table: You see a pair of `<tr></tr>` tags for each row, along with just the right number of data cells (usually denoted `<td></td>`). But because we're in the header section for this table, you can use table heading (`<th>`) markup to make up a complete table row by creating the proper number of cells.

You can say what you like about the Feds, but this is some of the most readable production HTML we've ever seen. Even if it isn't HTML5 (yet), it's incredibly clean, well laid out, and easy to read and follow. (Maybe all those taxpayer dollars aren't being wasted after all.)

Marching through the table body

If you look at the individual table rows in the markup, you can see the same regular, predictable structure repeating for each one. The difference between the Industry cells (which appear with alternating blue and white backgrounds) hinges on the alternating presence or absence of a `greenbar` class for the table row in which they reside. Each table row follows a regular structure, with a table heading (`<th>`) cell in the industry column at the far left, and table data (`<td>`) cells for all remaining data in the other ten cells in each row.

Here's the markup for one row in the body of Table B-9 to give you a taste of what it looks and reads like:

```
<tr>
  <th id="ces_table9.r.1"><p class="sub0">Total private</p></th>
  <td><span class="datavalue">103.5</span></td>
  <td><span class="datavalue">104.7</span></td>
  <td><span class="datavalue">105.5</span></td>
  <td><span class="datavalue">105.6</span></td>
  <td><span class="datavalue">0.1</span></td>
  <td><span class="datavalue">136.0</span></td>
  <td><span class="datavalue">139.7</span></td>
  <td><span class="datavalue">141.2</span></td>
  <td><span class="datavalue">141.3</span></td>
  <td><span class="datavalue">0.1</span></td>
</tr>
```

The special `datavalue` CSS class formats data value cells (columns 2 through 11) with a unique CSS identifier (`ces_table9.r.1`) for the left-most cell. A paragraph class (`sub0`) designates CSS for the heading that reads "Total Private" in the preceding HTML snippet. That's how detailed layout, positioning, and appearance controls are applied to table information throughout. But what's most noteworthy is how simple, regular, and predictable the overall markup is. Our best guess: A program is generating that HTML automatically, probably from a spreadsheet somewhere.

Finishing with the footer

We admit it once again: We expected to see a table footer (`<tfoot>` element) at the bottom of the table shown earlier in Figure 6-4. What we saw instead was a second table body (`<tbody>`) with a single table row (and yes, with a single data cell `<td colspan="11">`). However, within that lone table data cell, the content is laid out in a single paragraph (using the `<p>` element), with manual line breaks (`<br>`) between each individual footnote. Here's what that markup looks like:

```
<tbody>
  <tr class="footnotes">
    <td class="footnotes" colspan="11">
      <p class="footnotes">
      <span class="footnotestitle">Footnotes<br /></span>
<a id="ces_table9.f.1" name="ces_table9.f.1">(1) </a>Data relate to production
            employees in mining and logging and manufacturing, construction
            employees in construction, and nonsupervisory employees in
            the service-providing industries. These groups account for
            approximately four-fifths of the total employment on private
            nonfarm payrolls.<br />
<a id="ces_table9.f.2" name="ces_table9.f.2">(2) </a>The indexes of aggregate
            weekly hours are calculated by dividing the current month's
            estimates of aggregate hours by the corresponding 2002 annual
            average aggregate hours. Aggregate hours estimates are the product
            of estimates of average weekly hours and employment.<br />
<a id="ces_table9.f.3" name="ces_table9.f.3">(3) </a>The indexes of aggregate
            weekly payrolls are calculated by dividing the current month's
            estimates of aggregate weekly payrolls by the corresponding 2002
            annual average aggregate weekly payrolls. Aggregate payrolls
            estimates are the product of estimates of average hourly earnings,
            average weekly hours, and employment.<br />
<a id="ces_table9.f.p" name="ces_table9.f.p">(p) </a>Preliminary<br />
      </p>
    </td>
  </tr>
</tbody>
```

There's absolutely nothing wrong with this approach, but there's no reason why the designers couldn't have used the `<tfoot>` element instead, either. That's the nice thing about learning HTML: When you get acquainted with the structure and the syntax, you quickly discover that you have many ways to do what needs to be done. This one works quite nicely and is very readable.

7

Working with Forms in HTML

In This Chapter

▷ Using forms in your web pages

▷ Creating forms

▷ Working with form data

▷ Designing easy-to-use forms

▷ Making forms easy with a form framework

*M*ost of the HTML you write helps you display content and information for your users. Sometimes, however, you want a web page to gather information from users instead of giving static information to them. HTML *form markup elements* give you a healthy collection of tags and attributes for creating forms to collect information from visitors to your site.

This chapter covers the many uses for forms. It also shows you how to use form markup tags to solicit information from your users, reviews your options for working with data you receive, and gives you tips on creating easy-to-use forms that help users provide the information you're looking for.

Exploring Types of Web Forms

The web contains millions of forms, and every form is driven by the same set of markup tags. Web forms can be short or long, simple or complex, with myriad uses. But forms all fall into one of two broad categories:

✓ **Search forms** that let users search a site or the entire web

✓ **Data collection forms** that provide information for online shopping, technical support, site preferences, personalization, and more

Before you create any form, you must determine what kind of data your visitors will search for on your site and/or what kind of data you need to collect from visitors. Data drives the form elements that you use and how you put them together on a page.

Search forms

Search forms help you give visitors information.

The following search forms are from the friendly folks at the Internal Revenue Service (IRS). The difference between these search forms is the data the IRS site needs from you for its search:

- The IRS forms and publications search page (shown in Figure 7-1) is a simple, multifaceted search form featuring current IRS documents to help visitors search for tax forms and publications. This type of page can pinpoint relevant responses for searches by document number or title. Visitors can

  - Choose the best option to meet their search criteria.

  - Look at all relevant options.

- There's a whole list of File Fillable Forms that permit online filing for most of the common IRS tax forms, including Form 1040ES (estimated tax), Form 1040A (and all the related schedules, of which there are about two dozen), and many more.

- You can use the Online Payment Agreement (OPA) form to set up a payment plan with the IRS. It's a two-parter where you pick from a number of radio buttons to describe your status and situation in the first part, and then provide your taxpayer ID, date of birth, and so forth in the second part.

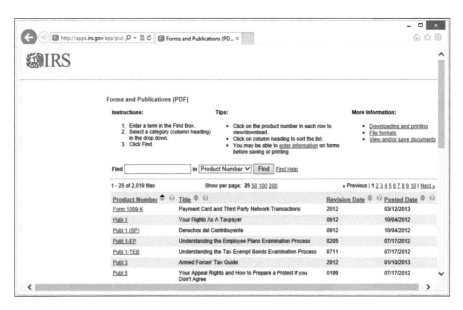

Figure 7-1: The IRS forms search page offers access to forms and related publications.

Searches come in all shapes and sizes, so the search forms that drive those searches come in all shapes and sizes, too. A short keyword search might do the trick, or you might need a more sophisticated search method.

Data collection forms

Data collection forms receive information you want to process or save. When you create a form that collects information, the information you need is what drives the structure and complexity of the form:

- **Just a little:** If you need just a little information, the form may be short and (relatively) sweet.

  Example: The Library of Congress (LoC) uses a form to collect information from teachers to subscribe to a free electronic newsletter, as shown in Figure 7-2. The LoC doesn't need much information to set up the subscription, so the form is short and simple.

Figure 7-2: A free subscription form collects basic information.

- **Lots:** If you need a lot of information, your form may be several pages long.

  Example: RateGenius uses long and detailed forms to gather the information it needs to help customers refinance a vehicle loan. The page in Figure 7-3 shows just the first two of numerous panes that a visitor must fill out to provide all the necessary information.

Figure 7-3: Some sites use many detailed forms to collect necessary data.

Creating Forms

HTML forms can present information to users, using text and images. But it can also proffer various types of other methods of presenting information, including the following:

- **Text input fields,** including in-line, single line, or multiple lines
- **Data selection tools,** such as radio buttons (which let you pick one option from a group)
- **Pick lists,** which let you fill in a value from a predefined set of options
- **Check boxes,** which enable you to pick zero, one, or more values from a predefined set of inputs

All in all, HTML form markup tags and attributes help you

- Define the overall form structure.
- Tell the web browser how to handle form data.
- Create input objects, such as text fields and drop-down lists.

Every form has the same basic structure. Also, which input elements you use depends upon the data you're presenting and collecting.

Structure

The <form> element is a content and input container: It works much like the paragraph (<p>) element, which contains paragraph text, or like the division (<div>) element, which contains various types of sub-elements in a logical document section. Thus, all input elements associated with a single form are

- ✔ Contained within a <form> element.
- ✔ Processed by the same form handler.

A *form handler* is a program on the web server (or a simple mailto: URL) that manages the data a user sends to you through the form. A web browser can only gather information through forms; it doesn't know what to do with the information after it has grabbed it. You must provide another mechanism to actually *do* something useful with data you collect in any form. (This chapter covers form handlers in brief later in the "Processing Data" section.)

Attributes

You always use these two key attributes with the <form> tag:

- ✔ action: The URL for the form handler
- ✔ method: How you want form data to be sent to the form handler

   Your form handler dictates which of the following values to use for method. (Your hosting or service provider probably has a document that describes how to invoke your local web server's form handler, including those oh-so-necessary details — and probably some examples, too.)

   - • get sends the form data to the form handler on the URL.
   - • post sends the form data in the HyperText Transfer Protocol (HTTP) header.

Webmonkey reviews the difference between get and post in its "Add HTML Forms to Your Site" article at www.webmonkey.com/2010/02/add_html_forms_to_your_site. You can also find a great discussion of HTML5 forms markup at http://msdn.microsoft.com/en-us/magazine/hh547102.aspx.

Markup

The markup in Listing 7-1 creates a form that uses the post method to send user-entered information to a form handler (guestbook.php) to be processed on the web server.

Listing 7-1: A Simple Form Processed by a Form Handler

```
<!DOCTYPE html>
<html>
<head>
    <title>Forms</title>
    <meta charset="UTF-8" />
</head>
<body>
    <form action="bin/guestbook.php" method="post">

    <!-- form input elements go here -->

    </form>
</body>
</html>
```

The value of the `action` attribute is a URL, so you can use absolute or relative URLs to point to a form handler on your server. Absolute and relative URLs are covered in more detail in Chapter 8.

Input tags

The tags you use to solicit input from your site visitors make up the bulk of any form. HTML supports a variety of input options, from text fields to radio buttons and from files to images.

Every input control associates some value with a name:

- ✔ When you create the control, you give it a name.
- ✔ The control sends back a value based on what the user does in the form.

For example, if you create a text field that collects a user's first name, you might name the field `firstname`. When the user types her first name in the field and submits the form, the value associated with `firstname` is whatever name the user typed in the field.

The whole point of a form is to gather values associated with input controls, so how you set the name and value for each control is important. The following sections explain how you should work with names and values for each of the input controls.

The `<input>` element (and by extension, the empty `<input ... >` tag) is the major player when it comes to using HTML forms to solicit user input. Inside the `<input>` element is where you define the kinds of input you want to collect, and how you package and present the input fields and cues you present to users so they can give you what you're asking for.

Input fields

You can use a variety of input field types in your forms, such as text, password, radio (button), checkbox, hidden, search, tel (telephone number), url, email (address), datetime, date, month, week, time, datetime-local, number, range (sets a range of numeric values), color, and more. Not all fields require values for name and type attributes (for example, text box or password fields), but it's a good idea to provide users with explanatory labels and examples of input data any time they might have questions about formats — such as when pondering whether to include dashes or spaces in credit card numbers. Check boxes and radio buttons, on the other hand, require such information so they can be properly labeled when the browser shows users what selections are available.

For input elements that require a user to select an option (a check box or radio button) rather than typing something into a field, you define both the name and the value. When the user selects a check box or a radio button and then clicks Submit, the form returns the name and value assigned to the element.

We discuss these two types of input fields in the upcoming section, "Check boxes and radio buttons."

Text fields

Text fields are single-line fields into which users type information. When you need to offer the user the opportunity to fill in more than one line, you use a text box, as we discuss in the upcoming section, "Multiline text boxes."

Here's how to create a single-line text field:

1. **Define the input type as a text field by using the** `<input />` **element with the** `type` **attribute set to** `text`.

   ```
   <input type="text">
   ```

2. **Then use the** `name` **attribute to give the input field a name.**

   ```
   <input type="text" name="firstname">
   ```

   The user supplies the value when she types in the field.

The following markup creates two text input fields, one for a first name and one for a last name:

```
<form action="bin/guestbook.php" method="post">
<ul style="list-style-type: none;">
  <li>First Name: <input type="text" name="firstname"></li>
  <li>Last Name: <input type="text" name="lastname"></li>
</ul>
</form>
```

In addition to the `<input >` elements, the preceding markup includes list (`<ul>` and `<li>`) elements and some text to label each input field. By themselves, most form elements don't give many clues about the type of information you want them to enter. Lists are covered in more detail in Chapter 5.

You must use HTML block and inline elements to format the appearance of your form and also to supply the necessary text. Figure 7-4 shows how a browser displays this kind of HTML. (To see the markup that produced this figure, visit `www.dummieshtml.com/html5cafe/ch07/07fig04.html`.)

Figure 7-4: Text entry fields in a form.

You can control the size of a text field with these attributes:

- ✔ `size`: The length (in characters) of the text field

- ✔ `maxlength`: The maximum number of characters the user can type into the field

The following markup creates a form that sets both fields to a `size` of 30 (characters long) and a `maxlength` of 25 (characters long). Even though each field will be about 30 characters long, a user can type only 25 characters into each field, as shown in Figure 7-5. (Setting the `size` attribute greater than `maxlength` ensures that the text field will always have some white space between the user input and the end of the field box on display; you don't have to do this yourself, but we find it visually pleasing.)

```
<form action="bin/guestbook.php" method="post">
<ul style="list-style-type: none;">
  <li>First Name: <input type="text" name="firstname" size="30"
      maxlength="25"></li>
  <li>Last Name: <input type="text" name="lastname" size="30"
      maxlength="25"></li>
</ul>
</form>
```

Figure 7-5: You can specify the length and maximum number of characters for a text field.

Password fields

A *password field* is a special text field that doesn't display what the user types. Each keystroke is represented on the screen by a placeholder character, such as an asterisk or a bullet, so that someone looking over the user's shoulder can't see what they type.

You create a password field by using the `<input>` element with the `type` attribute set to `password`, as follows:

```
<form action="bin/guestbook.php" method="post">
<ul style="list-style-type: none;">
  <li>First Name: <input type="text" name="firstname" size="30"
      maxlength="25"></li>
  <li>Last Name: <input type="text" name="lastname" size="30"
      maxlength="25"></li>
  <li>Password: <input type="password" name="psswd" size="30"
      maxlength="25"></li>
</ul>
</form>
```

Password fields are programmed like text fields.

Figure 7-6 shows how a browser replaces what you type with bullets. ***Note:*** Depending on the browser's default settings, some browsers replace the text with asterisks or some other character.

Figure 7-6: Password fields mask the text a user enters.

Check boxes and radio buttons

If only a finite set of possible values is available to the user, you can give him a collection of options to choose from:

- **Check boxes:** Choose more than one option.

- **Radio buttons:** Choose only one option.

  Radio buttons differ from check boxes in an important way: Users can select a single radio button from a set of options but can select any number of check boxes (including none, one, or more than one).

If many choices are available (more than half a dozen), use a drop-down list instead of radio buttons or check boxes. We show you how to create those in the upcoming section, "Drop-down list fields."

To create radio buttons and check boxes, take these steps:

1. **Use the `<input>` element with the `type` attribute set to `radio` or `checkbox`.**

2. **Create each option with these attributes:**

   - `name`: Give the option a name.

   - `value`: Specify what value is returned if the user selects the option.

You can also use the `checked` attribute (with a value of `checked`) to specify that an option should be already selected when the browser displays the form. This is a good way to specify a default selection.

This markup shows how to format check box and radio button options:

```
<form action="bin/guestbook.php" method="post">
<p>What are some of your favorite foods?</p>
<ul style="list-style-type: none;">
  <li><input type="checkbox" name="food" value="pizza" checked="checked">
    Pizza</li>
    <li><input type="checkbox" name="food" value="icecream">Ice Cream</li>
    <li><input type="checkbox" name="food" value="eggsham">Green Eggs
        and Ham</li>
</ul>

<p>What is your gender?</p>
<ul style="list-style-type: none;">
  <li><input type="radio" name="gender" value="male">Male</li>
    <li><input type="radio" name="gender" value="female" checked="checked">
    Female</li>
</ul>
</form>
```

The result is shown in Figure 7-7.

Figure 7-7: Radio and text buttons let users select from a list of predefined options.

In the preceding markup, each set of options uses the same name for each input control but gives a different value to each option. You give each item in a set of options the same name to let the browser know they're part of a set. If you want to, you can select as many check boxes as you like by default in the page markup — simply include `checked="checked"` in each `<input>` element you want selected in advance.

Hidden fields

A *hidden field* lets you collect name and value information that the user can't see along with the rest of the form data. Hidden fields are useful for keeping track of information associated with the form, such as its version or name.

If your Internet service provider (ISP) provides a generic application for a guest book or feedback form, you might have to put your name and e-mail address in the form's hidden fields so that the data goes specifically to you.

To create a hidden field, here's what you do:

1. **Use the `<input>` element with its `type` attribute set to `hidden`.**

2. **Supply the name and value pair you want to send to the form handler.**

Here's an example of markup for a hidden field:

```
<form action="bin/guestbook.php" method="post">
<input type="hidden" name="e-mail" value="me@mysite.com">
<ul style="list-style-type: none;">
  <li>First Name: <input type="text" name="firstname" size="30"
     maxlength="25"></li>
  <li>Last Name: <input type="text" name="lastname" size="30"
     maxlength="25"></li>
  <li>Password: <input type="password" name="psswd" size="30"
     maxlength="25"></li>
</ul>
</form>
```

As a rule, using an e-mail address in a hidden field is just asking for that address to be picked up by spammers. If your ISP says that this is how you should do your feedback form, ask for suggestions as to how you can mini-mize the damage. Surfers to your page can't see your e-mail address, but spammers' spiders can read the markup. At a minimum, you would hope that your ISP supports one of the many JavaScript encryption tools available to obscure e-mail addresses from harvesters.

File upload fields

A form can receive documents and other files, such as images, from users. When a user submits the form, the browser grabs a copy of the file and sends it with the other form data. To create a file upload field, this is what you do:

1. **Use the `<input>` element with the `type` attribute set to `file`.**

   The file itself is the form field value.

2. **Use the `name` attribute to give the control a name.**

Here's an example of markup for a file upload field:

```
<form action="bin/guestbook.php" method="post">
<p>Please submit your resume in Microsoft Word or plain text format:<br>
   <input type="file" name="resume">
</p>
</form>
```

Browsers render a file upload field with a Browse button (or a button simi-larly named) that allows a user to navigate a local hard drive and select a file to send, as shown in Figure 7-8.

Figure 7-8: A file upload field rendered as a Choose File button.

When you accept users' files through a form, you may receive files that are either huge or perhaps virus-infected. Consult with whomever is programming your form handler to discuss options to protect the system where files get saved. Several barriers can help minimize your risks, including the following:

- Virus-scanning software
- Restrictions on file size
- Restrictions on file type

Drop-down list fields

Drop-down lists are a great way to give users lots of options in a small amount of screen space. You use two tags to create a drop-down list:

- `<select>` creates the list.

  Use a `name` attribute with the `<select>` element to name your list.

- A collection of `<option>` elements identifies individual list options.

  The `value` attribute assigns a unique value for each `<option>` element.

Here's a markup example for a drop-down list:

```
<form action="bin/guestbook.php" method="post">
<p>What is your favorite food?</p>
  <select name="food">
    <option value="pizza">Pizza</option>
    <option value="icecream">Ice Cream</option>
    <option value="eggsham">Green Eggs and Ham</option>
  </select>
</form>
```

The browser turns this markup into a drop-down list with three items, as shown in Figure 7-9.

Figure 7-9: A drop-down list.

You can also enable users to select more than one item from a drop-down list by changing the default settings of your list:

- If you want your users to be able to choose more than one option (by holding down the Ctrl [Windows] or ⌘ [Mac] key while clicking options in the list), add the `multiple` attribute to the `<select>` tag. The value of `multiple` is `multiple`.

  If you give a stand-alone attribute a value, that value must be the same as the name for the attribute itself (that is, both `multiple` and `multiple="multiple"` are legal).

- By default, the browser displays only one option until the user clicks the drop-down menu arrow to display the rest of the list. Use the `size` attribute with the `<select>` tag to specify how many options to show.

  If you specify fewer than the total number of options, the browser includes a scroll bar with the drop-down list.

You can specify that one of the options in the drop-down list be already selected when the browser loads the page, just as you can specify a check box or radio button to be selected. Simply add the `selected` attribute for the `<option>` tag you want as the default. Use this when one choice is very likely, knowing that users can override your default selection quickly and easily.

Multiline text boxes

If a single-line text field doesn't offer enough room for a response, create a text box instead of a text field:

- ✔ The `<textarea>` element defines the box and its parameters.

- ✔ The `rows` attribute specifies the height of the box in rows based on the font in the text box.

- ✔ The `cols` attribute specifies the width of the box in columns based on the font in the text box.

The text that the user types into the box provides the value, so you need only give the box a name with the `name` attribute:

```
<form action="bin/guestbook.php" method="post">
  <p> Please include any comments here.</p>
  <textarea rows="10" cols="40" name="comments">
...comments here...
  </textarea>
</form>
```

Any text you include between the `<textarea>` and `</textarea>` tags appears in the text box in the browser, as shown in Figure 7-10. The user then enters information in the text box and overwrites your text.

Figure 7-10: A text box.

Submit and Reset buttons

Submit and Reset buttons help the user tell the browser what to do with the form. You can create buttons to either submit or reset your form, using the `<input>` element with the following `type` and `value` attributes:

- **Submit:** Visitors have to tell a browser when they're done with a form and want to send the contents. You create a button to submit the form to you by using the following markup:

  ```
  <input type="submit" value="Submit">
  ```

  You don't use the `name` attribute for the Submit and Reset buttons. Instead, you use the `value` attribute to specify how the browser labels the buttons for display.

- **Reset:** Visitors need to clear the form if they want to start all over again or decide not to fill it out. You create a button to reset (clear) the form by using the following markup:

  ```
  <input type="reset" value="Clear">
  ```

You can set the value to anything you want to appear on the button. In our example, we set ours to `Clear`. Of course, you can use something that's more appropriate to your website if you'd like.

Listing 7-2 shows an example of markup to create Submit and Reset buttons named Send and Clear, respectively.

Listing 7-2:   A Complete Multipart Form

```
<!DOCTYPE html>
<html>
<head>
    <title>Basic Form Markup</title>
    <meta charset="UFT-8" />
    <style type="text/css">
      h1 {background-color: silver;
          color: black;
          font-size: 1.2em;
          font-family: Arial, Verdana, sans-serif;}
      hr {color: blue;
          width: thick;}
      body {font-size: 12pt;
            color: brown;
            font-family: Tahoma, Bodoni, sans-serif;
            line-height: 0.8em;}
    </style>
```

```
    </head>
    <body>
      <h1>Multi-Part Form</h1>
      <hr />
        <div>
          <form action="bin/guestbook.php" method="post">
            <h1>Name and Password</h1>
              <p>First Name: <input type="text" name="firstname" size="30"
                maxlength="25"></p>
              <p>Last Name: <input type="text" name="lastname" size="30"
                maxlength="25"></p>
              <p>Password: <input type="password" name="psswd" size="30"
                maxlength="25"></p>
            <h1>Favorite Foods</h1>
              <p>What are some of your favorite foods?</p>
              <p><input type="checkbox" name="food" value="pizza"
                checked="checked">Pizza</p>
              <p><input type="checkbox" name="food" value="icecream">
                Ice Cream</p>
              <p><input type="checkbox" name="food" value="eggsham">
                Green Eggs and Ham</p>
            <h1>Gender Information</h1>
              <p>What is your gender?</p>
              <p><input type="radio" name="gender" value="male">Male</p>
              <p><input type="radio" name="gender" value="female">Female</p>

              <p style="line-height: 2em; margin: 2em;">
                <input type="submit" value="Send">
                <input type="reset" value="Clear">
              </p>
          </form>
        </div>
      <hr>
    </body>
  </html>
```

Figure 7-11 shows how a browser renders these buttons in a form.

Form validation

No matter how brilliant your site's visitors may be, there's always a chance that they'll enter data you aren't expecting or perhaps leave some important field unfilled. JavaScript to the rescue!

Figure 7-11: Submit and Reset buttons are labeled as Send and Clear.

Form validation is the process of checking data the user enters before it's put into your database. You can check the data either with local JavaScript or PHP scripts on your server.

JavaScript

You can validate entries in JavaScript before data goes to the server. This means that visitors don't wait for your server to check the data. They're told quickly (before they click Submit, if you want) if there's a problem.

If you want to use JavaScript in your forms and on your website, you can read more about it online at these sites:

- www.w3schools.com/js/default.asp
- www.quirksmode.org/js/forms.html
- www.webmonkey.com/2010/02/javascript_tutorial

PHP

You need to validate your form data on the server side because users can surf with JavaScript turned off. (They'll have a slower validation process.) Find out more about PHP at these sites:

- www.4guysfromrolla.com/webtech/LearnMore/Validation.asp
- ww35.php101.com/book

Processing Data

Getting form data is really only half the form battle. You create form elements to get data from users, but then you have to do something with that data. Of course, your form and your data are unique every time, so no single, generic form handler can manage the data for every form. Before you can find (or write) a program that handles your form data, you must know what you want to do with it. For example:

- If you just want to receive comments from a web form by e-mail, you might need only a simple `mailto:` URL.
- If a form gathers information from users to display in a guest book, you
  - Add the data to a text file or a small database that holds the entries.
  - Create a web page that displays the guest-book entries.
- If you want to use a shopping cart, you need programs and a database that can handle inventory, customer order information, shipping data, and cost calculations.

Your web-hosting provider — whether it's an internal IT group or an ISP you pay monthly — has the final say in what kind of applications you can use on your website to handle form data. If you want to use forms on your site, be sure that your hosting provider supports the applications you need to run on the server to process form input data (which normally uses the `post` or `get` method that we discuss earlier in this chapter). Chapter 3 includes more information on finding the right ISP to host your pages.

Processing forms on your pages

Typically, form data is processed in some way or another by some kind of program running on a web server. It might be a PHP script written in some programming language such as Perl, Java, or AppleScript, or a different handler program written using PHP, Apache, Java Server Pages (JSP), ASP, or other programs that run on web servers to process user input. These programs make data from your form useful by

- ✏ Putting it into a database or sharing it with some other kind of program.
- ✏ Creating customized HTML based on the data.
- ✏ Writing the data to a flat file.

Flat file is computer-geek speak for a plain, unadorned text file, or one that uses commas or tab characters on individual lines of text to separate field values (also known as CSV for *comma-separated values* or TSV for *tab-separated values*).

You don't have to be a programmer to make the most of forms. Many ISPs support (and provide) scripts for processing common forms, such as guest books, comment forms, and even shopping carts. Your ISP may give you

- ✏ All the information you need to get an input-processing program up and running
- ✏ HTML to include in your pages so they can interact with that program

You can tweak the markup that manages how the form appears in the canned HTML you get from an ISP, but don't change the form itself — especially the `<form>` tag names and values. The web-server program uses these to make the entire process work.

Several online script repositories provide free scripts that you can download and use along with your forms. Many of these also come with some generic HTML you can dress up and tweak to fit your website. You simply drop the program that processes the form into the folder on your site that holds programs (sometimes called `php-bin`, often something else), add the HTML to your page, and you're good to go. Some choice places on the web to find scripts you can download and put to work immediately are

- ✏ **Matt's Script archive:** `www.scriptarchive.com/nms.html`
- ✏ **The PHP Resource Index:** `http://php.resourceindex.com`
- ✏ **The Developer.com Network:** `www.developer.com`

Handling forms is beyond the scope of this book, but you can find out more about them from these friendly *For Dummies* titles:

- ✏ *PHP and MySQL For Dummies,* 4th Edition (2009)

    `www.dummies.com/store/product/PHP-and-MySQL-For-Dummies-4th-Edition.productCd-0470527587.html`

✏ *HTML5 Programming with JavaScript For Dummies* (2013)

```
www.dummies.com/store/product/HTML5-Programming-with-
       JavaScript-For-Dummies.productCd-1118431669.
       html
```

Designing User-Friendly Forms

Designing *useful* forms is a different undertaking from designing *easy-to-use* forms. Your form may gather the data that you need, but if your form is difficult for visitors to use, they may abandon it before they're done.

As you use the markup elements from this chapter, along with the other elements that drive page layout, keep the following guidelines in mind:

✏ **Provide textual cues for all your forms.** Be clear about the information you want and the format you need.

For example, tell users details such as whether

• Dates must be entered as mm/dd/yy (versus mm/dd/yyyy).

• The number of characters a field can take is limited.

As we explain earlier in this chapter, you can limit character by using the maxlength attribute.

✏ **Use field width and character limits to provide visual clues.** For example, if users should enter a credit card number as *xxxx-xxxx-xxxx-xxxx*, consider creating four text fields — one for each part of the number.

✏ **Group similar fields.** A logical grouping of fields makes filling out a form easier. It's confusing if you ask for the visitor's first name, then birthday, and then last name.

✏ **Break long forms into easy-to-manage sections.** Forms in short chunks are less intimidating and more likely to be completed.

Major online retailers (such as Amazon.com — www.amazon.com) use this method to get the detail they need for orders without making the process too painful.

✏ **Mark required fields clearly.** If some parts of your form *can't* be left blank when users submit the form, mark those fields clearly.

You can identify required fields by

• Making them bold

• Using a different color

• Placing an asterisk beside them

✏ **Write helpful, friendly error messages.** Make sure your form validation feedback makes sense to site visitors (check them with a group of testers just to make sure). Nothing turns visitors away like cryptic unhelpful message. ("Type 42 error" may mean something to a programmer, but not to anybody else.)

✔ **Tell users what kind of information they need for the form.** If users need any information in their hands before they fill out your form, a *form gateway* page can detail everything users should have before they start filling out the form.

TIP

The series of forms that RateGenius uses to gather information for car loans and loan refinancing are excellent examples of long forms that collect a variety of different kinds of data by using all the available form markup elements. Visit www.rategenius.com to review its form techniques.

Other Noteworthy Forms-Related Markup

Table 7-1 lists other forms-related HTML markup attributes that you might find in HTML files.

Table 7-1	Other Forms-Related (X)HTML Attributes		
Name	**Function/Value Equals**	**Value Types**	**Related Element(s)**
Accept	Lists acceptable MIME types for file upload	CS Media types	<form> <input />
accept-charset	Lists character encodings	Character set encodings	<form>
Checked	Preselects option for select lists	"checked"	<input />
Disabled	Disables form elements	"disabled"	<button> <input> <optgroup> <option> <select> <textarea>
Enctype	Specifies encoding method for form input data	Media type	<form>
For	Points to ID reference from other attributes	Idref	<label>
Label	Identifies a group of options in a form	Text	<optgroup>
Label	Specifies an option name in a form	Text	<option>

Name	Function/Value Equals	Value Types	Related Element(s)
Method	HTTP method to use when submitting a form	{"get"| "put"}	<form>
Multiple	Permits selection of multiple options in a form	"multiple"	<select>
Name	Names a specific form control	CDATA	<button> <textarea>
Name	Names a specific form input field	CDATA	<select>
Name	Names a form for script access	CDATA	<form>
Readonly	Blocks editing of text fields within a form	"readonly"	<input /> <textarea
Size	Specifies number of lines of text to display for a drop-down menu	Number	<select>
Tabindex	Defines tabbing order for form fields	Number	<a><area /> <button> <input /> <object> <select> <textarea>
Type	Defines button function in a form	{"button"| "reset"| "submit"}	<button>
Type	Specifies type of input required for form input field	{"button"| "checkbox"| "file"| "hidden"| "image"| "password"| "radio"| "reset"| "submit"| "text"}	<input />
Value	Supplies a value to send to the server when clicked	CDATA	<button>
Value	Associates values with radio buttons and check boxes	CDATA	<input />

Here's a key for the Value Types Column in Table 7-1:

- **CDATA:** SGML character data type permits all keyboard characters to be used.

- **CS Media Types:** Case-sensitive type names such as "text/html" "image/gif" or "text/css."

- **Character set encodings:** Usually UTF-8, ISO-LATIN-1, or ISO-8859-1. For a more complete list, see www.w3schools.com/TAGS/ref_charactersets.asp.

- **MIME:** Abbreviation for Multi-part Internet Mail Extensions, a standard method to encode various document and data types for e-mail attachments and for HTTP. For more info, see http://en.wikipedia.org/wiki/MIME.

Form Frameworks

Form frameworks basically put all the building blocks for building, validating, and processing forms data together into a single coherent collection of tools and code. When you know how to use a framework, it's trivial to build complex robust forms of your own — at least, as long as that framework is available on your web server.

- **Wufoo (**http://wufoo.com**):** Wufoo is an HTML form builder that helps you create contact forms, online surveys, and invitations so you can collect data, registrations, and online payments you need without writing a single line of code. Quick and easy!

- **jQuery Validation Plugins (**http://docs.jquery.com/Plugins/Validation**):** Even though jQuery makes it easy to write your own validation plugins, there are still a lot of subtleties you must worry about. For example, you need a standard library of validation methods. (Think of e-mails, URLs, and credit card numbers.) You need to place error messages into web documents and then show and hide them when appropriate. You want to react to more than just a submit event, like keyup or blur. You may need different ways to specify validation rules, based on the server-side environment in use for a particular project. And after all, you don't want to reinvent the wheel, do you?

- **Validatious (**http://validatious.org/learn/examples**):** Validatious offers easy form validation with unobtrusive JavaScript support, using a predefined CSS class named validate. This makes validations simply a matter of adding validator names to form elements, such as input, select, textarea, and so forth. It's not a complete forms framework but does make the validation part — often the trickiest for newbies and professionals alike — smooth and straightforward.

In addition, many web-oriented development environments (such as Visual Studio, Web Expressions, ASP.NET, and so forth) also include extensive form design and processing components. These work like frameworks, too, but generally require you to work within their overall environments to take advantage of their often awesome capabilities.

Part III
Adding Links, Images, and Other Media

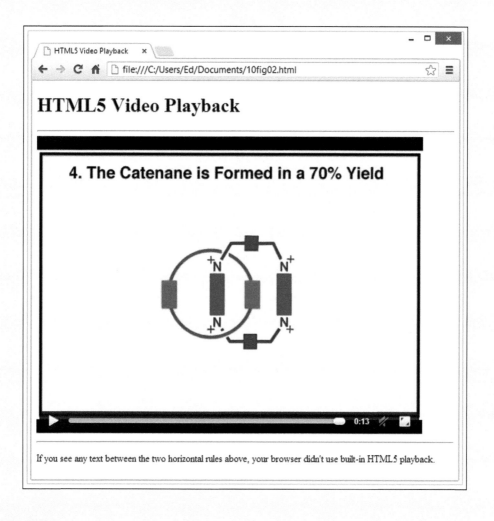

To explore some great resources on HTML links, web images, and media, visit www. dummies.com/extras/beginninghtml5css3. You can also find examples from the book by chapter at www.dummieshtml.com/html5cafe.

In this part . . .

- ✒ Following links is what interconnects the web
- ✒ Building and using better hyperlinks
- ✒ Using images to add visual interest to web pages
- ✒ Making the most of graphics and images online
- ✒ Driving HTML5 to new heights of media madness
- ✒ Crafting user-friendly web page controls and dashboards

8

Getting Hyper with Links in HTML

In This Chapter

▷ Creating simple links

▷ Opening linked pages in new windows

▷ Setting up links to locations within a web page

▷ Creating links to things other than web pages

*H*yperlinks, or simply *links,* connect HTML pages and other resources on the web. When you include a link on your page, you enable visitors to travel from your page to another website, another page on your site, or even another location on the same page. Without links, a page stands alone, disconnected from the rest of the web. With links, that page becomes part of the almost boundless collection of information that is the World Wide Web.

Basic Links 101

To create a link, you need

▷ **A web address** (called a Uniform Resource Locator; URL) for the website or file that's your link target. This usually starts with `http://`.

▷ **Some text** in your web page to label or describe the link. Make sure that the text you use says something useful about the resource being linked.

▷ **An anchor element** (`<a>`) with an href attribute to bring it all together. The element to create links is called an anchor element because you use it to anchor a URL to some text on your page. When users view your page in a browser, they can click the text to activate the link and visit the page whose URL you specified in that link. You insert the full URL in the `href` attribute to tell the link where to go.

You can think of the structure of a basic link as a cheeseburger (or your preferred vegan substitute). The URL is the patty, the link text is the cheese, and the anchor tags are the buns. Tasty, yes?

Anchor elements aren't block elements

Anchor elements are *inline elements* — that is, they apply to a few words or characters within a block of text (the text that you want to use as a link) instead of defining formatting for entire blocks of text. The anchor element typically sits inside a paragraph (`<p>`) or some other block element, such as a division (`<div>`), section (`<section>`), heading (`<h1>` through `<h6>`), or list item (`<li>`). When you create a link, you should always create it within a block element. Turn to Chapter 5 for more information on block elements.

Although many web browsers display anchors correctly even if you don't nestle them inside block elements, some browsers (such as the following) don't handle this breach of HTML syntax well:

- Text-only browsers for hand-held devices or mobile phones

- Text-to-speech readers for the visually impaired

Text-based browsers rely on block elements to divide up the sections of your page properly. Without a block element, these browsers might display your links in the wrong places!

For example, if you have a web page that describes HTML standards, you may want to refer web surfers to the World Wide Web Consortium (W3C) — the organization that governs all things related to HTML standards. A basic link to the W3C website, www.w3.org, looks like this:

```
<p>The <a href="http://www.w3.org">World Wide Web Consortium</a> is the
    standards body that oversees the ongoing development of the HTML
    specifications, and the WHATWG helps out with HTML5.</p>
```

You specify the link URL (`http://www.w3.org`) in the anchor element's `href` attribute. The text (`World Wide Web Consortium`) between the anchor element's opening and closing tags (`<a>` and `</a>`) describes the link.

Figure 8-1 shows how a browser displays this bit of markup.

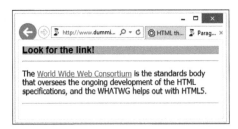

Figure 8-1: A paragraph with a link to the W3C.

You can also anchor URLs to images so that users can click an image to acti-vate a link. For more about creating images that link, see Chapter 9. For a detailed discussion of the ins and outs of URLs, see Chapter 1.

Exploring link options

You can link to a variety of online resources:

- Other HTML pages (either on your website or on another website)
- Different locations on the same HTML page
- Resources that aren't even HTML pages at all, such as e-mail addresses, pictures, and text files or downloads for visitors

Link locations, captions, and destinations exert a huge influence on how site visitors perceive links. Chapter 2 covers best practices for using links in your site design. The kind of link you create is determined by what you link to and how you formulate your link markup.

Absolute links

An *absolute link* uses a complete URL to connect browsers to a web page or online resource.

Links that use a complete URL to point to a resource are called *absolute* because they provide a complete, stand-alone path to another web resource. When you link to a page on someone else's website, the web browser needs every bit of information in the URL to find that page. The browser starts with the domain in the URL and works its way through the path to a specific file.

When you link to files on someone else's site, you must always use absolute URLs in the `href` attribute of the anchor element. Here's an example:

```
http://www.website.com/directory/page.html
```

Relative links

A *relative link* uses a kind of shorthand to specify a URL for a resource you're pointing to.

Use the following guidelines with relative links in your HTML pages:

- **Create relative links between resources in the same domain.**
- **Because both resources are in the same domain, you may omit domain information from the URL.**

    A *relative* URL uses the location of the resource you link **from** to identify the location of the resource you link **to** (for example, `page.html`).

A relative link is similar to telling someone that he or she needs to go to the Eastside Mall. If the person already knows where the Eastside Mall is, he or she doesn't need additional directions. Web browsers behave the same way.

If you use relative links on your site, your links still work if you change

- Servers.
- Domain names.

Simple links

You can take advantage of relative URLs when you create a link between pages on the same website. If you want to make a link from `http://www.mysite.com/home.html` to `http://www.mysite.com/about.html`, you can use this simplified, relative URL in an anchor element on `home.html`:

```
<p>Learn more <a href="about.html">about</a> our company.</p>
```

When a browser sees a link without a domain name, the browser assumes that the link is *relative* and uses the domain and path from the linking page to find the linked page. The preceding example works only if `home.html` and `about.html` are in the same directory, though.

Site links

As your site grows more complex and you organize your files into various folders, you can still use relative links. However, you must provide additional information in the relative URL to help the browser find files that don't reside in the same directory as the file from which you're linking.

Use `../` (two periods and a slash) before the filename to indicate that the browser should move up one level in the directory structure.

The markup for this directory navigation process looks like this:

```
<a href="../docs/home.html>Documentation home</a>
```

The notation in this anchor element instructs the browser to take these steps:

1. Move up one folder from the folder the linking document is stored in.
2. Find a folder called `docs`.
3. Inside that folder, find a file called `home.html`.

When you create a relative link, the location of the file *to* which you link is always relative to the file *from* which you link. As you create a relative URL, trace the path a browser takes if it starts on the page you're linking from to get to the page to which you're linking. That path defines the URL you need.

Avoiding common mistakes

Every web resource — site, page, or image — has a unique URL. Even one incorrect letter in a URL creates a *broken link,* which leads to an error page (usually the HTTP error `404 File or directory not found`).

URLs are so finicky that a simple typo — sometimes even a mistake in capitalization — breaks a link. Be sure to proofread your work and heed the following tips, which help you steer clear of avoidable missteps.

If a URL doesn't work, try these tactics:

- **Check the capitalization.** Some web servers (Linux and Unix, most notably) are *case-sensitive* (they distinguish between capital and lowercase letters). For example, such servers treat the filenames `Bios.html` and `bios.html` as different files on the web server. That means any browser looking for a particular URL *must* use uppercase and lowercase letters when necessary. Be sure that the capitalization in the link matches the capitalization for the URL.

  To avoid problems with files on your website, follow a standard naming convention. Often, using only lowercase letters can simplify your life.

- **Check the extension.** `Bios.htm` and `Bios.html` are two different files. If your link's URL uses one extension and the actual filename uses another, your link won't work.

  To avoid problems with extensions on your website, pick either `.html` or `.htm` *and stick to that extension.*

- **Check the filename.** For example, `bio.html` and `bios.html` are two different files.

- **Copy and paste.** Avoid retyping a URL if you can copy it. The best and most foolproof way to create a URL that works is as follows:

    a. *Load a page in your browser.*

    b. *Copy the URL from the browser's address or link text box.*

    c. *Paste the URL into your HTML markup.*

The copy-and-paste method for grabbing URLs presumes that you're grabbing them from a website somewhere. If you open a local file on your PC in a browser, you see something that looks like this: `file:///I:/H4D8e/html_ letter.html`. Here's how to decipher it:

- `file:///` is a common browser convention used to identify the document as a file in your local file system. It's used in Internet Explorer, Chrome, Firefox, and Safari but not Opera (we checked): It uses localhost/C: for local filesystem and drive designations instead.

- `I:/` is a drive letter.
- `H4D8e/` is a folder or directory on that drive.
- `html_letter.html` — the rightmost text element, in this case — is the name of the HTML file you opened.

You can't use URLs like this on a website, so please — don't try to!

Most people have had at least one letter returned and marked undeliverable because of an incomplete or inaccurate address. When the address isn't correct, the post office has no way to locate the intended recipient. The same is true for URLs. Without a fully formed URL, web servers don't know how to locate the target web page. URLs generally take the following form:

- **Protocol identifier followed by a colon (:)** — This is generally either `http` for Hypertext Transport Protocol, `https` for secure-server sites, or `ftp` for file transfer sites.
- **Hostname** — This is generally either a domain name such as `edtittel.com` or an IP address. The hostname is always preceded by two slashes (`//`).
- **Directory path** — Directory paths are preceded by a forward slash (`/`), and they direct the user to the specific web page being sought.

Thus, a fully formed URL takes this general form: `<protocolidentifier>://<hostname>/<directorypath>`. And, for example, a fully formed URL is `http://www.mywebsite.com/mywebpage`.

Customizing Links

You can customize links to

- Open linked documents in new windows
- Link to specific locations *within* a web page of your own
- Link to items other than HTML pages, such as
  - Portable Document Format (PDF) files
  - Compressed files
  - Word processing documents

Opening new windows

The web works because you can link pages on your website to pages on other people's websites by using a simple anchor element. When you link to someone else's site, though, you send users away from your own site.

The importance of http:// in HTML links

Browsers make surfing the web as easy as possible. If you type **www.sun.com**, **sun.com**, or often even just **sun** in your browser's address window, the browser obligingly brings up `http://www.oracle.com/us/sun/index.html`. Although this technique works when you type URLs into your browser window, it doesn't work when you're writing markup.

The URLs that you use in your HTML markup must be *fully formed* (complete in every detail). Browsers won't interpret URLs that don't include the page protocol. If you forget the `http://`, your link may not work!

To keep users on your site, HTML can open the linked page in a new window or in a new tab inside the same browser window. (Internet Explorer, Firefox, Chrome, and other browsers open new tabs. You can set Internet Explorer and other browser preferences to open in a new window instead of a new tab if you prefer.) The simple addition of the `target` attribute to an anchor element opens that link in a new browser window (or tab) instead of opening it in the current window:

```
<p>The <a href="http://www.w3.org" target="_blank">World Wide Web Consortium</a>
is the standards body that oversees the ongoing development of the XHTML
specification.</p>
```

When you give a `target` attribute a `_blank` value, this tells the browser to do the following:

1. Keep the linking page open in the current window.

2. Open the linked page in a new window or tab.

The result of using the `target="_blank"` attribute is shown in Figure 8-2, which depicts a new tab open for the W3C site.

Figure 8-2: Use the target attribute to open a new Internet Explorer window or tab for a linked file.

Pop-up windows irritate some users. Use them with care — and sparingly. You can use JavaScript to control the size, location, and appearance of pop-up windows as well as to put buttons on them to help users close them quickly. Check out Dr. Dobb's article "Introduction to JavaScript Pop-up Windows" for all the details on how to manage window appearance, size, and position on the screen when it appears. Find it online at:

```
www.drdobbs.com/web-development/introduction-to-
            javascript-pop-up-window/184412937
```

Specifying locations in web pages

Locations within web pages can be marked for direct access by links on

- The same page.
- The same website.
- Other websites.

We discuss each method in upcoming sections.

Keep these considerations in mind when adding links to web pages:

- Several short pages may present information more conveniently for readers than one long page with internal links.

  Links within large pages work nicely for quick access to directories, tables of contents, and glossaries.

- *Intradocument* linking works best on your own website, where you can create and control the markup.

When you link to spots on someone else's website, you're at its manager's mercy because that person controls linkable spots. Your links will break if a site designer removes or renames a spot to which you link.

Naming link locations

To identify and create a location within a page for direct access from other links, use an empty anchor element with the name attribute, like this:

```
<a name="top"></a>
```

The id attribute also works as an anchor element. It's often cleaner to use this method depending on your page design approach. (If you use id attributes for CSS, it may be easier to remember and more consistent overall.)

The anchor element that marks the spot doesn't affect the appearance of any surrounding content. You can mark spots wherever you need them without worrying about how your pages look (or change) as a result.

Linking within the same page

Links can help users navigate a single web page. Intradocument hyperlinks include such familiar features as

- ✏ Back to Top links.
- ✏ Tables of contents.

An *intradocument hyperlink,* also known as a named document link, uses a URL like this:

```
<a href="#top">Back to top</a>
```

The pound sign (#) indicates that you're pointing to a spot on the same page, not on another page.

Listing 8-1 shows how two anchor elements combine to link to a spot on the same page. (Documents that use intradocument links are usually longer. This document is short so you can easily see how to use the `top` anchor element.)

Listing 8-1:   Intradocument Hyperlinks

```
<!DOCTYPE html>
<html>
  <head>
    <title>Intradocument Hyperlinks at Work</title>
    <meta charset="UTF-8">
  </head>
  <body>
    <h1><a name="top"></a>Web-Based Training</h1>

    <p>Given the importance of the Web to businesses and other organizations,
       individuals who seek to improve job skills, or fulfill essential job
       functions, are turning to HTML and XML for training, particularly to
       HTML5. We believe this provides an outstanding opportunity for
       participation in an active and lucrative adult and continuing education
       market.</p>
    <p><a href="#top">Back to top</a></p>
  </body>
</html>
```

Figure 8-3 shows how this HTML markup appears in a web browser. If the user clicks the Back to Top link, the browser jumps back to the `top` spot — marked by `<a name="top"></a>`. The text for this example is short, but you can see how it works by resizing your browser window (making it tall and narrow) to display only two or three words per line of text.

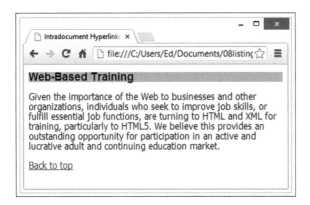

Figure 8-3: Use anchor elements to mark and link spots on a page.

Linking within the same website

You can combine intradocument and interdocument links to send visitors to a spot on a different web page on your site. Thus, to link to a spot named `descriptions` on a page named `home.html` on your site, use this markup:

```
<p>Review the <a href="home.html#descriptions">document descriptions</a>
    to find the documentation for your particular product.</p>
```

Linking on other websites

If you know that a page on another site has spots marked, you can use an absolute URL to point to a particular spot on that page, like this:

```
<p>Find out how to
<a href="http://www.yourcompany.com/training/online.htm#register">
register</a> for upcoming training courses led by our instructors.</p>
```

Be sure to check all links regularly to catch and fix the broken ones.

Gizmodo updated its "Best Free Web Site Link Checker" article in April 2013, just as we were writing this book. You can find the article here:

```
www.techsupportalert.com/best-free-web-site-link-
        checker.htm
```

Linking to non-HTML resources

Links can connect to virtually any kind of file, such as the following:

- Word processing documents
- Spreadsheets
- PDFs
- Compressed files
- Multimedia

Two typical uses for non-HTML links are software and PDF download pages.

File downloads

Non-web files must nevertheless be accessed via the Internet, so they possess unique URLs, just like HTML pages. Any file on a web server (regardless of its type) can be linked using a URL.

For instance, if you want your users to download a PDF file named `doc.pdf` and a Zip archive called `software.zip` from a web page, you use this HTML:

```
<h1>Download the new version of our software</h1>
<p><a href="software.zip">Software</a></p>
<p><a href="doc.pdf">Documentation</a></p>
```

You can't know how any user's browser will respond to a click on a link that leads to a non-web file. The browser may

- Prompt the user to save the file.
- Display the file without downloading it (common for PDFs).
- Display an error message (if the browser can't handle or doesn't recognize the type of file involved).

Because you can't know how a browser will respond, help users download files successfully by providing

- As much information as possible about the file formats in use
- Any special tools they need to work with the files
  - *Compressed files:* To work with the contents of a Zip file, the users need a compression utility, such as WinZip or ZipIt, if their operating systems don't support Zip files natively.
  - *PDFs:* To view a PDF file, users need the free Adobe Acrobat Reader (or some equivalent, such as Nitro PDF Reader).

You can make download markup more user-friendly by adding supporting text and links, like this:

```
<h1>Download our new software</h1>
     <p> <a href="software.zip">Software</a> (1.2 MB compressed ZIP file)</p>
     <p><b>Note:</b>
          You need a zip utility such as
       <a href="http://www.7-zip.org">7Zip</a> (Windows) or
       <a href="http://www.maczipit.com">ZipIt</a> (Macintosh)
          to open a ZIP file.</p>
     <p><a href="doc.pdf">Documentation</a> (440 KB PDF file) </p>
     <p><b>Note:</b>You need the free
       <a href="http://get.adobe.com/reader/">Adobe Reader</a>
          to view a PDF file.</p>
```

Figure 8-4 shows how a browser renders this HTML, and the dialog box it displays when you click the Software link.

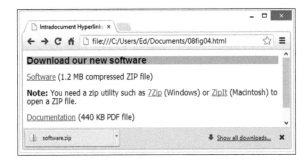

Figure 8-4: Chrome automatically downloads the Zip file.

E-mail addresses

A link to an e-mail address can automatically open a new e-mail addressed to exactly the right person.

This is a great way to help users send you e-mail with comments and requests.

An e-mail link uses the standard anchor element and an `href` attribute. The value of the `href` attribute is the target e-mail address, prefaced with `mailto:`.

```
<p>Send us your
  <a href="mailto:comments@mysite.com">comments</a>.</p>
```

The user's browser configuration controls how the browser handles an e-mail link. Most browsers follow these two basic steps automatically:

1. Open a new message window in the default e-mail program.

2. Insert the address from the `href` attribute into the To field of the message.

 Unfortunately, web page `mailto:` links are a prime source of e-mail addresses for spammers. Creating a form to receive feedback is often a better idea; better still, use JavaScript encryption on the e-mail address. (For more info, see Steven Chapman's great article "Hiding Your Email Address" at `http://javascript.about.com/library/blemail1.htm`.)

We generally tend to provide our e-mail addresses in the form: `ed at edtittel dot com`, knowing that people are smart enough to substitute @ for `at` and `.` for `dot`, and also knowing that address-harvesters usually aren't that canny. If you elect to use a form instead, be aware that this too can present security issues — always be sure to check your input, or take steps to avoid so-called SQL injection attacks. For more info, see Colin Mackay's article "SQL Injection Attacks and Some Tips on How to Prevent Them" at `www.codeproject.com/KB/database/SQLInjectionAttacks.aspx`.

Media links

One of the very coolest features about HTML5 is its greatly enhanced capability to grab and play back or display media files inside your web browser. Earlier HTML and XHTML versions usually required a specific player program to grab and interpret media files, but HTML5 brings audio, video, and multimedia playback right into the browser. A series of W3C specifications describes how this all works:

- The `<audio>` element takes a URL that points to some kind of audio file as the value of its `src` attribute. See this page:

  `www.w3.org/TR/html5/embedded-content-0.html#audio`

- The `<video>` element takes a URL that points to some kind of video file as the value for its `src` attribute. See this page:

  `www.w3.org/TR/html5/embedded-content-0.html#video`

- The `<source>` element can take a URL that points to some type of media (`src` attribute) and to a related player or codec to interpret that media (`type` and `media` attributes). See this page:

  `www.w3.org/TR/html5/embedded-content-0.html#the-`
  `         source-element`

9

Working with Images in HTML

▷ Determining the right format for your images

▷ Adding images to web pages

▷ Creating images and image maps that trigger links

*W*eb-page designers use images to deliver important information, direct site navigation, and contribute to overall look and feel on a web page. However, you have to use images properly, or you risk reducing their effectiveness.

This chapter is a crash course in using images on web pages. You find out which image formats are web-friendly and how to use HTML elements to add images to your web pages. You also discover how to attach links to an image and how to create image maps for a web page.

The Role of Images in a Web Page

Images in websites may be logos or clickable navigation aids, or they may display content; they can also make a page look prettier or serve to unify or illustrate a page's theme. A perfect example of the many different ways images can enhance and contribute to web pages is the White House home page at www.whitehouse.gov, shown in Figure 9-1, where the White House logo, photos, and a nice menu bar appear to good effect.

When used well, images are a key element of page design. When used poorly, though, they can make a page unreadable, unintelligible, or frustrating.

Figure 9-1: The White House web page uses images in a variety of ways.

Creating Web-Friendly Images

You can create and save graphics in many ways, but only a few formats are actually appropriate for images you intend to use on the web. As you create web-friendly images, you must pay attention to file formats and sizes.

Often, graphics file formats are specific to operating systems or software applications. Because you can't predict what a visitor's computer and software will be (other than he or she will use some sort of web browser), you need images that anyone can view with any browser. This means you need to use *cross-platform* file formats that users can view with any version of Microsoft Windows, the Mac OS, or Linux.

These three compressed graphics formats are best for general use on the web:

- **Graphics Interchange Format (GIF):** Images saved as GIFs often are smaller than those saved in other file formats. GIF supports up to 256 colors only, so if you try to save an image created with millions of colors as a GIF, you lose image quality. GIF is the best format for less-complex, non-photographic images, such as line art, clip art, or icons.

- **Joint Photographic Experts Group (JPEG):** The JPEG file format supports 24-bit color (millions of colors) and complex images, such as photographs. JPEG is cross-platform and application-independent. A good image editing tool can help you tweak the compression so you can strike an optimum balance between the image's quality and its file size.

✓ **Portable Network Graphics (PNG):** PNG is the latest cross-platform and application-independent image file format. It was created to combine the best aspects of GIF and JPEG. PNG has the same compression as GIF but supports 24-bit color (and even 32-bit color) like JPEG does.

Any good graphics editing tool, such as those mentioned in Chapter 23, lets you save images in any of these formats. Experiment with them to see how converting a graphic from one format to another changes its appearance and file size. Then choose whichever format produces the best results.

Table 9-1 shows guidelines for choosing a file format for images by type.

Table 9-1	Choosing the Right File Format for an Image	
File Format	*Best Used For*	*Watch Out*
GIF	Line art, icons, and images with few colors and less detail	Don't use this format if you have a complex image or photo.
JPEG	Photos or images with millions of colors and lots of detail	Don't use with line art. Compromises quality when you compress the file.
PNG	Photos or images with millions of colors and lots of detail	Don't use with line art. Offers best balance between quality and file size.

Each of the following sites offers a complete overview of graphics formats:

✓ W3C's "Graphics on the Web" article at `www.w3.org/Graphics`

✓ Quackit.com's Web Graphics Tutorial at `www.quackit.com/web_graphics/tutorial`

As you ponder your page design, consider this: General graphics effects such as colored or image-based backgrounds, gradients, buttons, and so forth may not require graphics at all. Before you leap to the conclusion that what your page needs is graphics, graphics, and more graphics, consult Chapters 15 and 16. Chapter 15 tackles buttons, boxes, and borders, and Chapter 16 covers use of color and backgrounds, all from a CSS perspective. You may not need as many graphics as you thought, and if you use CSS for such things, your pages will load faster, and your users will thank you for it. This goes double or triple for users on smartphones or tablets where lots of graphics could drive them to distraction (or to leave your site for good).

Optimizing images

As you build graphics for your web page, maintain a healthy balance between file quality and file size. If you poke around with your favorite search engine, you can find good tutorials on trimming image file sizes and optimizing entire sites for fast download. For tips and tricks to help you build pages that download quickly, review these handy resources:

- Optimizing images:

  www.yourhtmlsource.com/optimisation/imageoptimisation.html

- Optimizing web graphics:

  www.websiteoptimization.com/speed/12

Adding an Image to a Web Page

When an image is ready for the web, you need to use the correct markup to add it to your page, but you also need to know where to store your image.

Image location

You can store images for your website in several places. Image storage works best if it uses *relative* URLs stored somewhere on the website with your other HTML files. You can store images in the same root as your HTML files, which gets confusing if you have a lot of files, or you can create a `graphics` or `images` directory in the root file for your website.

Relative links connect resources from the same website. You use *absolute* links between resources on two different websites. Turn to Chapter 8 for a complete discussion of the differences between relative and absolute links.

Here are three compelling reasons to store images on your own site:

- **Control:** When images reside on your site, you have complete control over them. You know your images aren't going to disappear or change, and you can work to optimize them.

- **Speed:** If you link to images on another site, you never know when that site may go down or respond unbelievably slowly. Linking to images on someone else's site also causes the other site's owner to pay for bandwidth required to display it on your pages — on another site!

- **Copyright:** If you show images from another site on your pages, you may violate copyright laws. If you must do this, obtain permission from the copyright holder to store and display images on your website.

Using the <img> element

The image (`<img>`) element is an *empty element* (sometimes called a *singleton tag*) that enables you to specify the place on the page where you want your image to go.

An empty element uses only one tag, with neither a distinct opening nor a distinct closing tag.

The following markup places an image named `07fg02-cd.jpg`, which is saved in the same directory as the (X)HTML file, between two paragraphs:

```
<!DOCTYPE html>
<html>
<head>
  <meta charset="UTF-8">
   <title>Optical Disks at Work</title>
</head>
  <body>
  <h1>CD/DVD as a Storage Medium</h1>
  <p>CD-ROMs and DVDs have become a standard storage option in today's computing
     world because they are inexpensive and easy to use.</p>
  <img src="09fg02-cd.jpg" alt="line drawing of optical disk">
  <p>To read from a CD or DVD, you only need a standard CD-ROM drive, but to
     create CDs or DVDs, you need a DVD burner (all DVD burners can read
     and write CDs as well).</p>
  </body>
</html>
```

A web browser replaces the `img` element with the image file provided as the value for the `src` attribute, as shown in Figure 9-2.

The `src` attribute is like the `href` attribute that you use with an anchor (`<a>`) element. The `src` attribute specifies the location for the image you want to display on your page. The preceding example points to an image file in the same folder as the HTML file referencing it.

Adding alternative and title text

Alternative text describes an image so those users who can't see the images for some reason can access that text to find out more about the image. Adding alternative text (often referred to by developers as "alt text") is a good practice because it accounts for the following types of users:

- ✓ Visually impaired users who may not be able to see images and must rely on alternative text for a text-to-speech reader to read to them

- ✓ Users who access the website from a phone browser with limited graphics capabilities

- ✓ Users with slow Internet connections who choose not to display images

Figure 9-2: Use the <img> element to place graphics in a web page.

Some search engines and cataloging tools use alternative text to index images.

Most of your users will see your images, but be prepared for those who won't. The HTML specifications require that you provide alternative text to describe each image on a web page. Use the alt attribute with the img element to add this information to your markup, like so:

```
<!DOCTYPE html>
<html>
  <head>
    <meta charset="UTF-8">
    <title>Inside the Orchestra</title>
  </head>

  <body>
    <p>Among the different sections of the orchestra you will find:</p>
    <p><img src="09fg03-violin.jpg" alt="violin" title="violin"> Strings</p>
    <p><img src="09fg03-trumpet.jpg" alt="trumpet" title="trumpet"> Brass</p>
    <p><img src="09fg03-woodwinds.jpg" alt="clarinet and saxophone"
        title="clarinet and saxophone"> Woodwinds</p>
  </body>
</html>
```

When browsers don't display an image (or can't, as with text-only browsers such as Lynx), they display alternative text instead, as shown in Figure 9-3. (We turned images off in Internet Explorer because Chrome didn't cooperate.)

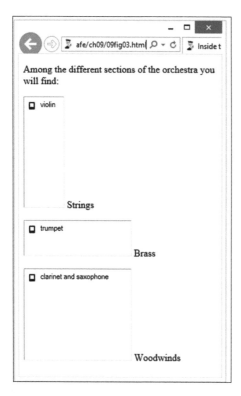

Figure 9-3: When a browser doesn't show an image, it shows alternative text.

When browsers show an image, browsers — including Internet Explorer, Firefox, Chrome, Safari, and Opera — show title text as pop-up tips when you hover your mouse pointer over an image for a few seconds, as shown in Figure 9-4. This requires adding a `title` attribute to each `<img>` element, which is why it's also included in the preceding markup. ***Note:*** `alt` text is required for a page to validate, but `title` text is not required.

Among the different sections of the orchestra you will find:

violin Strings

Brass

Woodwinds

Figure 9-4: A browser displays title text as a pop-up tip.

This means you can use alternative text to describe the image to those who can't see it and/or title text to provide useful (or amusing) information about the same image.

The W3C's Web Accessibility Initiative (WAI) includes helpful tips for creating useful and usable alternatives to visual content at this site:

```
www.w3.org/TR/WCAG10-TECHS/#gl-provide-equivalents
```

You may see suggestions to use alt text for so-called *keyword stuffing* from presumptive SEO experts. Search engines look for certain words in web pages and may sometimes use them to rank certain pages higher in their search results. Thus, some people take this to mean that using keywords in alt text improves page rankings. This is bogus. All we have to say is, "Don't do it!"

Specifying image size

Use the `height` and `width` attributes with the `<img>` element to let the browser know just how tall and wide an image is (the default unit is pixels, or px):

```
<p><img src="07fg03-trumpet.jpg"
    width="50" height="70" alt="trumpet" />Brass</p>
```

Most browsers download the HTML and text associated with a page before they download the page graphics. Instead of making users wait for the whole page to download, browsers typically display the text first and then fill in graphics as they become available. If you tell the browser how big a graphic is, the browser can reserve a spot for it in the page display. This speeds the process of populating graphics — and other stuff — on the web page.

You can check the width and height of an image in pixels in any image editing program or in the image viewers built into Windows and the Mac OS. (You may be able simply to view the properties of the image in either Windows or the Mac OS to see its height and width.)

Another good use of the height and width attributes is to create colored lines on a page by using just a small colored square. For example, this markup adds a 10-x-10-px blue box to a web page:

```
<img src="09fg05-blue-box.gif" alt="blue box" height="10" width="10">
```

Use the `<img>` element height and width attributes to set image height and width. Thus we use these values to create a 10-x-10-px blue box in a browser window (shown at the top of Figure 9-5) even though the original image is 600 x 600 pixels. In general, it's safe to reduce image dimensions using these attributes although you'll always want to check the results carefully during testing. With any kind of aspect sensitive image, you want to maintain its aspect ratio by dividing the original dimensions by some common value.

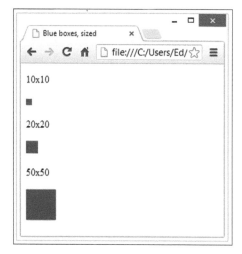

Figure 9-5: A series of small blue boxes.

Figure 9-5 also shows boxes with dimensions of 20 x 20 and 50 x 50 px. Here are the changes to the values for `height` and `width` in the markup to produce the other two boxes:

```
<img src="09fg05-blue-box.gif" alt="blue box" height="20" width="20">
<img src="09fg05-blue-box.gif" alt="blue box" height="50" width="50">
```

Using this technique, you can turn a single image like the blue box (only 2.39K in size) into a variety of lines and even boxes:

✔ This technique can ensure that all dividers and other border elements on your page use the same color because they're all based on the same graphic.

✔ If you decide you want to change all your blue lines to green, you just change the image. Every line you created changes colors.

When you specify an image's height and width that are different from the image's actual height and width, you rely on the browser to scale the image display. This trick works great for single-color images (such as the blue box), but it doesn't work well for images with multiple colors or images that contain actual photos. The browser doesn't size images well, and you wind up with a distorted picture. Figure 9-6 shows how badly a browser handles enlarging a trumpet image when the markup multiplies the image height by four and its width by two (note the resemblance to a flugelhorn!):

```
<p><img src="09fg03-trumpet.jpg" width="200" height="124" alt="trumpet"
Title = "trumpet" />Brass</p>
```

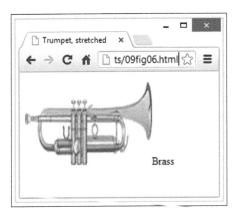

Figure 9-6: Don't use a browser to resize complex images; use a graphics editor!

If you need several sizes for the same image — as for a logo or navigation button — use a large image as the master for that graphic and make smaller versions. This trick gives you better control over the final look and feel of each image.

Image borders and alignment

You must use CSS to control image borders, positioning, alignment, spacing, text flow, and more. We cover those details in Chapters 14 and 15. In case we haven't made this sufficiently clear already, we strongly urge you to use CSS for borders, positioning, and alignment for both text and images, and let HTML do the job it does best: representing and pointing to actual content.

Images That Link

Web pages often use images for navigation. They're prettier than plain-text links, and you can add both form and function on your page with one element.

Triggering links

To create an image that triggers a link, you substitute an < img /> element in place of text to which you would anchor your link. This markup links text:

```
<p><a href="http://www.w3.org">Visit the W3C</a></p>
```

This markup replaces the text Visit the W3C with an appropriate icon:

```
<p><a href="http://www.w3.org"><img src="w3.jpg"
     alt="Visit the W3C Web Site"
     title = "Visit the W3C Web Site" height="75" width="131"
     style="border: solid blue; padding: 0.1em; margin: 2.0em;"></a></p>
```

The preceding markup creates a linked image to http://www.w3.org. In the preceding example, the alternative text now reads Visit the W3C Web Site, so users who can't see the image know where the link goes. When a user moves the mouse pointer over the image, the cursor changes from an arrow into a pointing hand (or any icon the browser uses for a link).

We include a blue border around this image as a visual cue to let users know it serves as a link. The border appears as a blue outline (shown in Figure 9-7).

Figure 9-7: Combine image and anchor elements to create a linked image.

A quick click of the image launches the W3C website. It's as simple as that.

You can set the border of any image you use in a link to 0 if you want to keep the browser from surrounding your image with a blue line. Without that line, however, users need other visual (or alternative text) clues so they know that an image is a link. Be sure images that serve as links scream to the user (tastefully of course), "I'm a link!" In all cases, if the automatic outline is eliminated, you should build an outline into the graphic itself or add a caption that indicates that the image serves as a link.

Building image maps

When you use an `<img>` element with an anchor element to create a linking image, you can attach only one link to that image. To create a larger image that connects links to different regions on the page, you need an *image map*.

To create an image map, you need two things:

- **An image** with distinct areas obvious to users

  For example, an image of a park might show a playground, a picnic area, and a pond area.
- **Markup** to map the different regions on the map to different URLs

Elements and attributes

Use the `<img>` element to add the map image into your page, just as you would any other image. In addition, include the `usemap` attribute to let the browser know that image map information should go with that image. The value of the `usemap` attribute is the name of your map.

You use two elements and a collection of attributes to define the image map:

✔ map holds the map information. The map element uses the name attribute to identify the map. The value of name should match the value of usemap in the <img> element that goes with the map.

✔ area links specific parts of the map to URLs. The area element takes these attributes to define the specifics for each section of the map:

- shape: Specifies the shape of the region (a clickable hot spot that makes the image map work). You can choose from rect (rectangle), circle, and poly (a triangle or polygon).

- coords: Defines the region's coordinates.

  A rectangle's coordinates include the left, right, top, and bottom points.

  A circle's coordinates include the x and y coordinates for the center of the circle as well as the circle's radius.

  A polygon's coordinates are a collection of x and y coordinates for every vertex in the polygon.

  To determine image coordinates, you can use an image map editor such as Mapedit from www.boutell.com/mapedit or a graphics editor such as PaintShop Photo Pro from www.corel.com. Mapedit also records those coordinates for you.

- href: Specifies the URL to which the region links (can be absolute or relative).

- alt: Provides alternative text for the image region.

Markup

The following defines a three-region map called NavMap linked to the graphics file named 09fg08-navmap.gif:

```
<img src="09fg08-navmap.gif" width="302" height="30" usemap="#NavMap"
      style="border: 0px; border: 2.0em;">
<map name="NavMap">
  <area shape="rect" coords="0,0,99,30" href="home.html" alt="Home"
      title="Home">
  <area shape="rect" coords="102,0,202,30" href="about.html" alt="About"
      title="About">
  <area shape="rect" coords="202,0,301,30" href="products.html"
      alt="Products" title="Products">
</map>
```

Figure 9-8 shows how a browser displays this markup.

When the mouse sits over a region in the map, the cursor turns into a pointing hand (just as it changes over any other hyperlink). So take advantage of the title text to include useful information about the link and to make the map more accessible to the visually impaired.

Figure 9-8: Image maps turn different areas of an image into linking regions.

A common use for image maps is to turn maps of places (states, countries, and such) into linkable maps. Here are some online resources you can use:

- The About.com image map tutorial at

      http://webdesign.about.com/od/imagemaps/a/aabg051899a.htm

   provides more details on building image maps by hand.

- HTMLGoodies has a great collection of image map tutorials and information at

      www.htmlgoodies.com/tutorials/image_maps/index.php

- For a more fully fleshed HTML file that implements the preceding image map example, see this book's website at

      www.dummieshtml.com/html5cafe/ch09/09fig08.html

Creating image maps by hand can be tricky. Use an image editor to identify each point in your map and *then* create the proper markup for it. Most HTML tools include utilities to help you make image maps. If you take advantage of such a tool, you can create image maps quickly and with few errors. Find out more about HTML tools in Chapter 23.

Exercise caution when using image maps. If you're creating a visual aid (something like a map with links to different countries shown therein, for example), using an image map makes perfect sense. On the other hand, you should never use a graphic with image maps for your main navigation. (Well, you *could,* but you wouldn't like the results!) Always use HTML and CSS for the main website navigation, or if you must use a graphical image map, include a text-based alternative along with that map so that visually impaired site visitors can also navigate by using the alternative controls instead.

In general, the best thing for navigation is to use text for button labels and to let CSS handle the work involved in making buttons look good. Chapter 15 discusses some truly great techniques to make text buttons pop.

10

Managing Media and More in HTML

In This Chapter

▷ Understanding media support in HTML5

▷ Working with audio, video, and more

▷ Crafting useful web page controls

▷ Working with frames in web pages . . . or not?

*I*ncreasingly, the web is becoming more than just a medium for accessing text and images. On the one hand, the web is embracing an ever-widening array of media, such as audio, video, and other forms of *streaming media* (video calls, video conferences, live audio, and so on). On the other hand, the web provides a platform for all kinds of interactive applications that provide services, crunch numbers, and do the kinds of things that people once called on computers to run locally and autonomously through their web browsers instead. Writing web-enabled software is beyond the scope of this book, but dealing with media in HTML5 is not.

HTML5 adds standard ways of playing media to the basic markup mix. Earlier versions of HTML had to rely on browser plug-ins to handle any kind of media. There was no guarantee that the right plug-in would be available for various specific kinds of media on *your* particular browser, even if plug-ins might be available for other browsers.

This chapter provides a quick tutorial on using various types of media in your web pages. You find out which media formats are web-friendly and how to use HTML5 elements to incorporate media into your web pages. You also discover how to use plug-ins for media, to support older browsers that may not accommodate the new media-handling capabilities in HTML5.

The long tail of web software

In statistics, the *long tail* refers to that portion of a distribution of numbers that follows the head or primary part of that kind of data. The head is where the bulk of the values concentrate, but there are also a lot of values distributed over a very long sequence at the tail end of the graph. In retail sales terminology, the long tail describes a strategy for selling a large number of unique or specialized items in fairly small quantities (the tail end of the distribution) in addition to a small number of popular items sold in very large quantities (the head of the distribution). This long tail adds to the overall market and increases sales overall.

For web browsers (and software in general), the long tail describes continued use of old software in smaller numbers over a long period of time, even after newer, more capable versions become available. That explains why, even though Internet Explorer is available in version 10 as we write this chapter, and Google Chrome is at version 27, some users are still running IE versions 6 or lower, and Chrome versions back in the teens. Web designers have to decide whether or not to support this long tail: If they do, they have to build pages that provide work-arounds when they want to use newer features, such as the built-in HTML5 media handling capabilities, but don't want to preclude users running older browsers from accessing such media, which requires running the right plug-in to play it back. Your call!

The Battle of the Media Formats

In getting HTML5 to the point where it could offer reasonable built-in media playback, there was quite a bit of discussion involved within the standards bodies' working groups that defined this kind of markup. This is a sport that Texans sometimes call *'cussin' and discussin'*, where the ratio of the former to the latter varies directly with the heat of the debate. And, given that the debate got pretty hot in this arena from time to time, there were no doubt meetings where the various interests involved turned the air blue!

Here's where things currently stand with media in HTML5. First, the current HTML5 specification recommends support for the royalty-free Ogg Vorbis (audio) and Ogg Theora (video) formats. But browser makers can choose to support whichever audio and video formats they like. Alas, this means that content authors (that's you) cannot assume any particular format will work in all browsers. That's a drag, as the upcoming Table 10-1 reveals.

The HTML Working Group (the folks who decide what goes into the HTML5 specification, also known as WHATWG at www.whatwg.org) believes it is desirable to specify at least one audio and video format for all browsers to support. What makes a media format ideal? An ideal format should do the following:

 ✓ **Support good compression** to keep file sizes and bandwidth consumption down

✏ **Support good image or sound quality** to deliver a positive media experience

✏ **Impose low decode processor overhead** to keep media from overwhelming the playback device

✏ **Be royalty-free** so browser makers and users don't need to worry about licensing issues or potential patent infringements

✏ **Include a hardware decoder for the format** because mobile devices often can't carry the processing load to decode media, especially video

Meet the major audio formats

A quick search of audio file formats shows that there are over 30 entries in this crowded field. For the purposes of this book, however, we focus on the major players supported in the most popular web browsers, as shown in Table 10-1 (which appears later in this chapter, in the "Comparing Traditional and HMTL5 Media Handling" section). As is also the case with video, you can find both royalty-free and proprietary formats in our short list. The name inside the first set of parentheses after each format name identifies a common file extension associated with that format.

✏ **Ogg Vorbis (Ogg; royalty-free):** A lossy audio compression format distributed free of royalty or licensing fees with other open and free media projects. Vorbis is a music-oriented format, but Ogg also supports Opus (a human speech compression format) and the lossless FLAC compression format. Ogg is distributed under the open BSD license. Both FLAC and Vorbis are extremely popular music formats, with Vorbis preferred for the web because its compression, whereas *lossy* (which means some sound fidelity is sacrificed in the interests of saving on bandwidth) is well suited for streaming online delivery. The file extension, .ogg, comes from the name of the container in which Vorbis files are most commonly carried. (The same extension is also used for Theora video as noted in the next section.)

✏ **MP3 (MP3; proprietary):** This proprietary lossy audio compression format is one of the most widely used formats for audio files at present — it's possibly even *the* most widely used format. MP3 stands for MPEG-2 Layer 3, which in turn identifies the efforts of the Motion Picture Experts Group to create a usable digital audio format that makes acceptable trade-offs between audio fidelity and file size. (An audio file created using a 128 kilobits per second streaming rate setting for MP3 produces a listenable file that is less than 10 percent of the size of its original CD audio counterpart.) MP3 files can be compressed at higher or lower bitrates to deliberately trade audio quality against file size (lower quality, smaller files) or file size against audio quality (higher quality, bigger files). The PC is a long-time supporter of MP3, which is very commonly used in Windows software of all kinds, including Internet Explorer for the web.

✔ **Waveform Audio File Format, or WAVE (WAV; royalty-free):** Usually known as WAV (thanks to its file extension), this audio format supports both compressed and uncompressed audio formats. WAV is a joint effort from IBM and Microsoft but requires no licensing or royalty payments. WAV works with numerous widely available audio codecs (encoders/decoders, which translate analog audio signals into digital patterns for storage, and digital patterns into analog audio signals for playback). The biggest issue with WAV is that its PC origin means it's not as widely supported on Mac OS, Linux/Unix, or mobile device operating systems.

Each of these audio formats has its pros and cons, but Vorbis appears poised to become most widely supported. In fact, the Web Hypertext Application Technology Working Group (WHATWG) recommends that all browser makers include Ogg Vorbis and Theora support in future offerings.

Meet the major video formats

As with audio, many, many potential video formats are available for use on the web. But for the purposes of this book, we focus on the major players that are supported in the most popular web browsers included in Table 10-1 (which appears in the next section, "Comparing Traditional and HTML5 Media Handling"). As with audio, you can find both royalty-free and proprietary formats here, too. Here's a list of the major players (the name inside the first set of parentheses after each format name identifies a common file extension associated with that format):

✔ **Ogg Theora (Ogg; royalty-free):** A free lossy video compression format distributed free of royalty or licensing fees with other open and free media projects. Ogg Theora is more or less the same in capability and bitrate efficiency as MPEG-4, or early versions of Windows Media Video (WMV), or RealVideo. Theora files make use of the Ogg container for delivery. (The same container also serves the Vorbis or FLAC audio formats.)

✔ **H.264 (MP4; proprietary):** More formally known as MPEG-4, H.264 or AVC (Advanced Video Coding) is a proprietary codec standard developed jointly by the ITU-T Video Coding Experts Group and the ISO/IEC JTC1 Motion Picture Experts Group (MPEG). This codec supports HD video and is widely used in

• Videos from Vimeo, YouTube, and the iTunes Store.

• Web software such as the Adobe Flash Player, Microsoft Silverlight.

• HDTV terrestrial, cable, and satellite feeds.

✔ **VP8/9 (WebM; royalty-free):** Free audio-video format designed for use with HTML5 video, a WebM file combines VP8 or VP9 video and Vorbis audio streams. It works natively with Firefox, Opera, and Chrome, and with plug-ins for Internet Explorer and Safari. The Google WebM hardware decoder is available to semiconductor companies at no cost, and it incurs no licensing or royalty fees.

Each of these video formats has its pros and cons, but Theora and WebM appear poised to become most widely supported, and WHATWG is recommending that all browser makers include Ogg Vorbis and Theora support in future offerings.

Comparing Traditional and HTML5 Media Handling

HTML5 supports a variety of media tags (and media formats) for media playback in web browsers. Because HTML5 remains something of a work in progress, not all formats work for all media in all browsers, as shown in Table 10-1. However, if you stick to the common denominators, you can find a way to deliver what you want to the biggest possible audience. And no matter what, given the WHATWG's recommendations, the Ogg formats (Vorbis, Theora, and so forth) look like good bets.

To read the discussions included in the HTML Living Standard document for audio and video elements in Section 4.8 "Embedded Content," please visit this page:

```
www.whatwg.org/specs/web-apps/current-work/
            multipage/#auto-toc-4
```

Table 10-1	**Media Support in Modern Browsers**					
Browser	**Video Formats**			**Audio Formats**		
	Ogg Theora	**H.264**	**VP8/9 (WebM)**	**Ogg Vorbis**	**MP3**	**WAV**
Internet Explorer 9.0+	MI*	9.0	MI*	No	Yes	No
Mozilla Firefox 3.6+	3.5	No	4.0	Yes	No	Yes
Google Chrome 6.0+	3.0	No	6.0	Yes	Yes	Yes
Safari 5.0+	MI*	3	MI*	No	Yes	Yes
Opera 10.6+	3.5	3.1	MI*	Yes	No	Yes

Sources: Developer.Mozilla.org "Using HTML5 audio and video"; MSDN Magazine "Working with Media in HTML5."

* MI means "manual installation required."

Mastering HTML5 Media Markup

Simply stated, there are two primary media elements for HTML5, both of which are absurdly easy to use. The audio element is named `<audio>`, and the video element is named `<video>`. In HTML5, the browser determines which players are built-in and thus available for use. You need to plan your use of audio and video accordingly, as you see in the sections on these two media elements that follow next, `<audio>` first, `<video>` second.

Making beautiful music with audio

Of course, there's more to the `<audio>` element than music — it happily plays back any kind of audio file, but we simply can't resist a good headline opportunity. Here's a simplified version of what audio markup looks like:

```
<audio src="sounds.ogg" controls>Alternatives</audio>
```

Here the `src` attribute points to the audio file you'd like to have played back. It specifies the location for the audio object for playback. The location must be a valid URI (Uniform Resource Identifier) that, just like a URL, identifies where the browser should look for the audio file.

The `controls` entry stands in for a number of control attributes you can use to manage audio playback and behavior, as follows (presented in alphabetical order):

✔ `autoplay`: Tells the browser to start playing audio as soon as the object file is loaded. The only legal value for this attribute is `autoplay` but no value is strictly required in HTML5.

✔ `controls`: Tells the browser to display an onscreen widget to control audio playback (usually with Pause/Play buttons, a progress bar, and volume controls). As with autoplay, the only legal value for this attribute is `controls`, but no value is strictly required in HTML5.

✔ `loop`: Tells the browser to go back to the beginning and keep playing when it gets to the end of the object file. Here, too, the only legal value for this attribute is `loop`, and no value is strictly required.

✔ `preload`: Tells the browser whether it should preload the object file, and if so how it should be preloaded. Possible values include

- `none`: Doesn't load any part of the audio file when the page loads

- `metadata`: Loads only the audio metadata when the page loads. It also sets up playback but doesn't have data loaded yet.

- `auto`: Loads entire audio file when the page loads

The `preload` attribute is ignored if `autoplay` is present.

The Alternatives section is very interesting and quite helpful in supporting older browsers. Page visitors see, or run, the content inside the `<audio>` `</audio>` tags only if their browser doesn't support the audio element (because their browser ignores tags it doesn't recognize), but HTML5-savvy browsers are smart enough to skip such alternative directions. This is where you can call plug-ins for specific players and different file formats because you know that only visitors who can't use the built-in HTML5 audio playback capabilities will encounter this markup. We take advantage of this in the example that follows to show you how to call other file formats in case your chosen format can't be played. As shown, a browser that lacks HTML5 audio support would display the word *Alternatives* onscreen!

Here's some markup that won't play back an `.ogg` audio file until the user triggers the Play button on the onscreen controls, with continuous looping as long as the page stays onscreen. We also provide WAV and MP3 alternatives for older browsers:

```
<audio controls preload="none" loop>
  <source src="sound.ogg" type="audio/ogg">
  <source src="sound.wav" type="audio/x-wav">
  <source src="sound.mp3" type="audio/mpeg">
  <p>Browser does not support HTML5 audio; alternate playback provided.</p>
</audio>
```

By default, if you don't include a `src` attribute in the opening `<audio>` tag, the target for the first `<source>` element is played in a browser that recognizes the HTML5 `<audio>` element. This setup makes it easy to stack up your playback options in the Alternatives section, starting with the one you want most, and so on. If players for the three formats are not available, no sounds will be played at all. As soon as the browser finds a player to match the type of sound file (`.ogg` first, `.wav` second, `.mp3` third), the browser uses the player to play the sound, and then the browser continues processing the remainder of the HTML document that follows.

Figure 10-1 shows what this page inside a properly constructed HTML file with some additional text and information looks like onscreen in Chrome.

Moving media with video

Unlike audio, which doesn't actually require much (or any) space on the screen, video requires an onscreen frame, as well as more sophisticated and more numerous controls. That's why although the two markup elements are similar, video comes with considerably more baggage, even though the basic structure of the element remains the same as before:

```
<video src="video.ogg" controls>Alternatives</video>
```

Play/pause   Time elapsed

Playback progress   Volume status

Figure 10-1: An audio control bar displayed in Chrome.

Here the `src` attribute points to the video file you'd like to have played back. It specifies the name of the video object file for playback and must be a valid URI. Example: `src="video.ogg"`.

The list of control attributes for video is considerably longer and a bit more complicated, too:

- `autoplay`: Tells the browser to start playing video as soon as the object file is loaded. Examples: `autoplay` or `autoplay="autoplay"`.

- `controls`: Tells the browser to display an onscreen widget to control video playback (usually with Pause/Play buttons, a progress bar, and volume controls). Examples: `controls` or `controls="controls"`.

- `height`: Sets the height, in pixels, of the box inside which the video will display. Example: `height="480"`.

- `loop`: Tells the browser to go back to the beginning and keep playing when it gets to the end of the object file. Examples: `loop` or `loop="loop"`.

- `mediagroup`: Used for synchronizing playback of multiple videos or media elements (such as a sign language track or an SAP track).

Takes a string value, where all items with the same `mediagroup` value are treated together as members of that group. Example: `mediagroup="movie"`.

✔ `muted`: Sets audio output state for playback; if present, audio is muted when playback begins. Use this when loud or startling audio might otherwise bother page visitors so that they can elect to turn on audio if they like. Examples: `muted` or `muted="muted"`.

✔ `poster`: Specifies an image to display while the video file is not available (hasn't loaded yet). Example: `poster="poster.jpg"`.

✔ `preload`: Tells the browser whether it should preload the object file, and if so how it should be preloaded. Possible values include:

- `none`: Does not load any part of the video file when the page loads

- `metadata`: Loads only the video metadata when the page loads. It also sets up playback but doesn't have data loaded yet.

- `auto`: Loads entire video file when the page loads

The `preload` attribute is ignored if `autoplay` is present.

✔ `width`: Sets the width, in pixels, of the box inside which the video displays. Example: `width="640"`.

The following markup displays a video snippet from Wikipedia:

```
<video controls poster="poster.png"
 src="http://upload.wikimedia.org/wikipedia/commons/5/5c/Cat.ogg"
 width="640" height="480">
  <source src="cat.webm" type="video/webm">
  <source src="cat.mp4" type="video/mp4">
  <p> Browser does not support HTML5 video; alternate playback provided.</p>
</video>
```

Figure 10-2 shows what this page inside a properly constructed HTML file with some additional text and information looks like onscreen in Chrome, just after the video concludes playback. The control bar for video is nearly identical to the control bar for audio. The difference is that the video control bar has a frame control at the far right. Please note also that alternatives for video playback work the same as they do for audio feedback, so you can stack your preferred player first for HTML5 browsers to use if they can, followed by other players in whatever order you prefer.

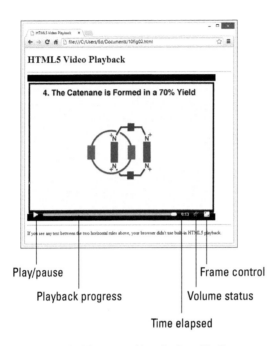

Play/pause

Playback progress

Time elapsed

Frame control

Volume status

Figure 10-2: A video control bar displayed in Chrome.

Undergoing the conversion experience

So, what if you want to follow our lead and provide alternative file formats for your audio or video files? To make them available in the big three formats of each kind (.ogg, .wav, and .mp3 for audio; and .ogg, .mp4, and .webm for video), you need some conversion tools. Here are some good resources to help you get started down that path so that when you make files available, you can reach the broadest possible audience:

- About.com, "4 Free Audio Converter Software Programs"

    ```
    http://pcsupport.about.com/od/fileextensions/tp/free-
        audio-converter.htm
    ```

- About.com, "5 Free Video Converter Programs and Online Services"

    ```
    http://pcsupport.about.com/od/fileextensions/tp/free-
        video-converter.htm
    ```

Thanks to these excellent articles, we're pretty sure you can find something suitable for either category. If you don't find what you need, you can do what we do when faced with such a dilemma: Simply search for *"free audio converter"* or *"free video converter"* and keep trying candidates until something sticks.

Mastering media in HTML5

After you start working with the audio and video elements (and the ever-helpful support source element, too), you'll get a feel for making good use of audio and video in your web pages. But what we present here is just the tip of an enormous and incredibly interesting iceberg of information and activity. For more details on the various audio and video formats, search online for this generic phrase:

`Play back` *format* `in HTML5`

where you substitute your chosen format name (Ogg, Vorbis, Theora, MP4, MP3, WebM, or WAV,) for the *format* element therein. When we tried that approach in researching this chapter, we found oodles of great material readily available. You should, too!

Working with Web Page Controls

The `controls` attribute that HTML5 so helpfully provides for both the audio and video elements sets the stage for our next discussion where we present the various onscreen progress bars, gauges, and meters that HTML5 makes available for on-page use. The following sections look at the markup elements involved — `meter`, `progress`, and `time` — and include online examples at the tail end of each element. The section ends with a quick tutorial on how to update controls in real time on your web pages.

Displaying a meter bar

The HTML5 `<meter>` element lets you display a meter bar for various counters that you might manage over time to show readings for various metrics. The `<meter>` element includes these numerical attributes, whose values may be integers (that is, whole numbers) or decimal numbers:

- `value`: The current measured value for your meter
- `high`: States a value considered to be high for readings on this meter
- `low`: States a value considered to be low for readings on this meter
- `max`: Sets the upper bound for readings on this meter and its display
- `min`: Sets the lower bound for readings on this meter and its display
- `optimum`: States a value considered to be optimal for readings on this meter

Here's a fully tricked-out markup example, shown in Figure 10-3 displayed in Chrome:

```
<meter high="90" low="10" max="100" min="0" optimum="50"
 value="44">Center-seeking meter</meter>
```

Figure 10-3 shows the meter in the context of a complete HTML file, with some use of CSS to set off the meter display. The meter's current value falls just below the optimal halfway mark.

Figure 10-3: A simple centering meter.

The `high`, `low`, and `optimum` attributes as well as the text enclosed between the opening `<meter>` and closing `</meter>` tags do not appear in the browser display of the meter. It's probably best to think of this information as a kind of built-in documentation to help explain how the meter works.

To see and play around with meter markup (and value settings), visit this page:

```
www.quackit.com/html_5/tags/html_meter_tag.cfm
```

For a nice demo of a meter at work (as you type into a text box, the character count goes up and the green meter bar gets longer), visit this page:

```
http://jsfiddle.net/RBUmQ/1/
```

The following is a snippet of HTML markup that shows three different meter bars: one for storage space consumption, one for voter turnout, and one for tickets sold. Don't scratch your head too much about it: It's just a contrived example.

```
<p>Storage space usage: <meter value="6" max="8">6 blocks used
   (out of 8 total)</meter> </p>
<p>Voter turnout:
  <meter value="0.75"><img alt="75%" src="graph75.png"></meter></p>
<p>Tickets sold: <meter min="0" max="100" value="75"></meter></p>
```

Tracking progress on activities

Whereas the meter element is designed to handle readings that can go up or down over time, the progress element is designed to report on activities that go one way only: up! Think of a typical progress bar that shows how far along you are on a software download, a file copy, or an install maneuver, and you've mastered the progress bar concept.

This simplicity makes the progress element something of a one-trick pony in the HTML5 world, and explains why it takes exactly two attributes:

  ✔ max: The value that represents completion of the task whose progress is being measured by this control

  ✔ value: The current value for the amount of progress achieved

Here's an example of some progress markup:

```
<progress max="100" value="44">progress bar</progress>
```

Figure 10-4 shows a static snapshot of the bar displayed in Chrome. At runtime, green in the progress bar fills in from left to right (that is, start to end), showing that something is — or should be — happening.

Figure 10-4: The progress element tracks completion of a task.

To fool around with progress bar markup online, visit this page:

`www.quackit.com/html_5/tags/html_progress_tag.cfm`

For a great demo (with access to underlying HTML5 markup and JavaScript for dynamic update of a progress bar), visit this page:

`http://developerdrive.com/demo/progress_bar/demo.html`

Here's a fun tutorial on what you can do with CSS and the `progress` element (see Parts IV and V of this book for many more details on working with CSS):

`http://css-tricks.com/css3-progress-bars`

Tracking and reporting on time

HTML5 adds a lot more data smarts to its repertoire, as compared with earlier HTML versions. Among these kinds of elements and their attributes, `<time>` permits content developers to use (and update) time values on their web pages in a variety of interesting ways.

The secret to `<time>` in HTML5 lies in understanding the kinds of values that this element's sole attribute — `datetime` — can take. This data type is called a *date or time string* and accommodates many forms for representing such information. The HTML5 specification explains how this works as follows:

> *The time element represents either a time on a 24 hour clock, or a precise date in the proleptic Gregorian calendar, optionally with a time and a time-zone offset.*

This explanation could use some *further* explanation. Here's a list of the formats time and date attributes embrace, including examples in case you prefer the "monkey-see, monkey-do" method of comprehension:

- ✔ **Valid time HH:MM[:SS][.fff]:** A 24-hour time where two-digit hours and minutes values are required, and seconds are optional, as are decimal fractions of a second. This means 8 a.m. is `"08:00"` but that 8 p.m. is `"20:00"`.

- ✔ **Valid date YYYY-MM-DD:** A complete date where four-digit year, two-digit month, and two-digit day of month values are all required.

- ✔ **Valid date and time with timezone offset:** Combines the previous two value types — date first and time second with a T in the middle — and then adds a timezone offset to include timezone information. Thus 4 p.m. on September 11, 2001 Central (US) Time is `"2001-09-11T16:00-06:00"`. Timezones range from –12:00 to +14:00, and you can use the capital letter *Z* (Zulu time) to denote +00:00 for Coordinated Universal Time (UTC) also known as Greenwich Mean Time (GMT).

What does the "proleptic Georgian calendar" stuff mean? It means that for <time> element values, time begins at 0 AD (no BC dates, in other words). But because <time> is intended to provide time stamps and time values, this shouldn't be a problem for most content developers who will use this element to keep track of things like publication dates, most recent update dates, and so forth. The nice thing about time in HTML5 is that the content between the opening <time> and closing </time> tags is intended to be human-readable, and the value of the datetime attribute is intended to be machine-readable, so both humans reading web pages and computers handling them can read and use time information included in such pages.

Who knew that dealing with <time> could take so much time? The following example markup shows the preceding example formats in HTML5:

```
<time datetime="20:00">eight PM</time>
<time datetime="2001-09-11">another day of infamy (adoi)</time>
<time datetime="2001-09-11T16:00">4 PM adoi</time>
<time datetime="2001-09-11T16:00-06:00">4 PM adoi Central (US) time</time>
```

The result is shown in Figure 10-5. Note that only HTML cares about the datetime attribute value; humans see the corresponding text enclosed within the <time> element instead.

One important take-away from this set of examples should be the idea that careful labeling of the content inside the <time> element is important because it tells page visitors about time in their web browsers. But of course, if that's not why you're recording time, you needn't put any text inside the <time> element at all.

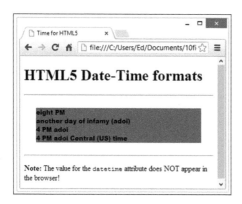

Figure 10-5: Example time markup displayed in Chrome.

To fool around with <time> markup online, visit this page:

www.quackit.com/html_5/tags/html_time_tag.cfm

There's no real reason to update the datetime attribute in a <time> element, so we skip the pointers to JavaScript updating techniques in this section. That doesn't stop us from returning to that subject in the next section, though.

Updating HTML5 controls

We can share the secret to updating HTML5 controls in one word: JavaScript. Though it's not the only scripting tool available to web content developers (that's you!), it is probably the most popular and widely used of such tools. To make a progress bar show progress or a meter measure change over time, you need some way to update the value associated with the value attribute as the web page is processed. JavaScript offers lots of good ways to do this, including responding to events in the browser environment, polling changes to local variables, counting time (or other values), and so forth.

To really understand how to use the <progress> or <meter> elements in HTML5, you have to understand JavaScript (or another web-friendly scripting language). That's outside the scope of this particular book, though we did include examples you can imitate to take the "monkey-see, monkey-do" approach to putting this markup to work. If you want to do it right, however, you'll want to add to your reading list. In particular, you might find these other *For Dummies* books of great interest:

- *HTML5 Programming with JavaScript For Dummies,* by John Paul Mueller (April 2013), more or less picks up where we leave off here.

- *PHP, MySQL, JavaScript & HTML5 All-in-One For Dummies,* by Steve Suehring and Janet Valade (April 2013), covers a full range of HTML5-related programming topics and tools. The book is designed as a comprehensive reference.

Part IV
Adopting CSS Style

```
/* =============================================
   Author's custom styles
   ============================================= */

#topnav {
    width:100%;
    text-align:center;
    background-color:#000000;
    height:24px;
    color:#FFFFFF;
    }

#topnav a {
    color:#FFFFFF;
    text-decoration: none;
    }

#topnav a:hover {
    text-decoration: underline;
    }

#container {
    width: 600px;
    margin: 10px auto 10px auto;
    border: 2px dotted #333333;
    }

#content {
    padding:10px;
    }

footer {
    font-size: .7em;
    text-align: right;
    }
```

To find out more about CSS markup and best practices, visit www.dummies.com/
extras/beginninghtml5css3. Find the examples for these chapters at www.
html4dummies.com/html5cafe in the sections labeled Ch11 through Ch13.

In this part . . .

- Understanding the oh-so-crucial distinction between content and appearance
- Working your way through CSS units of measure
- Digging into CSS syntax and structure by using selectors and declarations
- Using classes and IDs to focus style on elements or instances
- Working with inline, internal, and external style sheets
- Resolving multiple style selectors through the CSS cascade

Advantages of Style Sheets

In This Chapter

▸ Understanding the role of style sheets

▸ Discovering Cascading Style Sheets (CSS)

▸ Understanding the viewport

▸ Using different types of measurement units

*C*ascading Style Sheets (CSS) is the language web page authors use to tell a browser (or another user agent) how to format an HTML document. Remember: HTML5 is primarily a language for defining the structure (like the bones and muscles) of a document. The structural elements of a page, such as headings (`<h1>` through `<h6>`) and body text, don't affect how those elements look. By applying styles to those elements, though, you can specify an element's layout on the page and add design attributes (such as fonts, colors, and text indentation). CSS is the tool that lets you add skin (and even fancy clothing) to the structure created by your HTML markup and content.

Style sheets give you precise control over how structural elements appear on a web page. Better yet, you can create one style sheet for an entire website to keep the layout and look of your content consistent from page to page. And here's the icing on this cake: Style sheets are easy to build and even easier to integrate into web pages. In fact, with style sheets, you can

▸ Add style markup to individual HTML elements (called *inline style*).

▸ Create sequences of style instructions in the head of an HTML document (called an *internal style sheet*).

▸ Refer to a separate stand-alone style sheet via a link or other reference (called an *external style sheet*) inside your HTML document.

▸ Style an HTML document differently depending on whether it's being viewed on a desktop computer or a mobile phone.

In short, you can add style to a web page in lots of ways.

In the early days of HTML, you could add style and lay out an HTML document by using *presentational* HTML elements or by using certain HTML elements for purposes other than what they were designed for. Presentational HTML elements specify how content should look. You may occasionally still see some old HTML code that uses these presentational elements to do things that are better done with CSS. For example, prior to CSS, the only way to arrange elements in a grid was by using the `<table>` element. Today, CSS provides much more flexible ways to lay out a page (as we show you in Chapter 14). The `<font>` element (which is no longer a part of the HTML specification) used to be the only way to change the font face or size of HTML text. As the next few chapters demonstrate, designers can use CSS to do everything that the old `<font>` element used to do, and much, much more.

In HTML5, presentational elements and attributes were officially *deprecated* (made obsolete). As a result, there is no guarantee that certain old HTML4 and earlier presentational elements will continue to work in the future — not that you would ever consider using them anyway, right? We discuss deprecated markup in more detail on this book's website at `www.dummies html.com`.

Most modern browsers handle CSS3 well, but a few tricks are necessary in certain cases. We stick mostly to the safe stuff here, but we give you a taste of some of the cutting-edge features that are coming soon to a browser near you. Where necessary, we point you to resources on the web and tools that you can use to make sure that your web pages work correctly on nearly every web browser that is in use today.

Advantages of Style Sheets

HTML's formatting capabilities are limited by design. When you want tight control over the display of your web pages, style sheets are the way to go:

- Style sheets give you more flexibility than markup can.

- HTML5 no longer includes display-oriented (or presentational) elements and attributes, and these may cease to be supported by browsers in the future.

Style sheets supply lots of tools to format web pages with precise controls. With style sheets, you can

- **Control every aspect of page display.** Specify the amount of space between lines, character spacing, page margins, image placement, and more. You can also specify positioning of elements on your pages.

- ✓ **Apply changes globally.** Ensure consistent design across an entire website by applying the same style sheet to every web page.

  You can modify the look and feel of an entire site by changing just one document (the style sheet) instead of the markup on every page. Need to change the look for a heading? Redefine that heading's style attributes in the style sheet and save the sheet. The heading's look changes throughout your site.

- ✓ **Instruct browsers to control appearance.** Provide web browsers with more information about how you want your pages to appear than you can communicate using HTML.

- ✓ **Create dynamic pages.** With CSS3, anyone can easily animate HTML elements with just a couple lines of simple code.

The four steps to style

The gist of how style sheets work is as follows:

1. Select elements in a document (using *selectors*) that you want to add style to.

2. Write *declarations* that apply to the selectors. Each declaration consists of a property name and a value. The declarations specify how you want the selected markup to be styled.

   For example, you could specify that every first-level heading (`<h1>`) be displayed in yellow Garamond 24-point type with a purple background (not that you *would,* but you could).

3. Link style rules and markup.

4. The browser does the rest.

The combination of at least one selector and at least one declaration is called a *style rule.* Listing 11-1 shows a simple style rule that contains one selector and four declarations:

Listing 11-1:   A Simple Style Rule

```
h2 {
    font-face: Garamond;
    font-size: 24pt;
    color: yellow;
    background-color: purple;
    }
```

Understanding the C in CSS

Cascading is the process that browsers use to determine which style will apply to an element. Imagine, for example, that one style rule declares that paragraph text should be yellow, and then another rule declares that paragraph text should be purple. Through a somewhat complex set of rules, browsers decide which rule will actually apply to any single paragraph.

To visualize how cascading works, you can picture HTML elements falling down steps on their way to the viewer's browser. Along the way, they pick up styles such as size, color, weight, and so forth. All other things being equal, styles that the HTML element picks up later will be of higher importance to the browser.

When it's all said and done, the cascading rules are decided and the browser decides how to display a web page. Although the details of how the cascade works aren't important right now, it's very important for the web developer to know that every web browser follows the same rules (the cascading rules) in the event of conflicting styles.

What CSS can do for a web page

You can accomplish a (growing) list of tasks with CSS. You can:

- Specify font type, size, color, and effects.
- Set background colors and images.
- Control many aspects of text layout, including alignment and spacing.
- Set margins and borders.
- Control list display.
- Define table layout and display.
- Automatically generate content for standard page elements, such as counters and footers.
- Control cursor display.
- Create transitions.
- Animate the values of CSS properties by using keyframe animation.
- Design multicolumn layouts.
- Use any of thousands of fonts in your web pages.
- Define aural style sheets for text-to-speech readers.

Styling a Document with CSS

Listing 11-2 shows the HTML markup for the home page of the HTML5 Cafe. Notice that all the markup describes the purpose of the content — not how it should be presented.

Listing 11-2:   A Simple Semantic HTML5 Document

```
<!DOCTYPE html>
<html>
    <head>
        <meta charset="utf-8">
        <title>HTML5 Cafe: Home</title>
        <meta name="description" content="sample site for 9781118657201">
        <meta name="viewport" content="width=device-width">
    </head>
    <body>
        <div id="container">
          <nav id="topnav">
            <a href="index.html">HOME</a> |
            <a href="about.html">ABOUT US</a> |
            <a href="menu.html">MENU</a> |
            <a href="contact.html">CONTACT US</a>
          </nav>
        <div id="content">
          <h1>Welcome to HTML5 Cafe!</h1>
          <p>Here you will find all sorts of delicious HTML5 and CSS3 treats.</p>
          <figure id="home-image">
            <img src="img/pitr_Coffee_cup_icon.png"
                 width="400" height="400" alt="delicious coffee">
            <figcaption class="warning">powered by coffee.</figcaption>
          </figure>
        </div>
            <footer>
            copyright &copy; dummieshtml.com
            </footer>
        </div>
    </body>
</html>
```

Figure 11-1 shows the markup from Listing 11-2 rendered in a web browser. Notice that it's a very plain document with no styles applied other than the defaults.

It's not quite true to say that an HTML document with no CSS styles applied is unstyled. Even though you may not have applied styles to the document, each web browser contains a built-in style sheet that is called the *default style sheet.* This default style sheet is similar between browsers but not necessarily identical. The default style sheet sets the baseline styles that you can modify with your own CSS document. The default style sheet specifies that content in an <h1> element is bolded and 2em in size, for example.

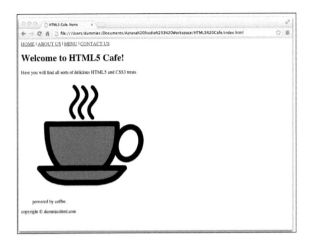

Figure 11-1: An unstyled HTML document uses the default browser styles.

Using HTML5 Boilerplate

For HTML5Cafe.com, we borrowed heavily from an open source project called HTML5 Boilerplate (www.html5boilerplate.com). HTML5 Boilerplate is a template for creating HTML5 websites. It combines the experience and knowledge of hundreds of web developers in order to make web development easier. Did we mention that it's free?

Normalize before you stylize

The default styles are meant to serve as a baseline from which you can add your own styles. However, you might notice something peculiar about these default styles: They're not very attractive! Also, some browsers don't quite follow the same rules as everyone else. (We're looking straight at you, Internet Explorer 6 and 7!) So, it's a good idea to establish your own baseline that fixes some of the ugliness of the default styles and addresses many of the inconsistencies between browsers.

Once again, our friends in the open source community came through with the perfect solution: `normalize.css`, a style sheet that seeks to eliminate many of the differences between browsers' default styles. You can download `normalize.css` from `http://git.io/normalize`. (It's also part of the HTML5 Boilerplate.) We don't explain the details of how `normalize.css` works, although you can certainly open it in Aptana Studio or any text editor and analyze it to your heart's content. The main thing about it is that it just works.

After you've saved a copy of `normalize.css` into your project, you can use an HTML `<link>` element to apply it to your web page. We talk more about the `<link>` element and the different ways to apply styles to a web page in the next few chapters. To apply `normalize.css` to the HTML5 Cafe home page, we simply add this element within the `<head>` element of the document:

```
<link rel="stylesheet" href="css/normalize.css">
```

After applying `normalize.css` to our web page, it looks like Figure 11-2.

Figure 11-2: The HTML5 Cafe's index.html with `normalize.css` applied.

If you compare Figure 11-2 with Figure 11-1, you can find a number of significant differences:

- The margins around the edges of the page are removed.
- The font has been changed to a sans-serif font. (Much easier on the eyes, don't you think?)
- The left margin has been removed from the image and its caption.
- The space has been removed from under the image caption.

What `normalize.css` does is give us a blank canvas upon which we can add our own styles. So, in this next step, we add styles!

HTML5 Boilerplate provides another style sheet in addition to `normalize.css` that's called `main.css`. This style sheet includes a few more styles that make a default web page look a bit better. Before you even add any of your own styles, simply including `main.css` in your document will make it look better. The `main.css` file also includes some *helper* CSS rules. Helper CSS rules define handy styles that are used fairly commonly in many different websites.

To include `main.css`, we use the following `<link>` element within the `<head>` element of `index.html`:

```
<link rel="stylesheet" href="css/main.css">
```

The result of adding the default `main.css` style sheet is shown in Figure 11-3.

Figure 11-3: HTML5 Cafe's `index.html` with HTML5 Boilerplate's default `main.css` applied.

The differences here are a bit more subtle than between Figure 11-1 and Figure 11-2. The main thing that happened is that the line height has been adjusted slightly. Other changes that were made affect only HTML elements that aren't currently used by HTML5 Cafe's home page.

Now (finally!) it's time to get to the good stuff: adding your own style to the web page. If you open up `main.css` in your code editor and scroll down a bit, you see a section labeled Author's Custom Styles. That's you it's talking about! This is where you can put your own CSS and really make HTML5 Cafe sparkle.

Figure 11-4 shows the CSS markup that we added to the custom styles section of `main.css`.

```css
/* ==========================================================================
   Author's custom styles
   ========================================================================== */

#topnav {
    width:100%;
    text-align:center;
    background-color:#000000;
    height:24px;
    color:#FFFFFF;
    }

#topnav a {
    color:#FFFFFF;
    text-decoration: none;
    }

#topnav a:hover {
    text-decoration: underline;
    }

#container {
    width: 600px;
    margin: 10px auto 10px auto;
    border: 2px dotted #333333;
    }

#content {
    padding:10px;
    }

footer {
    font-size: .7em;
    text-align: right;
    }
```

Figure 11-4: Our custom styles for HTML5 Cafe's `index.html`

Although we haven't yet talked about the syntax of CSS style rules, if you look at it for a moment, you can see that it's mostly pretty readable.

We get into much more detail about CSS selectors and properties in the next chapter. For now, just look it over and marvel at the results, as shown in Figure 11-5.

Figure 11-5: HTML5 Cafe's index.html with our custom styles applied.

What you can do with CSS

You have a healthy collection of properties to work with as you write your style rules. You can control just about every aspect of a page's display — from borders to font sizes and everything inbetween:

- **Background properties** control the background colors associated with blocks of text and with images. You can also use these properties to attach background colors to your page or to individual elements, such as horizontal rules.

- **Border properties** control borders associated with a page, lists, tables, images, and block elements (such as paragraphs). You can specify border width, color, style, and distance from element content.

- **Float and Alignment properties** control how elements (such as images) flow on the page relative to other elements. You can use these properties to integrate images and tables with the text on your page.

- **List properties** control how lists appear on your page, such as
  - Managing list markers
  - Using images in place of bullets

- **Margin properties** control the margins of the page and margins around block elements, tables, and images. These properties extend ultimate control over the white space on your page.

✔ **Padding properties** control the amount of white space around any block element on the page. When you use these with margin and border properties, you can create complex layouts.

✔ **Positioning properties** control where elements sit on the page; you can use them to put elements in specific places on the page.

✔ **Size properties** control how much space (in height and width) your elements (both text and images) take up on your page. They're especially handy for limiting the size of text boxes and images.

✔ **Table properties** control the layout of tables. You can use them to control cell spacing and other table-layout specifics.

✔ **Text properties** control how text appears on a page. You can set such properties as font size, font family, height, text color, letter and line spacing, alignment, and white space. These properties give you more control over text with style sheets than the `font` HTML element can.

✔ **Transition properties** create effects in which the value of another style changes smoothly over time. For example, with transitions you can specify that a button should grow when a user takes a certain action, or that an element should change colors, or appear to fade-in.

✔ **Transform properties** control rotation, skewing, scaling, and translation (or positioning) of 2D and 3D objects. Figure 11-6 shows an example of something that can be done with transform properties.

Figure 11-6: You can use transform properties to modify objects in 2D and 3D.

Entire books and websites are devoted to the fine details of using each and every property in these categories. We suggest one of these references:

- ✏ *CSS Web Design For Dummies* by Richard Mansfield
- ✏ *The Book of CSS3* by Peter Gasston
- ✏ *CSS: The Definitive Guide* by Eric A. Meyer
- ✏ Jens Meiert's continuously updated CSS properties references on the web at `http://meiert.com/en/indices/css-properties`

Although CSS syntax is straightforward, combining CSS styles with markup to fine-tune a page layout can get a little complicated. To become a CSS guru, you just need to:

- ✏ Know how the different properties work.
- ✏ Experiment to observe how different browsers handle CSS.
- ✏ Practice conveying your message on the web using CSS.

Putting CSS in Its Place

Before we go any further, we need to explain a few things about the environment in which CSS lives and does its work. CSS is most often used to apply styles to a web page when it's displayed in a web browser — whether that browser is on a desktop computer, a laptop computer, a tablet computer, or a mobile phone.

You can also use CSS to format HTML for printing, for text-to-speech devices, for projectors, or for any device that can read HTML content.

Because you'll most often be formatting HTML for display on some sort of screen, we focus on this scenario here. But, keep in mind that CSS is not limited to working just with screens.

Pixels, points, and dots — Oh my!

Except for their sizes, desktop, laptop, and mobile devices are all pretty similar. They all display text and images on color screens by changing the colors of tiny dots of light, called *pixels*. In fact, if you look closely enough at your computer's monitor (or perhaps use a magnifying glass if you have a very high-resolution monitor), you can probably see the individual pixels that make up every image your monitor or screen displays.

Even though the images on screens are made up of pixels, the size and the proximity of each dot to its neighbor (this is called the *pixel density*) varies between devices and monitors.

In addition, it's possible, and quite common, for computer users to change the number of pixels, known as the *resolution,* displayed on their screens. You may be familiar with the concept of resolution from adjusting it while setting up your computer or from purchasing a TV. Common resolution settings are 640 x 480, 800 x 600, and 1024 x 768. The first number typically refers to the width (in pixels) of the device, and the second refers to the height.

If you're following along, you may be wondering now how a device with a fixed number of physical pixels can sometimes display 800 x 600 pixels and sometimes 1024 x 768 pixels. The key is in a concept called *display pixels,* or, for our purposes, *CSS pixels.*

CSS pixels are a layer on top of the actual physical dots of light that make up images on your screen and the dots as they are presented to you. When you make a picture on your screen be 300 pixels wide, you're talking about CSS pixels. This distinction is good to know, especially when you're working with mobile devices, where it's common to zoom in or out on content. An object that is 300 display pixels wide may actually be 600 device pixels wide if the user's zoom level is 200 percent.

Display pixels are also sometimes referred to as *points* or *dots,* but we encourage you to not use these terms, because they're typically used to describe sizes for printing and only cause confusion on the web.

Fully understanding all the inner workings of display resolution and pixel density and the like isn't necessary in order to write CSS, or even to be a very good web designer. We mention these concepts here so that you're aware of them and so that you know that when we talk about pixels, we're not actually talking about the physical dots of light on your monitor (device pixels), but rather, a unit of measurement equal to at least one device pixel, but usually more — depending on the user's device.

Now that you know the difference between a device pixel and a CSS pixel, we talk briefly about how to measure things on the web.

Understanding the viewport

The *viewport* is the window through which a person sees your awesome web pages. In its simplest terms, it's the area of the web browser in which web pages are displayed. Like a window, the viewport is just a space through which you can view something else (a web page, in this case).

There are two big differences between how physical windows work and how the viewport works, however:

- On a desktop computer, users can resize the viewport by resizing the browser window. This would be like changing the size of a window in your home based on how much of the scene outside you want to be able to see at any time. (Another option would be to move closer to or farther away from the window, which is called *zooming* in the web browser world.)

- The viewport tells the web page its width, which allows the web page to rearrange itself to fit the window. Imagine rearranging objects outside and resizing them so that you can see them from within your room. It's like that.

Newer ways of laying out web pages depend on knowing the viewport width and rearranging elements in the browser dynamically to provide a great user experience to people using differently sized viewports. Using viewports and dynamic arrangement of elements is the main idea behind a type of web design called *responsive design*.

Responsive design came about in response to the increasing number of people who are surfing the web with their smartphones or tablet computers. The idea is that rather than forcing the user to resize or zoom in on your web page, the web page itself should respond to the size of the device viewing it and dynamically reflow content to improve the reading experience on a wider variety of devices.

Property measurement values

Many HTML properties use measurement values. We tell you which measurement values go with which properties throughout this book. Standard property measurements dictate the size of a property in two ways: absolute value measurements and relative value measurements.

Absolute value measurements dictate a specific length or height using one of these values:

- **Inches,** such as `.5in`
- **Centimeters,** such as `3cm`
- **Millimeters,** such as `4mm`
- **Picas,** such as `1pc`

  There are six picas in an inch.

✔ **Points,** such as 16pt. As previously mentioned, pt is a unit that is typically used for print, and you should refrain from using it in CSS that is styling HTML displayed on a screen.

There are 12 points in a pica.

✔ **Pixels,** such as 13px. (Defined as the smallest possible visible point of light that can be displayed, the pixel maps to at least 1 physical pixel on your screen.)

Keep in mind that a measurement of 1in does not necessarily mean 1 inch on the screen. The CSS specification defines an inch to be 96 device pixels. If your screen has a resolution lower than 96 pixels per inch, such as the very common 72 pixels per inch, a CSS inch won't actually be a screen inch.

The most commonly used absolute method for specifying widths and heights, as well as for positioning elements on the screen is px, and that's what we recommend. Although you can use inches or centimeters, it's best to stay away from them when you're designing for the web.

Relative value measurements base length or height on the current value of the element being measured. Relative values have the ability to scale based on factors such as the user's browser size or default font size, so using them for font sizes is considered a best practice . Relative values include the following:

✔ p%: A percentage of the current font-size value, such as 150%.

For example, you can define a font size of 75% for all paragraphs. The default style sheet for most browsers defined the base font size as 16px. So, a setting of 75 percent would cause the paragraph font size to be 12px (16 × 0.75=12).

✔ ex: A value that is relative to the x-height of the current font. An *x-height* is the equivalent of the height of the lowercase character of a font, such as 1.5ex.

✔ em: A value that is relative to the current font size, such as 2em. For any given typeface, 1em is equivalent to its point size. (Thus, a 16pt font has an em size of 16pt. Get it?)

In fact, both 1em and 100% equal the current font size.

When you're specifying the size of type in your web pages, we recommend sticking with using relative sizes specified with em, which we discuss further in the "A clever em trick" sidebar.

A clever em trick

To make em easier to work with and to calculate, many professional web developers use a clever trick. Employ this trick, and you will be among the font size elite.

Recall that the default base font size in the browser is equal to `16px`. In other words, if you don't apply any styling to a document, text in paragraphs will be 16 pixels tall. So, by default, `1em` is equal to `16px`. This is way too large for most web page designs. Most web pages are designed with a base font size of `12px` or `10px`. If you want to specify a `10px` font size using ems, you can say `.625em`. This requires math, however. Math is hard.

An easier way is to simply adjust the value of `1em` to be `10px`. You can do this by globally adjusting the size of the base font to 62.5 percent using the following CSS rule:

```
body {font-size:62.5%;}
```

Now, you can use em measurements just as a designer might use px measurements, but just shift the decimal point over one spot to the left. For example, if you want `<h1>` elements to be `24px`, that will be `2.4em` (2.4 times the base font size of `10px`).

This approach to font sizing gives you the best of both worlds: the ability to know exactly how large your fonts will be and to work with them easily in relation to absolutely sized objects on the screen, while also making sure that users who want or need to increase the font size will have the ability to do so.

About the CSS3 Standard

Whereas both CSS1 and CSS2 were proposed, debated, and finally recommended as big, monolithic standards for Cascading Style Sheets, CSS3 is a collection of many individual modules. If you visit the CSS Level 3 (the formal name for what we and others blithely call CSS3 instead) works-in-progress page at the W3C website (`www.w3.org/Style/CSS/current-work.html`), you can see a list of all the CSS modules in various levels of completion. In Table 11-1, we present these modules with brief descriptions.

Table 11-1 CSS Level 3 Modules, Descriptions, and Standards Status

Name	Description
Grid Template Layout	Describes a new method for positioning elements using constraints on their mutual alignment and flexibility of motion, where a layout grid defines the basic template
CSS Speech	An audio module that enables authors to control how documents are rendered using speech synthesis

Name	Description
Backgrounds and Borders	Describes background colors and images and describes border styles, including background image stretch, images for borders, rounded corners, and shadows
Basic User Interface	Features for styling interactive, dynamic web page aspects, including form element appearance to denote state, plus cursors and colors for GUI use
Box Model	Describes block-level content in normal flow, where document elements are laid out as rectangular boxes in sequence or nested orders that together comprise a horizontal or vertical (for Chinese and Japanese) flow
Marquee	Contains properties to control speed and direction of a marquee area, a scrolling mechanism that moves text through a region with no user intervention involved; used mostly on mobile devices
Cascading and Inheritance	Describes how values are assigned to properties, where cascading describes how multiple style sheets are combined, and inheritance involves parent value assignments or initial value settings
Color	Specifies color-related CSS controls, including transparency and notations for the `color` value-type
Fonts	Properties to select and adjust fonts, including emboss and outline effects, kerning, smoothing, and anti-aliasing
Generated Content for Paged Media	Advanced printing properties that go beyond the Paged Media module, including creating footnotes, cross-references, and generation of running headers from section titles
Image Values and Replaced Content	Defines how to deposit content on a page before, after, or instead of some element, where content can be text or an image or some other external object
Hyperlink Presentation	Properties to control how hyperlinks are presented, including controls on which hyperlinks are active, where targets are shown when a user traverses a link, and more
Line Layout	Describes alignment of text and other boxes on a line; expands `vertical-align` property for CSS1/2 to support alignment of multiple script types, including non-Roman alphabets and ideographs
Lists	Properties for styling lists, especially for bullet types, numbering systems, and use of images (especially for bullets) within list displays
Math	Properties for styling mathematical formulae, based on the presentational elements in the XML-based MathML application

(continued)

Table 11-1 *(continued)*

Name	Description
Multicolumn Layout	New properties to flow content into flexibly defined columnar layouts
Namespaces	Explains how CSS selectors can be extended to select elements based on XML-derived namespaces that can distinguish among multiple uses of the same element name from one another across multiple style sheets
Object Model	The Document Object Model (DOM) specifies functions used in programming libraries and web browsers to manipulate HTML, XML, and CSS documents; addresses functions for adding and deleting rules and changing properties in CSS style sheets, for APIs called the CSS Object Model or CSSOM
CSSOM View Module	Tool APIs to enable authors to inspect and manipulate document view information, including position data for element layout boxes, width of script viewports, and element scrolling
Paged Media	Extends print control properties from CSS2 with controls for running headers, footers, and page numbers
Positioning	Covers properties for absolute, fixed, and relative positioning of elements, to take them out of normal document flow and place them elsewhere on a page
Presentation Levels	Tools for stepping forward and backward through multiple renderings of a document, especially useful for slide presentations, outline views, and so forth
Ruby	Properties to manipulate Ruby positions, for small annotations on top of or next to ideograms or words in Chinese and Japanese (often used to hint pronunciation or meaning for difficult ideograms)
Style Attribute Syntax	Rules for expressing CSS markup as part of HTML and other markup language attributes (SVG)
Syntax	Generic, forward-compatible grammar which all levels of CSS must follow; value syntax restrictions for specific properties are addressed in other modules
Tables	Table layout controls, including rows, columns, cells, captions, borders, and alignment (same as in CSS2 but described in more detail in CSS3)
Text	Text-related properties from CSS2 with new properties for dealing with text in different languages and scripts with special emphasis on International Layout; text properties also covered in the Text Layout and Line Grid modules

Name	*Description*
Line Grid	Describes text where symbols in a line are aligned to an invisible grid, so all symbols line up vertically, commonly used for text composed of ideographs as in Japanese
Values and Units	Describes common values and units associated with CSS properties, along with describing how specified values from a style sheet get processed into computed values or actual values at runtime
Fonts	Describes how to download fonts for use within a document (also used within SVG, an XML-based stroke graphics rendering markup application)
Behavioral Extensions	Defines the binding property from the XML-based XML Binding Language, or XBL, to CSS, for associating elements in a document with scripts, event handlers, and CSS
Flexible Box Layout	Defines the `box` and `inline-box` keywords for the CSS `display` property, which causes an element to be displayed as a row or column of child elements, with controls over order and space distribution
Transforms	Defines properties to apply rotations, translations, or other visual transformations to an element box (same as in SVG)
Transitions	Properties to animate transitions between pseudo-classes, as when an element enters or leaves the hover state, with values for delay and value transitions between pairs of values (old/new, on/off, and so on)
Animations	Specifies properties that change their values during an animation, what sequence of values they take, and how long they hold each value

If you're interested in more information about current work on CSS3 (or other related efforts), please visit the W3C's Current Work page at `www.w3.org/Style/CSS/current-work.html`.

12

CSS Structure and Syntax

In This Chapter

▷ Using selectors and declarations

▷ Creating style rules

▷ Discovering CSS properties

▷ Understanding inheritance and the style cascade

*I*n this chapter, we talk about the rules, or syntax, of CSS. Once you understand how CSS goes about locating elements and applying styles to them, we'll get into more details about the important topic of cascading. So far, we've only touched on the topic of cascading but it's vital to understanding how to use CSS.

Exploring CSS Structure and Syntax

A style sheet is made of *style rules*. Each style rule has two parts:

▷ **Selector:** Specifies the markup element to which style rules apply

▷ **Declaration:** Specifies how content described by the markup looks

You use a set of punctuation marks and special characters to define a style rule. The syntax for a style rule always follows this pattern:

```
selector {declaration;}
```

A semicolon always follows each declaration to make it easier for computers to distinguish them. As we explain later in this chapter, a single selector may include one or more declarations. Furthermore, each declaration breaks down into two subitems:

✔ **Properties** are aspects of how the computer displays text and graphics (for example, font size or background color).

✔ **Values** provide data to specify how you want text and images to look on your page (for example, a 24pt font size or a yellow background).

You separate the property from the value in a declaration with a colon, and each declaration ends with a semicolon:

```
selector {property: value;}
```

The CSS specification lists exactly which properties you work with in your style rules and the different values they take. Most properties are pretty self-explanatory (color and border, for example). See Chapter 11 for a quick rundown of properties included in CSS.

Style sheets override a browser's internal (default) display rules; your style declarations affect the final appearance of the page in the user's browser. This means that you control how your content looks and create a more consistent and appropriate experience for visitors.

Figure 12-1 shows a simple HTML page with all three heading levels (plus some body text) without the style sheet applied. The browser uses its default settings to display the headings in different font sizes.

Figure 12-1: An HTML page without style specifications.

To spruce things up a bit, you might apply the following style rules to this page:

```
body {font-family: Arial;}

h1 {color: teal;
     font-size: 3em;}

h2 {color: maroon;
     font-size: 2em;}

h3 {color: black;
     font-size: 1.5em;}

p {font-style: italic;}
```

Figure 12-2 shows the same web page with the styles applied. Things look very different because the body text is changed to a sans-serif font, header titles are set for different colors, paragraph text is italic, and heading sizes are magnified beyond their usual settings.

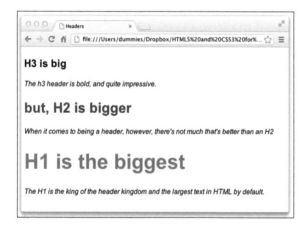

Figure 12-2: An HTML page with custom style rules in effect.

Users can change their preferences so that their browsers ignore your style sheets (although most users will use your sheets). For example, a person who has trouble reading small text may override your style sheet to make the text larger. If you don't anticipate this in your design, a larger font size may cause your site to look bad or even to not work at all. Test web pages with style sheets turned off to be sure they look good (or acceptable) without your style sheets.

For detailed instructions on disabling or altering style sheets, see Jim Thatcher's discussion "Reading Web Pages without CSS" at www.jimthatcher.com/ webcourseb.htm. The instructions vary by web browser, but you can use accessibility plug-ins to manage or disable style sheets.

Font family

When assigning values to the `font-family` property, you can use a list of comma-separated font names. These names must match fonts available to a user's web browser. If a font name includes spaces — such as Times New Roman — enclose it in quotation marks.

```
h1 {font-family: Verdana, "Times New Roman", serif;}
```

In the preceding rule, the browser knows to use Verdana first; if that's not available, it looks for Times New Roman, and then it uses a generic serif font as its last option. Chapter 17 covers the use of fonts in CSS.

Selectors and declarations

You probably want a style rule to affect the display of more than one property for any given selector. You can create several style rules for a single selector, each with one declaration, like this:

```
h1 {color: teal;}
h1 {font-family: Arial;}
h1 {font-size: 3em;}
```

However, such a large collection of style rules can be hard to manage. CSS allows you to combine several declarations in a single style rule that affects multiple display characteristics for a single selector, like this:

```
h1 {color: teal;
    font-family: Arial;
    font-size: 3em;}
```

All the declarations for the `h1` selector are within the same set of brackets (`{}`) and are separated by semicolons (`;`). You can put as many declarations as you want in a style rule; just end each declaration with a semicolon.

From a purely technical standpoint, white space is irrelevant in style sheets (just as it is in HTML), but you should use a consistent spacing scheme to make it easy to read and edit your style sheets. One exception to this white space rule occurs when you declare multiple font names in the `font-family` declaration. See the "Font family" sidebar for more information.

You can make the same set of declarations apply to a collection of selectors, too: You just separate the selectors with commas. The following style rule applies the declarations for text color, font family, and font size to the `h1`, `h2`, and `h3` selectors:

```
h1, h2, h3 {color: teal;
            font-family: Arial;
            font-size: 2.5em;}
```

Style sheet syntax relies heavily on punctuation, so mind your colons and commas or a style rule might not work exactly as you expect. If that happens, make sure that you're not using a semicolon where you need a colon, or a parenthesis where you need a curly bracket. Watch out for semicolons, too! Validation tools help catch these lapses: Use them. The W3C CSS validation service at http://jigsaw.w3.org/css-validator helps find problems in your style sheets.

The selectors

Before you can style an element, you need to tell the browser which element you want to style. This is where the selector comes in. CSS contains several ways to select elements, ranging from the very broad (select everything) to the very specific (select only one particular instance of an element).

The universal selector

The most basic selector of all is the *universal selector*. The universal selector matches any element type. The symbol for the universal selector is the asterisk (*). Here's the universal selector being used to set the margin on every element in the document to 0:

```
* {margin: 0px;}
```

The universal selector is useful as a tool for taking a shortcut through the thickets of complex selectors that are sometimes required to address elements that are nested deep within a document. For example, suppose it's St. Patrick's Day and you want to change the color of every element to green. You can do this, and override the base color of every element, by using a universal selector:

```
* {color: green;}
```

That's some powerful stuff! To see the universal selector in action, follow these steps:

1. **Open Aptana Studio if it isn't already open.**

2. **Open `index.html` for editing.**

   This is the home page of the HTML5 Cafe site, and it should look something like the markup in Listing 12-1.

Listing 12-1: The HTML Markup for the HTML5 Cafe Home Page

```
<!DOCTYPE html>
<html>
    <head>
        <meta charset="utf-8">
        <title>HTML5 Cafe: Home</title>
        <meta name="description" content="sample site for 9781118657201">
        <meta name="viewport" content="width=device-width">
        <link rel="stylesheet" href="css/normalize.css">
        <link rel="stylesheet" href="css/main.css">
    </head>
    <body>
        <div id="container">
            <nav id="topnav">
                <a href="index.html">HOME</a> | <a href="about.html">ABOUT US</a> | <a
href="menu.html">MENU</a> | <a href="contact.html">CONTACT US</a>
            </nav>
            <div id="content">
                <h1>Welcome to HTML5 Cafe!</h1>
                <p>Here you will find all sorts of delicious HTML5 and CSS3 treats.
                </p>
                <figure id="home-image">
                    <img src="img/pitr_Coffee_cup_icon.png"
                    width="400" height="400" alt="delicious coffee">
                    <figcaption class="warning">
                        powered by coffee.
                    </figcaption>
                </figure>
            </div>
            <footer>
                copyright &copy; dummieshtml.com
            </footer>
        </div>
    </body>
</html>
```

If you preview the home page in a browser at this point, it should resemble Figure 12-3.

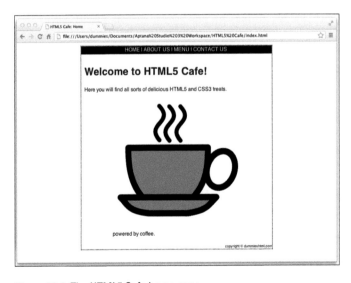

3. **Insert a new line right before `</head>`.**

4. **Type the following:**

```
<style>
    * {color: green;}
</style>
```

5. **Save your changes to `index.html` and open the file in your web browser.**

   You see something similar to Figure 12-4.

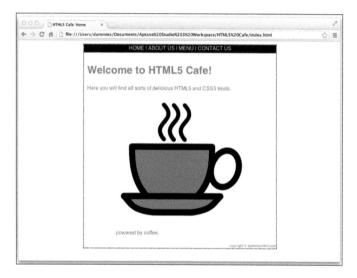

Figure 12-4: Top o' the mornin' to ya! That's a lot of green.

You may be surprised that more things didn't turn green in Figure 12-4. For example, the border around the page and the navigation links kept their old colors. The reason is in the definition of the universal selector:

   The universal selector selects any element type.

In other words, styles rules with the universal selector are applied to every element, but any element in the document may be styled differently if you use one of the other, more specific, selectors. This is what's happening here.

Here's a more interesting example of the universal selector. In this example, we add a CSS transform effect to every element in the document:

1. **Assuming that you still have `index.html` open in Aptana Studio, delete the previous CSS rule you created (but leave the beginning and ending `<style>` tags in place).**

2. Type the following rule between the `<style>` and `</style>` tags.

```
* {-webkit-transform: rotate(100deg);
   -moz-transition: rotate(100deg);
   -ms-transition: rotate(100deg);
   -o-transition: rotate(100deg);}
```

This rule rotates every element in the document 100 degrees. When you preview the document in your browser, you now see something like the web page in Figure 12-5.

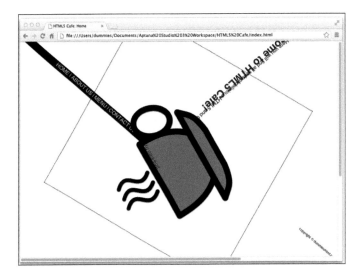

Figure 12-5: Who jumbled up the web page?

The universal selector is the most blunt tool in our shed. For more precise CSS work, additional selectors are available.

You may occasionally see CSS declarations containing `property:value` pairs that are identical except for a few characters at the beginning that start with a dash, as in the last example.

```
-webkit-transform: rotate(100deg);
-moz-transition: rotate(100deg);
-ms-transition: rotate(100deg);
-o-transition: rotate(100deg);
```

These characters — such as `webkit` and `moz` — at the beginning of the property name are called *browser prefixes*. Because some of the CSS3 properties are not yet final, browser creators implemented their own versions of these CSS3 features, and named them with browser prefixes to indicate that they aren't the standard versions of the properties.

Each declaration in the preceding rule is targeted at a different web browser, or type of web browser. The first browser prefix, -webkit, is used with Google Chrome and Apple Safari (among others). The second browser prefix, -moz, is used by Mozilla's Firefox browser. The -o prefix belongs to the Opera browser. The -ms prefix is for Microsoft's Internet Explorer.

In most cases, vendor-specific properties work the same (or close to the same) as one another, and as the latest version of the unfinished standard property. As CSS3 properties become standards, browser prefixes will become unnecessary. For now, however, it's a good idea, and required in many cases, to use them for certain CSS3 properties.

Element type selectors

Element type selectors select a particular type of element. For example, you may want to change the size of every <h1> element in your document or change the font style of paragraph text. Here's an example of an element type selector in a rule that changes the font size of the <h1> element to 3em.

```
h1 {font-size: 3em;}
```

The element type selector works the same as the universal selector, except only with one element type. For example, if you wanted to only rotate the coffee cup image on the HTML5 Cafe home page, you could do so by simply changing the universal selector from the previous example to img. Here's the new declaration:

```
img {-webkit-transform: rotate(100deg);
     -moz-transition: rotate(100deg);
     -ms-transition: rotate(100deg);
     -o-transition: rotate(100deg);}
```

When you preview the page, it looks like Figure 12-6.

But, what if you had multiple images on this page and wanted only one of them to be rotated? For that, you need yet another, more specific, selector.

ID selectors

ID selectors select an element according to its ID attribute. Because the ID attribute is designed to be unique within an HTML document, the ID selector is a good way to address just one particular element.

For example, if you look at the HTML for the HTML5 Cafe home page, you see that it contains two <div> elements. One of these elements encloses the entire contents of the <body> and has an ID value of container. The other element surrounds just the center content area (excluding the navigation and the footer) and has an ID value of content.

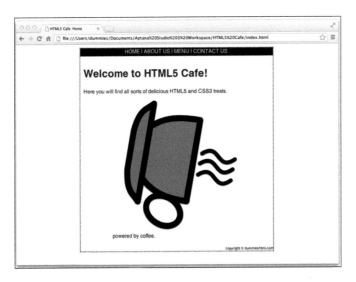

Figure 12-6: The cup spilleth over.

To use an ID selector, you preface the value of the ID you want to select with a # symbol. For example, if you want to change the background color on the div with the ID of content, you would use the following declaration:

```
#content {background-color: aquamarine;}
```

Class selectors

Sometimes you need style rules that apply only to specific instances of an HTML markup element. For example, if you want a style rule that applies only to paragraphs that hold copyright information, you need a way to tell the browser that a rule has a limited scope.

To target a style rule closely, combine the class attribute with a markup element. The following examples show HTML for two kinds of paragraphs:

- ✒ A regular paragraph (without a class attribute)

    ```
    <p>This is a regular paragraph.</p>
    ```
- ✒ A class attribute with the value of copyright

    ```
    <p class="copyright">This is a paragraph of class
            copyright. &copy; 2013.</p>
    ```

To create a style rule that applies only to the copyright paragraph, follow the paragraph selector in the style rule with

- ✒ A period (.)
- ✒ The value of the class attribute, such as copyright

The resulting rule looks like this:

```
p.copyright {font-family: Arial;
            font-size: 12px;
            color: white;
            background: teal;}
```

By combining an element type selector (p) with a class selector (.copyright), we can specify that the following rules apply only to p elements with this class attribute. This style rule specifies that all paragraphs of class copyright display white text on a teal background in 12px Arial font.

To test out this new copyright class, add a paragraph tag with a copyright class to the copyright info in the footer of HTML5 Cafe's index.html:

```
<footer>
    <p class="copyright">copyright &copy; dummieshtml.com</p>
</footer>
```

Figure 12-7 shows how a browser applies this style only to a paragraph where class equals copyright and not to the other paragraph on the page.

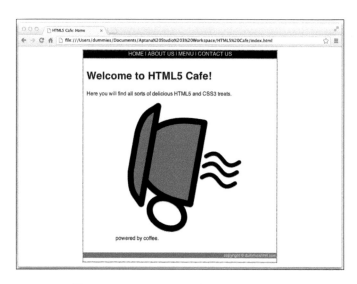

Figure 12-7: Classes can target your style rules more precisely.

You can also create style-rule classes that aren't associated with any element, like the following example:

```
.warning {color: red;
          font-weight: bold;
          font-size: 1.5em;}
```

You can use this style class with any element by adding `class="warning"` to that element. Figure 12-8 shows how a browser applies the warning style to the paragraph and heading, but not to the block quote, as in this HTML:

```
<p>This is a paragraph without the warning class applied.</p>
<blockquote>This is a block quote without a defined class.</blockquote>
<h1 class="warning">Warnings</h1>
<p class="warning">This is a paragraph with the warning class applied.</p>
```

Figure 12-8: You can use class selectors to create style rules that work with any element.

You can also use the `span` element to selectively apply custom styles to inline content (or to create arbitrary content containers that extend from the opening `<span>` tag to its closing `</span>` counterpart):

```
<p>This is a paragraph without the <span class="warning">warning class</span>
            applied only to the words "warning class."</p>
```

To see this declaration in action, add it inside the `<style>` element in `index.html` and then place `class="warning"` within the starting tag of one of the elements containing text in `index.html`.

```
<figcaption class="warning">powered by coffee.</figcaption>
```

When you preview the document in a browser, the text inside of `<fig caption>` should now be red, bold, and larger, as shown in Figure 12-9.

Other selectors

CSS includes other selector types as well, which are somewhat more advanced and less commonly used than the four we cover in the preceding sections. These are:

- **Adjacent sibling selector:** Selects elements only when they are next to another specified element.

    ```
    h1 + p {font-style: italic; }
    ```

    The preceding example applies to any `<p>` that directly follows an `<h1>`.

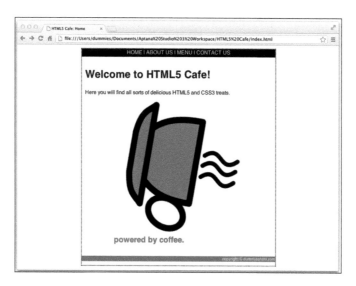

Figure 12-9: Using a class selector to apply style to an element.

- **Attribute selector:** Selects elements based on the values of their attributes.

  ```
  img[src="chris.jpg"] {border: 6px solid purple;}
  ```

  This rule applies a thick purple border to any `<img>` with a `src` attribute equal to `chris.jpg`.

- **Child selector:** Selects elements that are a direct child of another element. For example, in this HTML, the `<em>` is a direct child of `<p>`, but the `<a>` is not.

  ```
  <p>It is <em>important</em> to remember this <a
          href="picture.jpg">picture</a>.</p>
  ```

  To use a child selector, type > between the parent and its direct child that you want to target.

  ```
  p>em {color:red;}
  ```

- **Descendant selector:** Selects elements that are lower on the document tree than a specified element. For example, this rule targets any `<p>` that is nested within a `<footer>`:

  ```
  footer p {font-size: 50%;}
  ```

  Note that descendant selectors apply to all descendants that match the selector, not just to the first descendant. So, the preceding example matches the `<p>` in this HTML:

  ```
  <footer><p>copyright 2013</p></footer>
  ```

as well as the one in this HTML:

```
<footer><div><p>copyright 2013</p></div></footer>
```

✔ **Pseudo-classes:** Selects elements based on properties that aren't in the document tree. For example, you can use a pseudo-class to apply a style to an element when the user hovers the mouse over the element, or to change the style of a link that has been visited previously.

```
a:hover{text-decoration:none;}
```

In this example, the underline is removed from links when the user points at the link with the mouse.

The list of possible pseudo-classes includes the following:

- :first-child
- :link
- :visited
- :hover
- :active
- :focus
- :lang(n)

Inheriting styles

A basic concept in HTML (and markup in general) is nesting tags:

✔ Every valid HTML document nests within <html> and </html> tags.

✔ Everything a browser displays in a window is nested within <body> and </body> tags. (That's just the beginning, really.)

The CSS specification recognizes that you often nest one element inside another and wants to be sure that styles associated with the parent element find their way to the child element. This mechanism is called *inheritance*.

When you assign a style to an element, the same style applies to all elements nested inside that element. For example, a style rule for the body element that sets page background, text color, font size, font family, and margins looks like this:

```
body {background: teal;
      color: white;
      font-size: 18px;
      font-family: Garamond;
      margin-left: 72px;
      margin-right: 72px;
      margin-top: 72px; }
```

Pay attention to inheritance!

When you build complex style sheets to guide the appearance of every aspect of a page, keep inheritance in mind. For instance, if you set margins for a page in a body style rule, all margins you set for every other element on the page are based on margins set for the body. If you know how your style rules work together, you can use inheritance to minimize style rule repetition and create a cohesive display for your page.

This chapter covers basic CSS syntax, but you can fine-tune your style rules with advanced techniques. A complete overview of CSS syntax rules is available in the "CSS Structure and Rules" tutorial by the Web Design Group at www.htmlhelp.com/reference/css/structure.html.

To set style rules for the entire document, set them in the body element. Changing the font for the entire page, for example, is much easier to do that way; it beats changing every single element one at a time.

When you link the following HTML to the preceding style rule, which applies only to the body element, that formatting is inherited by all subordinate elements:

```
<body>
  <p>This paragraph inherits the page styles.</p>
  <h1>As does this heading</h1>
  <ul>
      <li>As do the items in this list</li>
      <li>Item</li>
      <li>Item</li>
  </ul>
</body>
```

Understanding the Cascade

Multiple style sheets can affect page elements and build upon each other. It's like inheriting styles within a web page. This is the *cascading* part of CSS.

Cascading is how CSS deals with situations in which two or more style rules have declarations that apply to the same element and property. The three principles of cascading to keep in mind are:

- **Origin:** Did the user specify one of the style rules? If so, this is the most important one and wins in a conflict.

- **Specificity:** ID selectors beat class selectors. Class selectors beat element type selectors.

✔ **Proximity:** How close is the style to the element being styled? The next chapter shows you that there are three places where style rules can be defined. The one that's closest to the element being styled, or that is read last by the browser, wins in a conflict.

For example, here's a simple bit of HTML markup with a couple of elements:

```
<body>
    <div id="content">
        <p class="information">This is the content.</p>
    </div>
</body>
```

Here's part of a style sheet that's applied to this HTML:

```
body {font-family: Arial;}
div {color: green;}
p {font-size: 18px;
   color: blue;}
.information {font-size: 16px;}
```

Notice that these style rules apply two different font sizes and two different colors to the <p> element. The browser needs to resolve this conflict, and it does so by using the principles of origin, specificity, and proximity. In this particular case, after all the conflicts are resolved the text inside the <p> element has the following rules applied to it:

```
font-family: Arial;
color: blue;
font-size: 16px;
```

Even though two different font sizes and two different colors apply to the paragraph text in this example, text can only be one color and one size at a time. By applying the three principles of the cascade, the browser has resolved the conflict and the winning styles have been chosen.

13

Using Different Kinds of Style Sheets

In This Chapter

▷ Using inline styles

▷ Styling a page with the `<style>` element

▷ Using external style sheets

▷ Styling a site with external style sheets

*W*hen you finish creating your style rules, you're ready to connect them to your HTML page by using one of these options:

✓ **Insert style information into your document.** You can either

• Use the `style` attribute to add style information directly to a tag. This is an *inline style*.

• Use the `<style>` element to build a style sheet into a web page. This is an *internal style sheet*.

✓ **Use an external style sheet.** You can either

• Use the `<link>` tag to link your web page to an external style sheet.

• Use the CSS `@import` statement to import an external style sheet into the web page.

Applying Inline Styles

Each element in an HTML document has a special, optional attribute named `style`. Web page authors use the `style` attribute to apply CSS rules to that single element without having to worry about using a selector. Style rules applied in this way are called *inline styles*.

Listing 13-1 shows a sample HTML document that has been styled entirely with inline styles.

Listing 13-1:   An HTML Document Styled with Inline Styles

```
<!DOCTYPE html>
<html>
    <head>
        <meta charset="utf-8">
        <title>HTML5 Cafe: Home</title>
        <meta name="description" content="sample site for 9781118657201">
        <meta name="viewport" content="width=device-width">
    </head>
    <body style="font-family: Arial;">
        <div id="container" style="width: 600px; margin: 10px auto 10px; border: 2px dotted
#333333;">
            <nav id="topnav" style="width: 100%;text-align: center;background-color: #000000;height:
24px;color:#FFFFFF;">
                <a href="index.html" style="color:white;text-decoration: none;">HOME</a> |
                <a href="about.html" style="color:white;text-decoration: none;">ABOUT US</a> |
                <a href="menu.html" style="color:white;text-decoration: none;">MENU</a> |
                <a href="contact.html" style="color:white;text-decoration: none;">CONTACT US</a>
            </nav>
        <div id="content" style="padding: 10px;">
            <h1>Welcome to HTML5 Cafe!</h1>
            <p>Here you will find all sorts of delicious HTML5 and CSS3 treats.</p>
            <figure id="home-image">
                <img src="img/pitr_Coffee_cup_icon.png"
                        width="400" height="400" alt="delicious coffee">
                <figcaption class="warning">powered by coffee.</figcaption>
            </figure>
        </div>
            <footer style="font-size: .7em; text-align: right;">
              copyright &copy; dummieshtml.com
            </footer>
        </div>
    </body>
</html>
```

One thing you may notice about this document is that it's wordy. Because inline styles apply only to the element they're inside of, using inline styles requires a lot of typing.

The result of all this typing is a web page that looks exactly like the original HTML5 Cafe home page.

Inline styles are also difficult to maintain. Imagine if you wrote the document from Figure 13-1 and then wanted to change the color that's applied to the link elements. You'd need to carefully go through the markup and change the color for each link to the new value. In this particular example, that might take only a few moments. But what if the document had many more links?

For example, what if it was a hyperlinked index for a book? You could spend hours going through and modifying the inline styles for each link.

Welcome to HTML5 Cafe!

Here you will find all sorts of delicious HTML5 and CSS3 treats.

powered by coffee.

Figure 13-1: The result of styling the HTML5 Cafe home page with inline styles.

Of course, no one would actually build a website this way.

In fact, if there's any chance that you'll ever want to reuse or modify a style, you shouldn't use inline styles. So, when *should* you use inline styles? Practically never.

As always, there are exceptions to our opinion that you should never use inline styles. However, most of them have to do with working around bugs in programs that will be using the CSS. For example, if you're writing an HTML e-mail, it's necessary to use inline styles to ensure compatibility with certain e-mail programs. For normal day-to-day web development, do your future self a favor (as well as anyone else who might need to edit your markup) and don't use inline styles.

The one thing that's good about inline styles is that they're nearly at the top of the CSS cascade. In other words, a style applied using an inline style takes precedence over any other style that may apply to that element.

Once again, there are exceptions to our statements about inline styles taking precedence over every other style. The exceptions are as follows:

✔ **User style sheet:** These are styles defined by someone inside of their own web browser. For example, users with vision disabilities may universally adjust font sizes in their browsers to make web pages easier to read.

✔ **The !important attribute:** The !important attribute is like an escape hatch from the cascade. To use !important, put it after the value in a CSS declaration, immediately before the semicolon. For example:

```
p {color: purple !important;}
```

When you use !important, you bypass the normal cascade, and the style with the !important attribute is applied. Period.

Okay. We know of one small exception to the !important exception. When a user's style sheet also specifies the same declaration as !important, the declaration marked as !important can lose the cascade battle. This situation is really rare, however, and applies only to that one user's browser. So, effectively, you can count on !important to mean "do it, no matter what!"

Getting to Know Internal Style Sheets

Like inline styles, an internal style sheet lives inside your HTML page. Unlike inline styles, the rules in an internal style sheet use selectors and can apply to multiple elements within a document.

Understanding the <style> element

To create an internal style sheet, just add style rules to the <style> element in the document header. You can include as many (or as few) style rules as you want in an internal style sheet.

The style element doesn't require any attributes in HTML5. In previous versions of HTML, a type attribute was required, which explicitly specified that the style rules were CSS style rules. This was pretty much always redundant, however, because CSS was the only type of style rule anyone was using in HTML. The elimination of such silly and redundant requirements is just one of the beautiful things about HTML5.

Figuring out internal style sheet scope

Rules defined in an internal style sheet apply to just the HTML document in which they appear. It's common to use internal style sheets when your entire website is just that one page, or when a single page needs to have some styles that are different from the rest of the pages in the site.

Listing 13-2 shows how you can rewrite the example from Listing 13-1 using an internal style sheet. Notice how much cleaner the HTML is in this example.

Listing 13-2: Internal Style Sheets Use Selectors and Apply to a Single Document

```html
<!DOCTYPE html>
<html>
    <head>
        <meta charset="utf-8">
        <title>HTML5 Cafe: Home</title>
        <meta name="description" content="sample site for 9781118657201">
        <meta name="viewport" content="width=device-width">
        <style>
            #topnav {
                width:100%;
                text-align:center;
                background-color:#000000;
                height:24px;
                color:#FFFFFF;
                }

            #topnav a {
                color:#FFFFFF;
                text-decoration: none;
                }

            #topnav a:hover {
                text-decoration: underline;
                }

            #container {
                width: 600px;
                margin: 10px auto 10px auto;
                border: 2px dotted #333333;
                }

            #content {
                padding:10px;
                }

            footer {
                font-size: .7em;
                text-align: right;
                }
        </style>
    </head>
    <body>
        <div id="container">
          <nav id="topnav">
            <a href="index.html">HOME</a> |
            <a href="about.html">ABOUT US</a> |
            <a href="menu.html">MENU</a> |
            <a href="contact.html">CONTACT US</a>
          </nav>
        <div id="content">
          <h1>Welcome to HTML5 Cafe!</h1>
          <p>Here you will find all sorts of delicious HTML5 and CSS3 treats.</p>
          <figure id="home-image">
            <img src="img/pitr_Coffee_cup_icon.png"
                 width="400" height="400" alt="delicious coffee">
            <figcaption class="warning">powered by coffee.</figcaption>
          </figure>
        </div>
          <footer>
            copyright &copy; dummieshtml.com
          </footer>
        </div>
        </body>
</html>
```

If you need to change the color of the top navigation links in this document to red, you can do so by just making one edit: Simply change the value of the color property. So, the `#topnav a` rule before the change looks like this:

```
#topnav a {
    color:#FFFFFF;
    text-decoration: none;
    }
```

and after the change, it might look like this:

```
#topnav a {
    color:#FF0000;
    text-decoration: none;
    }
```

In this example, we specify the color using what's called *hexadecimal notation*. We talk more about the different ways of naming colors in HTML in Chapter 16. For now, just know that the first two characters (after the #) specify the amount of red, the third and fourth characters specify the amount of green, and the fifth and sixth specify the amount of blue. By combining different amounts of each color, you can create exactly 16,777,216 different colors.

The benefit of using an internal style sheet is convenience: Your style rules are on the same page as your markup, so you can tweak both quickly. If you want the same style rules to control the appearance of more than one HTML page, move those styles from individual web pages to an external style sheet.

Working with External Style Sheets

An external style sheet holds all your style rules in a separate text document that you can reference from any HTML file on your site. You must maintain a separate style sheet file, but an external style sheet offers benefits for overall site maintenance. If your site's pages use the same style sheet, you can change any formatting characteristic on all pages with a change to the style sheet.

CSS files

External style sheets follow the same format as internal style sheets except that they aren't enclosed within a `<style>` element. Instead, external style sheets are made up of one or more CSS rules in a file saved with the extension `.css`.

In earlier chapters, we present a couple of examples of external style sheets. For example, in Chapter 11, we look at `normalize.css` and `main.css`.

Link element attributes

Listing 13-3 shows the `<head>` element from a page in the HTML5 Cafe site, which includes both the `normalize.css` and `main.css` style sheets. Any number of external style sheets may be included in the `<head>` of a document.

Listing 13-3:   The `<head>` Element from a Page in the HTML5 Cafe Site

```
<head>
    <meta charset="utf-8">
    <title>HTML5 Cafe: Home</title>
    <meta name="description" content="sample site for 9781118657201">
    <meta name="viewport" content="width=device-width">
    <link rel="stylesheet" href="css/normalize.css">
    <link rel="stylesheet" href="css/main.css">
</head>
```

Notice the two `<link>` elements in this markup. The `<link>` element is most often used to link to style sheets. Two attributes are required when you use `<link>` to link to an external style sheet.

The `rel` attribute indicates the relationship between the linked document and the document that's linking to it. When you're linking to a style sheet, the `rel` attribute should always have a value of `stylesheet`.

The other required attribute is `href`. As with the `<a>` element, the `href` attribute contains the path to the linked file. The `href` attribute in the `<link>` element can take either of the following:

- ✔ A relative link (a style sheet on your own site)
- ✔ An absolute link (a style sheet that doesn't reside on your own site)

To quickly add style to your web page (or to experiment to see how browsers handle different styles), use an absolute URL to point to one of the W3C's Core Style sheets. Read more about them at `www.w3.org/StyleSheets/Core`. Chapter 8 covers the difference between relative and absolute links.

Usually, you shouldn't use a style sheet that doesn't reside on your website, because you want control of your site's look and feel.

We recommend using an external style sheet for every website. Even if your website currently contains only one page, it will likely grow in the future, and you'll be glad that you had the foresight to set things up the right way in the first place. Then you'll remember that we advised you to do just that, and you'll turn to your co-worker and say, "I need to buy Ed and Chris a beer.

That advice they gave me was exactly right!" Of course, we're not going to share a single beer, so we'll do our best to provide you with at least one more beer-worthy tip in this book — and hopefully many more than that.

Importing and when to use @import

Another way to include CSS in your HTML document is with the @import statement. The @import statement instructs the browser to load an external style sheet and use its styles. You use it within the <style> element but before any of the individual style rules, like so:

```
<style>
    @import "http://www.somesite.edu/stylesheet.css";
</style>
```

You can also use the @import statement within external style sheets to create a sort of super-external style sheet. For example, you can have an external style sheet that references other external style sheets. However, just because you *could* do something doesn't mean that it's the best thing to do.

The truth is that @import is convenient but otherwise not good for much. You could organize your CSS styles into multiple external style sheets and then link them together or import them into the <style> element in a page. Unfortunately, this added complexity can have a negative impact on the performance of your web pages.

Most experts agree that the best way to use style sheets is to have as few external style sheets as possible and use the <link> element to include them in the <head> of each HTML page in your site.

Part V
Enhancing Your Pages' Look and Feel

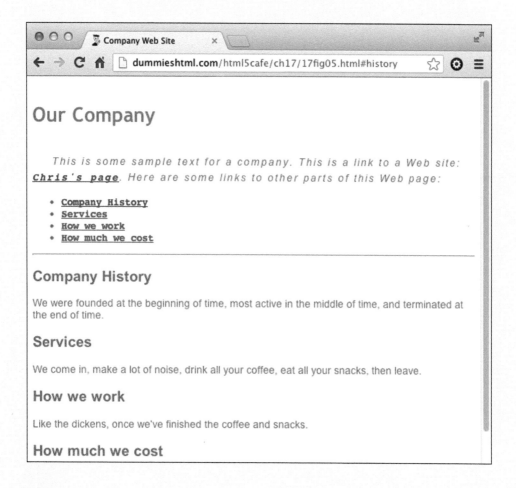

To access some great CSS resources for buttons, colors, fonts, and text effects, visit www.dummies.com/extras/beginninghtml5css3. Also, all links and markup examples are available online at www.dummieshtml.com/html5cafe/menu.html in the sections labeled Ch14 through Ch19.

In this part . . .

- Breaking into CSS box models for HTML elements
- Perfecting HTML element positioning with CSS markup
- Building page elements with CSS buttons, borders, and backgrounds
- Working with color in CSS to add contrast, drama, and readability to your pages
- Managing typography on web pages with CSS
- Crafting careful and dramatics text effects with CSS
- Creating animations with CSS, including using colors and objects

14

Managing Layout and Positioning

In This Chapter

▷ Understanding the box model

▷ Positioning objects on a page

▷ Floating elements

▷ Using a layout generator

*I*t's time to start getting the details of how CSS helps you format a web page. In this chapter, we cover the important issue of how to position elements in a web page. We also discuss the two categories of elements where CSS is concerned. Finally, we show you an online tool that you can use to create complex website layouts easily.

If you need a refresher on CSS style rules and properties, read Chapter 12 (a high-level overview of CSS and how it works). Then you can return to this chapter and put CSS into action.

Managing Layout

You can use CSS to lay out your pages so that images and blocks of text

▷ Appear exactly where you want them to.

▷ Fit exactly within the amount of space you want them to occupy.

As is the case with every CSS change you make to a web page, positioning elements is all about changing the default behavior of HTML elements in the browser.

Tiny boxes

CSS treats each visible element in an HTML document as a rectangle. A line of text is a rectangle. An image of a circle is a rectangle. A picture of your cat is a rectangle. Figure 14-1 illustrates this point by drawing rectangles on a web page in approximately the places where CSS does.

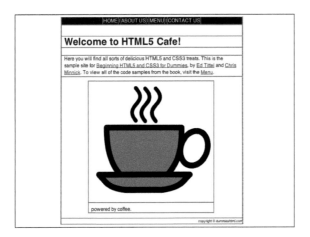

Figure 14-1: CSS draws a rectangular box around each element.

If you ever want to see the box that an HTML element lives in, one way is by putting a border on it using CSS. Figure 14-2 shows a `<p>` element with a red 2-pixel wide border around it. For convenience, and so we can show you everything in the same screen, we've used inline styling here.

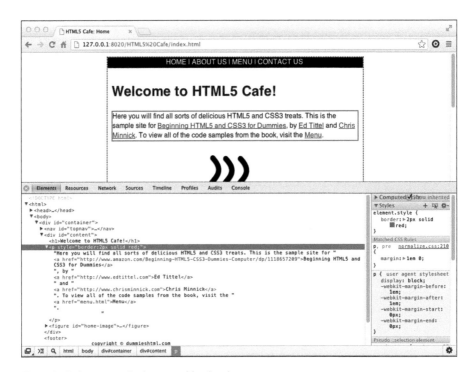

Figure 14-2: A paragraph element with a border.

In Figures 14-2 and Figure 14-3, we're using the Chrome DevTools, which are built into Google's Chrome web browser, to show the markup and the browser window at the same time. The Chrome DevTools are extremely helpful for testing, debugging, analyzing, and building web pages. If you want to see and work with the tools, you can press Ctrl+Shift+I in Windows or Option+Control+I on the Mac OS when you have the Chrome browser open.

Figure 14-3 shows a red border around another element — the <a> element around Chris Minnick's name.

Well, now. That's certainly interesting. Notice that the border around Chris Minnick wraps from one line to the next. The rectangle is there, but it's been broken into two parts.

To understand what's going on here, we need to explain the difference between inline and block-level elements.

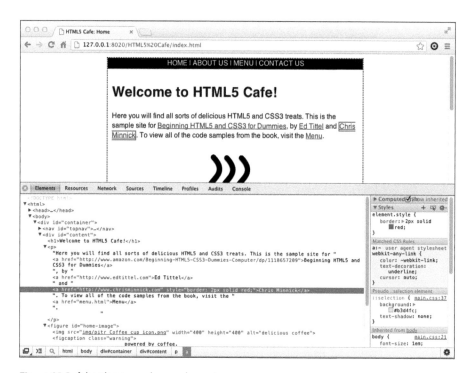

Figure 14-3: A border around an a element.

Block versus inline elements

For the purpose of laying out a web page, HTML elements that get displayed in a browser all fall into one of two categories:

✔ **Block elements,** such as `<p>` and `<div>`, form a block on the page. They take up the full width available to them and begin on a new line. Block-level elements may contain other block-level elements as well as inline elements.

✔ **Inline elements,** such as `<span>` and `<a>` do not start a new line. They are used inside of block elements. It's not valid HTML to put block-level elements within inline elements.

There is a third basic type of element where the elements aren't displayed. This list includes `<meta>`, `<link>`, and other elements that serve a function in the web page but don't show up when you view it in a browser.

Listing 14-1 shows a block-level element, `<p>`, with several inline elements inside of it.

Listing 14-1:   Block-Level Elements May Contain Inline Elements

```
<!DOCTYPE html>
<html lang="en">
    <head>
        <meta charset="utf-8" />
        <title>HTML</title>
    </head>

    <body>
        <p>
        The <a href="http://docs.webplatform.org/wiki/html/elements/p">p</a> element is a block-
level element. It starts on a <em>new line</em>, it takes up the full width available to it, and it
may contain other block-level and inline elements.
        </p>
    </body>
</html>
```

In HTML5, the terms block-level and inline have been replaced with a more complex set of categories. HTML5's equivalent term for block-level is *flow content,* and inline elements correspond to HTML5's *phrasing content.* HTML5 has several other categories of content that aren't important as we talk about CSS layout.

CSS uses the terms block and inline, and so even though HTML no longer contains these terms, it's still the best way to understand and group HTML elements for the purpose of arranging them in a browser.

Table 14-1 lists all of HTML5's block-level elements.

Table 14-1	HTML5's Block-Level Elements	
`<address>`	`<figure>`	`<hr>`
`<article>`	`<footer>`	`<noscript>`
`<aside>`	`<form>`	`<ol>`
`<audio>`	`<form>`	`<output>`
`<blockquote>`	`<h1>`	`<p>`
` `	`<h2>`	`<pre>`
`<canvas>`	`<h3>`	`<section>`
`<dd>`	`<h4>`	`<table>`
`<div>`	`<h5>`	`<tfoot>`
`<dl>`	`<h6>`	`<ul>`
`<fieldset>`	`<header>`	`<video>`
`<figcaption>`	`<hrgroup>`	

Table 14-2 lists all of the inline elements.

Table 14-2	HTML5's Inline Elements	
`<a>`	`<em>`	`<small>`
`<abbr>`	`<i>`	`<span>`
`<b>`	`<kbd>`	`<strong>`
`<bdi>`	`<mark>`	`<sub>`
`<bdo>`	`<q>`	`<sup>`
` `	`<rp>`	`<time>`
`<cite>`	`<rt>`	`<u>`
`<code>`	`<ruby>`	`<var>`
`<data>`	`<s>`	`<wbr>`
`<dfn>`	`<samp>`	

For complete details on what each of these elements does, visit the HTML reference at `dev.w3.org/html5/html-author/`.

By default, with no CSS applied by the web pages' author, HTML elements appear on the screen in the same order as you type them into your markup in what's called normal flow, which we discuss next.

Normal flow

Normal flow specifies that blocks are stacked upon each other vertically, starting at the top of the block that contains them. Inline elements flow horizontally from left to right.

Figure 14-4 illustrates normal flow.

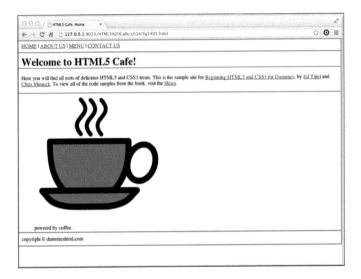

Figure 14-4: An example of normal flow.

If normal flow is how you want your page to be laid out, you're in luck: There's nothing more that you need to do than to just write your HTML markup, then stand back and admire the logic and simplicity of normal flow.

There are many times, however, when normal flow just won't cut it. For that, CSS provides plenty of tools for overriding and readjusting elements in an HTML page. Much of the rest of this chapter is dedicated to demonstrating non-normal flow, or *out of flow* elements.

Compare the section of the home page of www.nasa.gov as shown in Figure 14-5 with the same section, minus all of the CSS shown in Figure 14-6. Can you see how the elements in the plain version match up with the elements in the styled version?

Figure 14-5: An example of what's possible by taking elements out of flow.

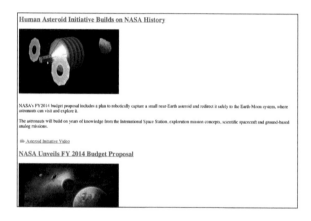

Figure 14-6: Remove the CSS, and everything flows normally, if not beautifully or efficiently.

The HTML5 Cafe website is much less complicated than the NASA site (it's not rocket science, after all), and it was designed to work pretty well even without any external style sheets, as shown in Figure 14-4.

However, if you compare Figure 14-7 with the styled version of the page in Figure 14-8, it's clear that we did some work to a few of the elements to position them just where we want them on the page:

- The content block has been centered in the window.
- The navigation has been centered in the content block.
- The coffee cup image and its caption have been centered in the content block.
- The copyright statement has been right-aligned in the content block.

Figure 14-7: The normal flow version of HTML5 Cafe.

Figure 14-8: The styled version of HTML5 Cafe.

Putting absolute and relative in perspective

Think about how you might answer the question "Where are you?" There are several ways to answer this question (besides with "None of your business!", of course.)

The first way is by telling your location in regards to something else. For example, you might say,

"Walking my dog."

or

"In my car."

This type of location information is *relative* to something else (your dog or your car, in these examples). When the dog and car move, you move.

The other type of location information that you might give is an actual address or a specific, unchanging location. For example, you could say,

"In San Jose."

or even

"At 1313 Mockingbird Lane."

This type of information is absolute. You're at this location, and the location is a fixed place on the map.

Of course, we can get philosophical on you here and remind you that everything is relative and that there are no absolutes — and it's just a matter of what it's relative to. In the first case ("walking my dog"), your position is relative to the dog. In the second case ("1313 Mockingbird Lane"), your position is relative to the city. In another case ("California"), your position is relative to the United States.

Keep this example in mind as we go through this chapter. CSS positioning works much the same way.

Before we move on to explaining just how these elements were positioned (which we do in Chapter 15), we need to explain how CSS positioning works.

Managing Positioning

CSS provides several ways to specify exactly where an element should appear on a page. The kinds of properties involved are discussed in the following sections.

How a browser positions an element in a browser is determined by the `position` property. Position has 5 possible values:

- ✔ `static`: Static is the default. When position is set to static, elements flow according to the rules of normal flow.
- ✔ `inherit`: Specifies that the current element should use the same value for position as its parent element.

✔ `fixed`: Specifies that the element should be fixed to the background and not move, even if the page is scrolled.

✔ `absolute`: The element is positioned relative to its first positioned ancestor element.

✔ `relative`: The element is positioned relative to its normal position.

CSS positioning is a little tricky to understand at first, but when you get it, it's very powerful. So we spend a bit of time explaining the `position` element, and specifically its two most important values: `relative` and `absolute`.

About coordinates and offsets

When you position an object using fixed, absolute, or relative positioning, you do so by specifying an *offset*. The offset tells the browser the distance to move the object. The four offset properties — top, right, bottom, and left — correspond with the four edges of the box that you're positioning.

Relative positioning

When you use relative positioning, you're offsetting the element from its current position, relative to its parent element. To demonstrate relative positioning, Figure 14-9 shows a document with a `<div>` element containing text that's relatively positioned within another `<div>`.

Figure 14-9: The paragraph is positioned relative to its parent element.

Listing 14-2 shows the HTML markup for this page.

Listing 14-2: The HTML Markup for Figure 14-9

```html
<!DOCTYPE html>
<html>
    <head>
        <title>relative positioning</title>
        <style>
            #main-box {
                width: 300px;
                height: 300px;
                border: 1px solid red;
                margin-left: 40px;
            }
            #my-para {
                width: 200px;
                position: relative;
                top: 40px;
                left: 20px;
                border: 1px solid blue;
            }
        </style>
    </head>
    <body>
        <div id="main-box">
            <div id="my-para">This div is positioned with position:relative.</div>
        </div>
    </body>
</html>
```

Notice that the inside box (containing text) has been moved down and to the left of the upper-left corner of the containing box (with the id="main-box" attribute).

If you were to move the outside (containing) box in this example by changing the value of the margin property or through another means, the resulting configuration of these two elements would remain the same. They would just be in a different place in the browser window.

Absolute positioning

Sometimes, you just want to position something in a particular location on your web page, not relative to another element. This is the function of position: absolute.

Take a look at the CSS in Listing 14-3. This is the same markup we show you in Listing 14-2, except with the value of the position property changed to absolute.

Listing 14-3:   The Position Has Been Changed to Absolute

```
<style>
    #main-box {
        width: 300px;
        height: 300px;
        border: 1px solid red;
        margin-left: 40px;
    }
    #my-para {
        width: 200px;
        position: absolute;
        top: 40px;
        left: 20px;
        border: 1px solid blue;
    }
</style>
```

When viewed in a browser, the result is Figure 14-10. Notice that the inner box is now positioned relative to the upper-left corner of the browser window, not the parent `<div>`. In fact, the parent `<div>` has no effect on the positioned `<div>` at all here. We can move the parent `<div>` completely out of the picture, and the absolutely positioned `<div>` stays right where it's at.

Figure 14-10: The inner box is now absolutely positioned.

Floating

Another way to take boxes out of the normal flow of the web page is by using the `float` property. You can float a box to the left or to the right, which will take the box out of the normal flow and push it as far as possible in the specified direction. Because it's no longer in the normal flow, objects and text that are still in the normal flow will flow around it. The About Us page on the

HTML5 Cafe website uses the float property to wrap text around the author pictures, as shown in Figure 14-11.

Figure 14-11: The `float` property can be used to wrap text around images.

The `float` property has four possible values:

- ✔ `float: left` moves the selected element as far left as possible and forces other content to wrap to the right of it.
- ✔ `float: right` moves the selected element as far right as possible and forces other content to wrap to the left of it.
- ✔ `float: none` is the default setting and specifies that the element will follow the normal flow.
- ✔ `float: inherit` specifies that the element should be floated the same as its parent element.

Remember that block elements take up as much horizontal space as they have available to them, unless you specifically set the `width` property. This fact has caused many web developers hours and hours of problems while they try to figure out why a floated element doesn't work the way they expect. Simply remember to always specify a width when you float an element, and you'll thank us later.

Using a Layout Generator

By combining CSS positioning and floats, you can do amazing things with web page layouts. For example, you might want to have a website with a left or right column for navigation. Or, you might want to have a three-column layout with the main content in the middle of the page. Or, you might want to use a grid system so that you can position elements pretty much where ever you want in the browser.

Each of these different options is shown in Figure 14-12.

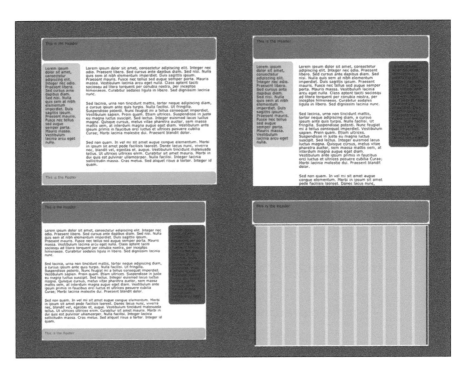

Figure 14-12: Examples of different types of web page layouts.

All of these are possible and are commonly done with CSS. Because they're so common, people have created tools, called *layout generators,* for automatically generating the CSS necessary to create different layouts. One such layout generator is the one created by Generate It!, which resides at www.generate it.net/layout-generator.

Figure 14-13 shows the interface for the Generate It! Layout Generator.

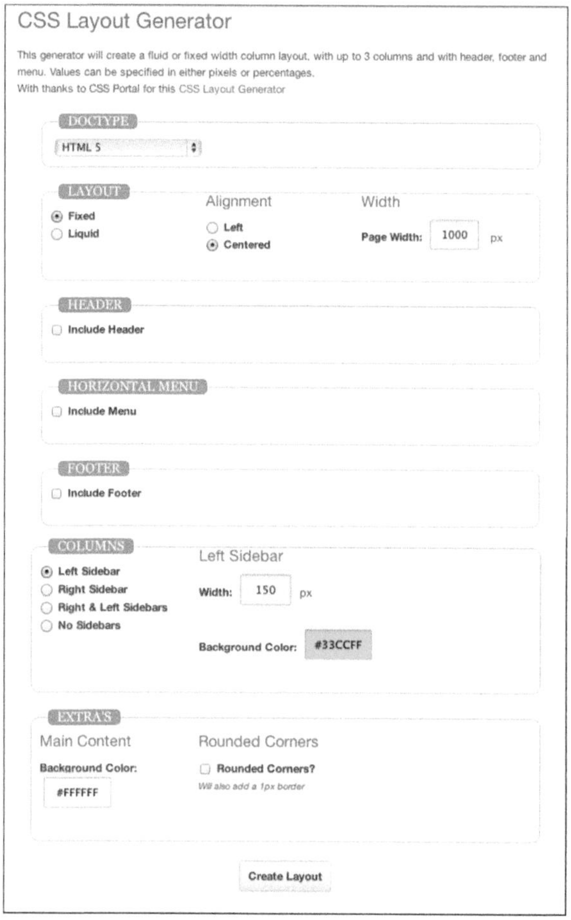

Figure 14-13: An example of a CSS layout generator.

This layout generator uses a series of forms where you can specify different attributes of the layout that you want to generate. These include the following:

- Whether the layout should be fixed (always the same width), or liquid (the width changes based on the width of the browser)

- Whether the layout should be left-aligned in the browser window, or centered (if it's set to a fixed width)

- The default width of the layout

- Whether to include a header, horizontal menu, and footer as well as the attributes of each

✔ The number of columns in the layout

✔ The width of each of the columns

✔ Background colors for the columns and the page as a whole

When you're done filling out the form, click the Create Layout button, and the CSS and HTML for the layout you designed appear, as shown in Figure 14-14.

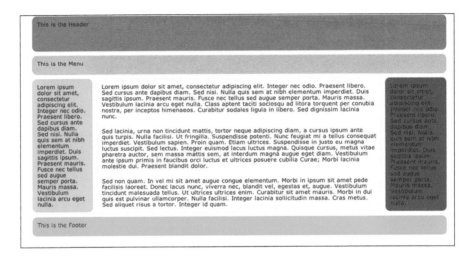

Figure 14-14: A layout generated by the layout generator.

If you're happy with this layout (and who wouldn't be happy, with all those happy colors?), click the Download Layout link and download a `.zip` file containing starter HTML and CSS files. You can customize these and insert your own content, and away you go!

15

Building with Boxes, Borders, and Buttons

In This Chapter

▷ Working with the CSS box model

▷ Positioning blocks

▷ Aligning text

▷ Indenting text

▷ Creating buttons with CSS

*C*hapter 14 describes the difference between block and inline elements, and how to arrange both in the browser window. In this chapter, we go inside those elements to show you how to change the spacing between elements, change the spacing inside of elements, assign borders to elements, align the content of elements, and more!

Meeting the Box Model

As we show you in Chapter 14, each element in an HTML document is represented as a rectangular box. You also see how these boxes stack up depending on whether they're inline or block-level elements. In this section, we talk about those rectangles and the ways in which you can change them using CSS.

Figure 15-1 shows what is known as the CSS box model.

The box model has four types of space, or to put it another way, four edges. These four spaces/edges are as follows:

- **Content:** Content is the rectangle that's filled up by your text, image, video, or whatever.

- **Padding:** Padding is the space between the edge of your content and the border. You can control the width of the padding with the `padding-top`, `padding-right`, `padding-bottom`, and `padding-left` properties or with the shorthand `padding` property, as you see shortly.

- **Border:** The border area lies beyond the padding. To change the width of the border, you use the `border-width` property or the shorthand `border` property.

- **Margin:** Margin is outside of the element's border and is what separates one box from another. To control the width of the margin, you use the `margin-top`, `margin-right`, `margin-bottom`, and `margin-left` properties or the shorthand `margin` property.

Figure 15-2 makes it all real by showing how it applies to a picture of a cute cat on a web page. Throughout the rest of this chapter, we show you how to implement elements of the box model.

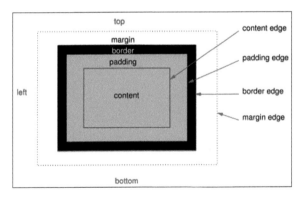

Figure 15-1: A diagram of the CSS box model.

Figure 15-2: The CSS box model in practice.

Putting the Box Model into Practice

To demonstrate the box model, we once again visit the HTML5 Cafe. Look again at the markup for the home page, shown in Listing 15-1. Find the `<figure>` element, which we've highlighted for you.

As you may recall from Chapter 14, `<figure>` is a block-level element.

The coffee cup image and its caption are the content of the `<figure>` element. Content takes up as much space as is needed to draw a rectangle around it. In this case, the image is 400 pixels wide and 400 pixels tall. Below the image, the caption has a certain line height, which is determined by the size of the caption text and the value of the line height. The total height of the `<figcaption>` element in this case is 22px. The combined height of the coffee cup image and the caption, then, is 422px. The width of the figure is still 400px.

Listing 15-1:   The Markup for the HTML Café Home Page

```
<!DOCTYPE html>
<html>
    <head>
        <meta charset="utf-8">
        <title>HTML5 Cafe: Home</title>
        <meta name="description" content="sample site for 9781118657201">
        <meta name="viewport" content="width=device-width">
        <link rel="stylesheet" href="css/normalize.css">
        <link rel="stylesheet" href="css/main.css">
    </head>
    <body>
        <div id="container">
            <nav id="topnav">
                <a href="index.html">HOME</a> | <a href="about.html">ABOUT US</a> | <a
href="menu.html">MENU</a> | <a href="contact.html">CONTACT US</a>
            </nav>
            <div id="content">
                <h1>Welcome to HTML5 Cafe!</h1>
                <p>Here you will find all sorts of delicious HTML5 and CSS3 treats. This is the
sample site for <a href="http://www.amazon.com/Beginning-HTML5-CSS3-Dummies-Computer/dp/
1118657209">Beginning HTML5 and CSS3 for Dummies</a>, by <a href="http://www.edtittel.com">Ed
Tittel</a> and <a href="http://www.chrisminnick.com">Chris Minnick</a>. To view all of the code
samples from the book, visit the <a href="menu.html">Menu</a>.
                </p>
                <figure id="home-image">
                    <img src="img/pitr_Coffee_cup_icon.png"
                    width="400" height="400" alt="delicious coffee">
                    <figcaption class="warning">
                        powered by coffee.
                    </figcaption>
                </figure>
            </div>
            <footer>
                copyright &copy; dummieshtml.com
            </footer>
        </div>
    </body>
</html>
```

The actual amount of space taken up by the figure element is greater than 400px, however. Remember that figure is a block-level element and that block-level elements take up the entire width available to them if you don't explicitly specify a width.

So, the width of the figure element here is actually determined by the width of the `<div>` element that holds it.

Figure 15-3 shows your good friend the Chrome DevTools Elements Panel with the `<figure>` element highlighted. Notice that the coffee cup picture has been highlighted in two colors and that a tiny box model diagram appears in the lower-right corner of the screen.

If you match the colors overlaid on and around the coffee cup image with the colors in the box model diagram, you find that the coffee cup icon represents the most inner part of the box model (the content), as we already determined. The space around the coffee cup matches up with the margin color in the box model.

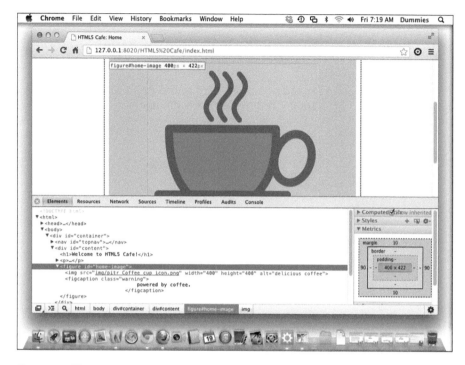

Figure 15-3: The <figure> element inside the Chrome DevTools.

The top and bottom margins around the image are set to 10px. This is a direct result of the style rule that we applied to the figure element (by selecting its ID):

```
#home-image {width: 400px;
             margin: 10px auto;}
```

In this case, we chose to apply the style to the coffee cup by selecting its ID, home-image. It would have also worked to select this image using an element type selector, figure. If we had selected it that way, however, these styles would be applied to every figure element on the site, which may not be exactly what we want. A combination of an element selector and an ID selector would perhaps be the most complete way to select this particular image. The resulting selector would be figure#home-image.

Notice also that the border and padding colors are missing from around the coffee cup. Because we haven't set a border or padding on the figure element, they are set to 0.

We can add a border and padding to the coffee cup picture by adding a couple of new declarations:

```
#home-image {width: 400px;
             margin: 10px auto;
             padding: 10px 10px 10px 10px;
             border: 10px solid black;}
```

With a border and padding added to the #home-image CSS rule, the box model diagram in Chrome DevTools changes, as shown in Figure 15-4.

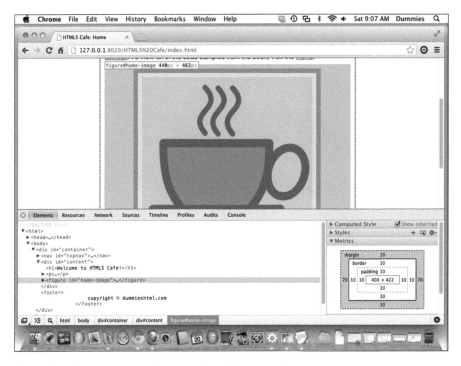

Figure 15-4: The <figure> element with padding and a border.

Note that several properties in the previous CSS rule, called *shorthand properties,* take multiple values, such as margin and padding. Shorthand properties collect values from multiple related CSS properties (such as margin-top, margin-right, margin-bottom, and margin-left, for example). As far as CSS is concerned, there is no difference between writing a separate declaration for each of the properties in a shorthand property, or using the shorthand property. If you learn and use the shorthand properties consistently, you save yourself some typing, and your CSS files will be somewhat smaller. We show you some of the shorthand properties in this chapter and the next as they come up.

Specifying padding and margin widths

Padding and margin are both names for spacing around content. `margin` creates an empty zone around the box (outside of the border), and `padding` defines the space between the border of the box and the content inside the box.

Margin

The margin of an element is the space between the element and another element. It can be set as a fixed length, as a percentage, or as *auto*. These are the important things to know about margin:

- The margin doesn't have a background color.
- The margin is outside of the border.
- Margins "collapse" in certain cases.

Margin collapsing is the property of margins when two elements are stacked on top of each other, only one of the margins will actually be used. For example, if two `<div>` elements — each with the top and bottom margins set to 10px — are stacked on top of each other, you would expect the margin between the bottom of the first element and the top of the second element to be 20px, as shown in Figure 15-5.

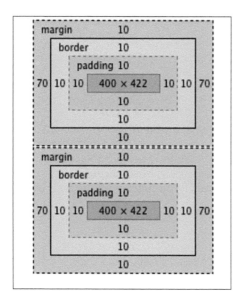

Figure 15-5: What you would expect. But, not what happens!

In reality, however, what happens by default is that only the larger margin will be used. In this case, both margins are 10px, so the combined margin will be 10px, as shown in Figure 15-6.

margin	10						
	border	10					
		padding 10					
70	10	10	400 × 422	10	10	70	
		10					
		10					
		10					
	border	10					
		padding 10					
70	10	10	400 × 422	10	10	70	
		10					
		10					
		10					

Figure 15-6: What actually happens. The smaller margin collapses.

But, if the first element had a 20px bottom margin and the second element had a 40px margin, the combined margin on the touching edge would be 40px wide.

Collapsing margins seems like a simple enough concept. But, as always, there are some exceptions to the rule and complicating scenarios. Margins collapse only for block-level elements that are in the normal flow of the document. So, if an element is absolutely positioned or floated, margin collapse doesn't happen. Also, if one element has a negative top or bottom margin, the negative and positive margins will be added together to come up with the final combined margin. Confused yet? Don't worry about it. It actually will make sense after you practice and gain experience working with margins.

Each element has four margin properties, which correspond to the four edges of the element's box model:

- margin top specifies the top margin.
- margin-right specifies the right margin.
- margin-bottom specifies the bottom margin.
- margin-left specifies the left margin.

A value of `auto` for any of the margin properties causes the browser to calculate the margin width automatically, depending on the space available.

TIP

You can use the `auto` value of the margin property to center elements horizontally. The trick is to set both the right and left margins of the element to `auto`. The browser splits the available space between them, which leaves the element centered in its container. Cool trick, huh?

Padding

Padding is the space between an element's content and its border. If a background color or image is set for an element, padding takes on the background.

You can specify the amount of padding for each edge of an element as a fixed measurement or as a percentage.

As with margin, there are four individual properties, which correspond to each of the four edges:

- ✔ `padding-top` sets the padding on the top.
- ✔ `padding-right` sets the padding on the right.
- ✔ `padding bottom` sets the padding on the bottom.
- ✔ `padding-left` sets the padding on the left.

Shortcut properties

Padding and margin both have shorthand properties that can save you a bit of typing. The shorthand property for setting the margins is simply `margin`. The shorthand property for setting the padding is `padding`.

The following rules explain how to set shorthand properties for padding and margin:

- ✔ If all the sides have the same value, a single value works. For example, `margin: 10px;` sets the values of `margin-top`, `margin-right`, `margin-bottom`, and `margin-left` to 10px.
- ✔ If top and bottom margins are the same, and if left and right margins are also the same, you can use just two numbers for the margin or padding shortcut. For example: `margin: 10px 20px;` sets the top and bottom margins to 10px and the right and left margins to 20px.
- ✔ If the top and bottom values are different but the right and left values are the same, you can use three values. For example, `padding: 10px 30px 20px;` sets the top padding to 10px, the right and left padding to 30px, and the bottom padding to 20px.

 ✔ All other cases require you to use four values with the shorthand property. For example, `padding: 3px 2px 18px 4px;` sets the padding
on each side of the content to one of the values. Of course, it's always
fine to use four values, even if it's not required. For example, there's
nothing wrong with writing `padding: 3px 3px 3px 3px;`, even
though it would be shorter to write just `padding: 3px;`.

To remember what's what, think of the edges of an element box in clockwise
order, starting with the top edge: `top`, `right`, `bottom`, and then `left`. One
easy way to remember the order of the edges in shortcut properties is to
remember that the first letters are the consonants in the word TRouBLe.
As in, "You'll be in big TRBL if you don't remember the order of the edges
correctly!"

Here are some examples of margin and padding rules and the effect they have
in the Chrome DevTools box model diagram. First, set top and bottom padding
to 0px and left and right padding to 10px:

```
padding: 0px 10px;
```

Figure 15-7 shows the resulting diagram for the element containing this
declaration.

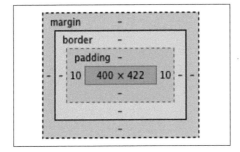

Figure 15-7: The result of using the padding
shortcut property with two values.

Next, here's how you would set the top and bottom margins to 20px and
40px, respectively, and set the left and right margins to 15px:

```
margin: 20px 15px 40px;
```

Figure 15-8 shows the resulting diagram for the element containing this
declaration.

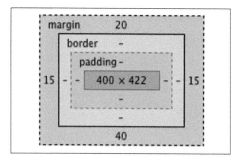

Figure 15-8: The result of using the margin shortcut property with three values.

And how about if you want to set all of the margins to 12px? That's easy:

```
margin: 12px;
```

Figure 15-9 shows the resulting diagram for the element containing this declaration.

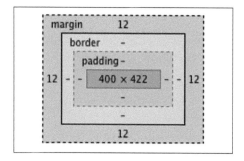

Figure 15-9: The result of using the margin shortcut property with one value.

Adding borders

Between the padding and the margin is the border. Borders are like a picture frame for your content. They can be very simple — perhaps just a thin black line — or they can be quite ornate. With CSS3, you can even use images for borders and create rounded corners on you borders!

The simplest way to create a border is by using the three basic border properties: border-width, border-style, and border-color.

border-width

border-width is a shorthand property for the four longhand properties that determine the thickness of the border: border-top-width, border-right-width, border-bottom-width, and border-left-width.

You can set the border width using a keyword or an explicit value. The three keywords that you can use to set the border width are

- thin.
- medium.
- thick.

If you require more precision than just what a certain browser decides is thin, medium, or thick, you can set the border-width property in pixels, ems, or another measurement unit.

border-style

border-style is a shorthand for the four properties used to set border styles: border-top-style, border-right-style, border-bottom-style, and border-left-style. By using the border-style property, you can set them all at one time, just as you did with the margin and padding shorthand properties. The border-style property has nine possible values. The following list describes how each border looks, as shown in Figure 15-10:

- border-style: none: The border has no style. In other words, it isn't displayed.
- border-style: dotted: The border is made up of dots. This is the style of border used on the HTML5 Cafe website.
- border-style: dashed: The border is made up of dashes. Dashes are similar to dots, but longer.
- border-style: solid: The border is a solid line.
- border-style: double: The border is made up of two lines that add up to the total width of the border you set.
- border-style: groove: The border has a 3D groove effect. It's the opposite of the ridge style.
- border-style: ridge: The border has a 3D ridge effect. It will appear to come out of the page.
- border-style: inset: The border makes the box appear to be inset, or embedded.
- border-style: outset: The border makes the box appear to be raised up, or embossed.

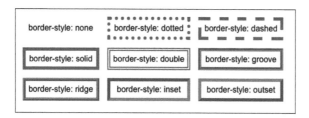

Figure 15-10: Each of the different styles of border.

As with the `padding` and `margin` properties, it's possible to have different border widths and border styles on each of the four sides of a box. You can accomplish this by setting the longhand properties for each edge separately or by using multiple values in the shorthand property. For example, `border-style: solid dotted;` puts a solid border on the top and bottom of the box, and a dotted border on the left and right.

border-color

As with the previous two properties, `border-color` is actually a shorthand combination of the four longhand properties: `border-top-color`, `border-right-color`, `border-bottom-color`, and `border-left-color`.

You can specify the color using any one of the ways to name colors in CSS (which we talk about in detail in Chapter 16).

The border shorthand property

If three separate border-related properties are too many for you, you're in luck! The `border` property is a super shorthand property that lets you set the `border-width`, `border-style`, and `border-color` all at once.

Here's the format for the border property:

```
border: width style color;
```

So, if you wanted a blue, 1 pixel wide, solid border, you could use the following declaration:

```
border: 1px solid blue;
```

Easy as that! The `border` shorthand property comes in very handy when you just need a simple border.

Aligning text

If you examine the CSS that's responsible for styling the center-aligned content in the HTML5 Cafe style sheet, a pattern emerges. Here's the CSS for the navigation:

```
#topnav {width:100%;
        text-align: center;
        background-color: #000000;
        height: 24px;
        color: #FFFFFF;}
```

Here's the CSS for the coffee cup image:

```
#logo {font-size: 2em;
       text-transform: uppercase;
       font-weight: bold;
       text-align: center;}
```

Here's the CSS for the copyright notice:

```
footer {font-size: .7em;
        text-align: right;}
```

Notice that in each of these three cases, the text-align property is present and responsible for the positioning of the element.

The text-align property does just what it sounds like — it aligns text within another element. The truth, however, is that CSS doesn't much care whether content is text, images, video, or another type of content when it comes to how the text-align property works. The text-align property just aligns all of the content in a block, horizontally, in one of four ways, depending on the value that you give the property. You may also just tell the current element to do the same thing as its parent element. Here are all the possible values of text-align:

- text-align: left aligns content with the left edge of the block.

- text-align: center centers content in the block.

- text-align: right aligns content with the right edge of the block.

- text-align: justify stretches lines of text so that each line has an equal length.

- text-align: inherit specifies that the current element should have the same text-align value as its parent element.

Indenting text

You can define the amount of space that should precede the first line of a paragraph by using the `text-indent` property.

Using the `text-indent` property doesn't indent the whole paragraph, only the first line. To accomplish indenting a whole paragraph, you need to use CSS box properties, such as `margin-left` and `margin-right`.

Syntax for indenting text

The style declaration used to indent text is

```
selector {text-indent: value;}
```

Here, *value* must be one of the standard length-property measurement values (listed in Chapter 11).

Markup for indenting text

To create a class that can be used to indent quotations by 2em, you may write a CSS rule like the following:

```
.quotation {font-style: italic; text-indent: 2em;}
```

Creating buttons with CSS

CSS, and especially CSS3, is capable of doing many jobs that you previously needed to use images for. One of these is the job of making really good-looking buttons.

CSS3 has several great new properties for rounding box corners, creating gradient effects, and adding shadows to boxes and text. We show you some of the great new capabilities and how they work in the next chapters. Right now, however, we take a look at what they're capable of doing.

As we show with the layout generator in Chapter 14, there are services on the web that make the job of creating complex CSS effects very easy. Another such service is a button generator. The button generator that we look at here is the CSS3 Button Generator at `http://css3button.net`. When you first arrive at `http://css3button.net`, a random button color and style is presented to you, as shown in Figure 15-11.

Preview of button

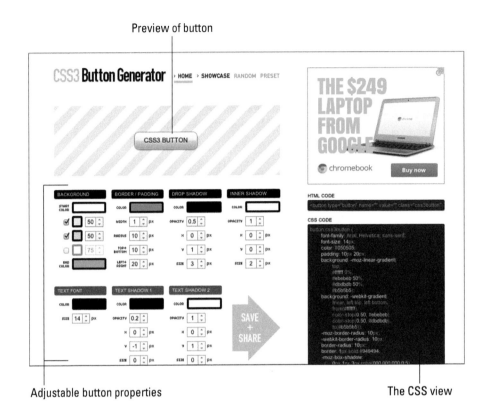

Adjustable button properties   The CSS view

Figure 15-11: The home screen for http://css3button.net.

The upper-left portion of the interface shows a preview of your button. The site presents the button on a background to make it easier to see light-colored borders and shadows.

Below the preview are the various properties of the button that you can adjust. When you change any of these properties, the button preview is instantly updated. Go ahead and try changing some of them!

The best part of the CSS Button Generator is in a dark gray box in the lower right: the CSS view. When you're happy with your button, you can select and copy the HTML and CSS for the button and paste them into your own HTML and CSS documents. Because it's just CSS, you can reuse this button style over and over in your website for different buttons with only a minimal effect on page load time.

Figure 15-12 shows the CSS markup for a custom button that we came up with. Figure 15-13 shows several instances of that button with different labels on them.

HTML CODE

```
<button type="button" name="" value="" class="css3button">
```

CSS CODE

```
button.css3button {
        font-family: Arial, Helvetica, sans-serif;
        font-size: 14px;
        color: #43733f;
        padding: 10px 20px;
        background: -moz-linear-gradient(
                top,
                #32f8ff 0%,
                #ebebeb 50%,
                #dbdbdb 50%,
                #3269ff);
        background: -webkit-gradient(
                linear, left top, left bottom,
                from(#32f8ff),
                color-stop(0.50, #ebebeb),
                color-stop(0.50, #dbdbdb),
                to(#3269ff));
        -moz-border-radius: 10px;
        -webkit-border-radius: 10px;
        border-radius: 10px;
        border: 1px solid #ff0000;
        -moz-box-shadow:
                0px 1px 3px rgba(196,43,196,0.5),
                inset 0px 0px 2px rgba(84,70,84,1);
        -webkit-box-shadow:
                0px 1px 3px rgba(196,43,196,0.5),
                inset 0px 0px 2px rgba(84,70,84,1);
        box-shadow:
                0px 1px 3px rgba(196,43,196,0.5),
                inset 0px 0px 2px rgba(84,70,84,1);
        text-shadow:
                0px -1px 0px rgba(000,000,000,0.2),
                0px 1px 0px rgba(255,255,255,1);
}
```

Figure 15-12: The CSS for our wild and crazy button.

Figure 15-13: Our wild and crazy button in action.

16

Using Colors and Backgrounds

In This Chapter

▶ Using color keywords

▶ Reading hex codes

▶ Working with backgrounds

*T*he web would be a pretty drab place without color. Imagine watching your favorite cat videos in grayscale. Life on the web just wouldn't be nearly as much fun. This book, in fact, wouldn't be as much fun in black and white, which is the primary reason it's printed in full color.

Fortunately, we don't need to live in a gray world. Your computer, laptop, tablet, or smartphone is capable of displaying millions of different colors. CSS is capable of instructing it to display those colors in infinite combinations. In this chapter, we show you the different ways to specify colors in CSS, how to assign colors to elements, and how to work with backgrounds.

Defining Color Values

CSS defines color values in two ways:

✓ **Name:** You choose from a limited list.

✓ **Number:** Pick the exact amounts of each of the primary colors to create the precise colors that you need.

Color names

The CSS3 Color specification includes 16 basic color names that you can use to define colors in your pages. Figure 16-1 shows these colors. The numbers that start with a pound sign (#) are in *hexadecimal* notation. Hexadecimal notation is a system of numbering that starts at 00 (which is the same as 0 in the decimal system we're more familiar with) and ends at FF (which is equivalent to 255 in the decimal system).

Name	#RGB Code	Color	Name	#RGB Code	Color
Black	#000000		Silver	#C0C0C0	
Gray	#808080		White	#FFFFFF	
Maroon	#800000		Red	#FF0000	
Purple	#800080		Fuchsia	#FF00FF	
Green	#008000		Lime	#00FF00	
Olive	#808000		Yellow	#FFFF00	
Navy	#000080		Blue	#0000FF	
Teal	#008080		Aqua	#00FFFF	

Figure 16-1: Basic Named Color Values in CSS.

You can safely use color names in your CSS markup and be confident that browsers will recognize them and use the correct colors in your web pages. You can also compare the colors onscreen to those on this printed page to see how print and digital displays can sometimes differ. (In some cases, it may be the color balance on your screen that's off; in others, the color the printer tried to match on the page may not be precisely correct — it's not as easy as you might think!)

Visit www.htmlhelp.com/reference/html40/values.html#color to see how your browser displays these colors. If you can, view this page on two or three different computers to see how a different browser, operating system, graphics card, and monitor can subtly change the display.

The following CSS style declaration says that all text within <p> tags should be blue:

```
p {color: blue;}
```

In addition to these 16 basic colors, the CSS3 Color specification defines a much longer list of *extended* color keywords that are supported by web browsers. This list includes such lovely colors as bisque, burlywood, mintcream, and thistle.

Visit `www.w3.org/wiki/CSS3/Color/Extended_color_keywords` to see the full list of extended color keywords.

Color numbers

Even the list of extended color keywords can be pretty limiting. To allow you to use any color you want, CSS provides additional methods for web page designers to specify their own colors.

Hexadecimal color codes

One way to specify colors in CSS is by using a *hex triplet*. A hex triplet (often called a *hex code* for short) is a series of three numbers, written in hexadecimal notation. The first number represents the color red. The second number represents green. The third number represents blue. The amount of each primary color that goes into the mix is determined by the size of the number, with 00 indicating that there should be none of that color, and FF indicating that there should be as much of that color as possible.

For example, the following hex triplet indicates pure blue:

```
#0000FF
```

This hex triplet is exactly equivalent to the CSS keyword `blue` that you met earlier. Hex code can represent many more colors than just the basic ones, however. For example, here's a shade of blue that has more complexity, looks more serious, and is serene, but not sad:

```
#386F96
```

Lovely color, isn't it? A fun party game that we web developers sometimes play after we've had too much coffee is "name that color." The goal of the game is to guess the numeric value for a color just by looking at it. After you've been working with web colors for a while, you may find yourself getting pretty good at this game. Try it out with this fairly easy example, shown in Figure 16-2.

Figure 16-2: See if you can guess the approximate hex code of this color.

The correct answer is #FF00FF, which is also known as Fuchsia. Fuchsia is the result of combining maximum parts red and blue, with no green.

You can play the HTML color guessing game in the privacy of your own home or office by visiting http://mallory.jemts.com.

If you know a color's hex code, you have all you need to use that color in your HTML page.

When you use hex code to define a color, you should always precede it with a pound sign (#). Otherwise, it may not display properly in some web browsers.

The following CSS style declaration makes all text contained by <p> tags blue:

```
p {color: #0000FF;}
```

RGB values

If hex codes just confuse you, fear not! You can also use decimal RGB values to define color. These value types aren't as common as hexadecimal values, but they're just as effective, and you don't need to grow six more digits to count them on your fingers:

- ✔ rgb(r,g,b): The r, g, and b are integers between 0 and 255 that (respectively) represent the red, green, and blue levels of the color.

- ✔ rgb(r%,g%,b%): The r%, g%, and b% represent (respectively) the percentage of red, green, and blue of the color.

Finding any color's hex code

You can't just wave your magic wand and come up with the hex code for any color, but that doesn't mean that you can't find the hex code through less magical means. Color converters follow a precise formula that changes a color's standard RGB notation into hexadecimal notation. Because you have better things to do with your time than compute hex codes, you have several options for figuring out the code for your color of choice, including web-safe colors shown on this book's online Cheat Sheet (www.dummies.com/cheatsheet/beginninghtml5css3). None of these make you use a calculator:

✎ **On the web:** Some good sources for hexadecimal color charts are

    www.webmonkey.com/2010/02/color_charts

    www.colorschemer.com/online.html

You simply find a color you like and type the hex code listed next to it into your HTML.

✎ **Using image editing software:** Many image editing applications, such as Adobe Photoshop or Adobe Fireworks, display the hexadecimal notation for any color. Even the Microsoft Word color picker shows you hex codes for colors in an image. If you have an image you like that you want to use as a color source for your web page, open the image in your favorite editor and find out what the colors' hex codes are.

Every color can be defined as a mixture of red, green, and blue (RGB). You can use either an RGB value or the equivalent hex code to describe a color's RGB value to a web browser. For more information about hexadecimal notation, please visit the "Tutorial on Hexadecimal Color" at www.lts.com/class/hextoc.htm.

Defining Color Definitions

You can define individual colors for any text on the web page, as well as define a background color for the entire web page or some portion thereof.

CSS uses the following properties to define colors:

✎ color defines the font color and is also used to define colors for links in their various states (link, active, focus, visited, and hover; see the upcoming section, "Links").

✎ background or background-color defines the background color for the entire page or defines the background for a particular element (for example, a background color for all first-level headings, similar to the idea of highlighting something in a Word document).

Text

You can change the color of text on your web page with three steps:

1. **Determine the selector.**

   For example, will the color apply to all first-level headings, to all paragraphs, or to a specific paragraph?

2. **Use the `color` property.**

3. **Identify the color name or hexadecimal value.**

The basic syntax for the style declaration is

```
selector {color: value;}
```

Here is a collection of style declarations where we use the `color` property to assign text color to the `body` element (and hence, to all other subsidiary HTML elements that can occur in a document body, except where other specifications override that selection as with the `h1` element):

```
body {color: olive; font-family: Verdana, sans-serif;
      background-color: #FFFFFF; font-size: 85%;}
hr {text-align: center;}
.navbar {font-size: 75%; text-align: center;}
h1 {color: #808000;}
p.chapternav {text-align: center;}
.footer {font-size: 80%;}
```

Note that in the preceding CSS rules, the color for all text on the page is defined by using a `body` selector. Color is applied to all text in the body of the document unless otherwise defined. To illustrate this at work, the first-level heading is defined as forest green, using hexadecimal notation.

Links

HTML links often have different colors based on their current *state*. By state, we don't mean Michigan or Texas, but rather the link's current status with regard to the particular user — whether the current user has visited the link previously, for example.

Normal CSS selectors aren't capable of styling elements based on their current state, so we need to employ a special type of selector here.

Pseudo classes allow you to define style rules based on information outside the document tree.

The *document tree* is a hierarchical representation for all elements in a document, much like a family tree, where every element has a parent and may contain a child. The document tree doesn't — and can't — contain information about whether a user has previously visited a certain link (for example). This is what we mean when we say that something is *outside the document tree.*

The five common pseudo classes that you can use with hyperlinks are

- :link defines formatting for links that haven't been visited.
- :visited defines formatting for links that have been visited.
- :focus defines formatting for links that are selected by the keyboard (for example, by pressing Tab) and are about to be activated by pressing Enter.
- :hover defines formatting for links when the mouse cursor hovers over them.
- :active defines formatting for links when they are selected (clicked by the mouse, or activated by pressing Enter).

The pseudo class name is preceded by a colon (:).

Pseudo classes can be used with

- Elements (such as the <a> element that defines hyperlinks).
- Classes.
- IDs.

For example, to define the style rules for visited and unvisited links, use the following syntax:

- The following sets the color of any hyperlink pointing to an unvisited URL to red by using its hexadecimal value:

  ```
  a:link {color: #FF0000;}
  ```
- The following sets any hyperlink that points to a visited URL to appear in the named color green:

  ```
  a:visited {color: green;}
  ```
- The following designates unvisited links with a class of internal to appear in (named color) yellow (see Chapter 12 for a discussion of CSS classes):

  ```
  a.internal:link {color: yellow;}
  ```

Links can occupy multiple states at one time. For example, a link can be visited and hovered over at the same time. Always define link style rules in the following order: `:link`, `:visited`, `:visible`, `:focus`, `:hover`, `:active`.

CSS applies "last rule seen" to display your page. Thus, if you put the pseudo class selectors in the wrong order, your results may not be what you want. For example, if `visited` follows `hover` and the two have overlapping rules, hover effects apply only to links that haven't yet been visited.

The following CSS rules render the document with olive, as the color for links that haven't been visited, and with yellow, as the color of visited links:

```
body {color: #808000; font-family: Verdana, sans-serif; font-size: 85%;}
a:link {color: olive;}
a:visited {color: yellow;}
```

The CSS specification defines `:link` and `:visited` as mutually exclusive, and it's up to the browser application to determine when to change the state (visited versus unvisited) for any given link. For example, a browser might determine that a link is unvisited if you clear your history data.

Backgrounds

To change the background color for your web page, or for a section of that page, follow these steps:

1. **Determine the selector.**

   For example, will the color apply to the entire background, or will it apply only to a specific section?

2. **Use the `background-color` or `background` property.**

3. **Identify the color name or hexadecimal value.**

The basic syntax for the style declaration is

```
selector {background-color: value;}
```

In the following collection of style declarations, the first style declaration uses the `background-color` property and sets it to light green by using hexadecimal notation:

```
body {color: #808000; font-family: Verdana, sans-serif;
      background-color: #EAF3DA; font-size: 85%;}
```

You can apply a background color to a block of text — for example, a paragraph — just like you define a background color for the entire page.

You use `background` as a shorthand property for all individual background properties, or use `background-color` to set just the color, like this:

```
selector {background: value value value;}
```

For more about shorthand properties, see Chapter 15.

Advanced backgrounds

Lining up multiple elements so that their backgrounds align perfectly and, likewise, mixing and matching multiple backgrounds can be difficult to achieve. It might take many lines of markup to get this job done right, especially working with CSS1 or CSS2. However, with CSS3, you can apply multiple backgrounds to a single element easily, and then use it to provide a backdrop for an element or a group of subsidiary elements. For example, on the backgrounds example page at www.dummieshtml.com/html5cafe/ch16/backgrounds/index.html, we combine three background images and apply them to one <div>.

The relevant CSS3 markup looks like this:

```
.customBackground {
    margin: 0px auto;
    width: 400px;
    height: 200px;
    border-radius: 10px;
    background:
    url(images/top.gif) top left repeat-x,
    url(images/bottom.gif) bottom left repeat-x,
    url(images/middle.gif) center repeat;
    }
```

The trick to this markup lies in the `background` specification, where we reference URLs for images for the three different backgrounds named `top.gif`, `bottom.gif`, and `middle.gif`, respectively. We use the `repeat-x` attribute to repeat the top and bottom horizontally. Using `repeat` means that `middle.gif` is repeated both horizontally and vertically. The `top.gif` background applies the dark to medium blue shading at the top of the frame, `bottom.gif` does likewise from the bottom, and `middle.gif` supplies the dots. The result is the image shown in Figure 16-3.

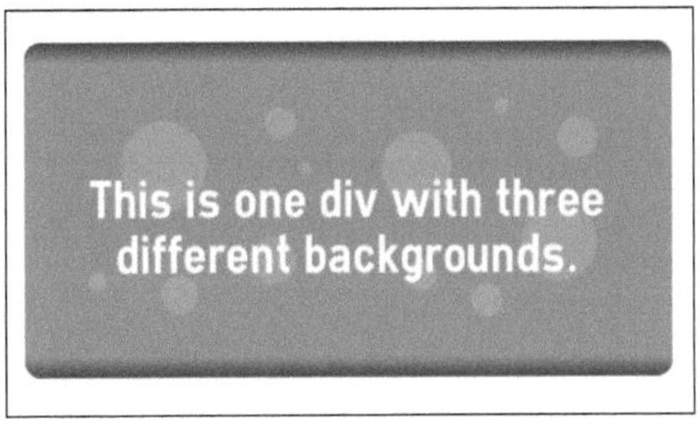

This is one div with three different backgrounds.

Figure 16-3: Here we artfully repeat three backgrounds to blend dots against two shaded backgrounds.

If you want to explore advanced multiple background techniques in more detail, CSS3.info has some excellent coverage of multiple backgrounds at www.css3.info/preview/multiple-backgrounds.

17

Web Typography

In This Chapter

▷ Changing font sizes

▷ Emboldening with bold

▷ Emphasizing with italic

▷ Changing capitalization

▷ Using web fonts

▷ Working with online font libraries

Typography is defined as the art and technique of arranging type in order to make language visible. Even more than just making language visible, however, typography has been shown to have a dramatic impact on whether people believe and assign value to what an author is saying. Despite the growing amount of video, images, and audio on the Internet, most websites are still primarily focused on conveying information through text. How the text looks has a major impact on how a website looks and how easy it is for people to read.

When you get the hang of working with text, the options for making your website more readable and more expressive are endless!

Finding Out about Fonts

A *font* is a set of characters that share a similar design. Examples of fonts include Times New Roman, Helvetica, Arial, and the dreaded Comic Sans. Cascading Style Sheets (CSS) gives you many different techniques for working with fonts. These techniques range from selecting a font, to making text bold or italic, to changing the color and size of text, and much more.

As you saw with border, margin, and padding, you can define individual font properties for different HTML5 elements with

- ✔ Individual CSS properties, such as `font-family`, `line-height`, and `font-size`
- ✔ A group of font properties in the catchall shorthand `font` property

Keep this in mind as you journey into the sometimes mind-boggling array of font properties. We show you the long way of doing things first, but the shorthand properties are often more commonly used.

Font family

To define the font face by using the CSS `font-family` property:

1. Identify the selector for the style declaration.

For example, making p the selector defines a font family for all `<p>` tags.

2. Add the property name `font-family`.

Browsers can access a limited number of font families by default. Different browsers on different operating systems can access different sets of font families. To deal with this situation, CSS allows you to specify multiple font families in case a browser doesn't support the font family you prefer. You can list multiple font family names, separated by commas. For example, it's common to see `font-family` declarations that look like this:

```
font-family: Arial, Helvetica, sans-serif;
```

This declaration lists, in order, the designer's preference for which font family should be used. The browser uses the first name in the list available on the computer on which it's running.

If a limited number of available font families sounds like a real bummer to you, hang on! With CSS3, this limitation has been lifted, as you see later in this chapter.

3. Define a `value` for the property (the name of the font family).

Use single or double quotation marks around any font family names that include spaces.

To format all first-level headings to use the Verdana font, use a style rule like this:

```
h1 {font-family: Verdana, Helvetica, sans-serif;}
```

In the preceding declaration, two more font families appear in case someone's browser doesn't support the Verdana font family.

We recommend including these font families in your style declarations:

⮡ **Common:** At least one of these common font families:

Arial: ABCDEFGHIJKLMNOPQRSTUVWXYZ abcdefghijklmnopqrstuvwxyz

Helvetica: ABCDEFGHIJKLMNOPQRSTUVWXYZ abcdefghijklmnopqrstuvwxyz

Times New Roman: ABCDEFGHIJKLMNOPQRSTUVWXYZ abcdefghijklmnopqrstuvwxyz

Verdana: ABCDEFGHIJKLMNOPQRSTUVWXYZ abcdefghijklmnopqrstuvwxyz

⮡ **Generic:** At least one of these generic font families:

Serif: ABCDEFGHIJKLMNOPQRSTUVWXYZ abcdefghijklmnopqrstuvwxyz

Sans serif: ABCDEFGHIJKLMNOPQRSTUVWXYZ abcdefghijklmnopqrstuvwxyz

Cursive: *ABCDEFGHIJKLMNOPQRSTUVWXYZ abcdefghijklmnopqrstuvwxyz*

Fantasy: *ABCDEFGHIJKLMNOPQRSTUV WXYZabcdefghijklmnopqrstuvwxyz*

Monospace: ABCDEFGHIJKLMNOPQRSTUVWXYZ abcdefghijklmnopqrstuvwxyz

Different elements may be formatted using different font families. These rules define a different font family for hyperlinks (see Figure 17-1):

```
body {color: #808000; font-family: Arial, sans-serif; font-size: 85%;}
hr {text-align: center;}
a {font-family: Courier, "Courier New", monospace;}
```

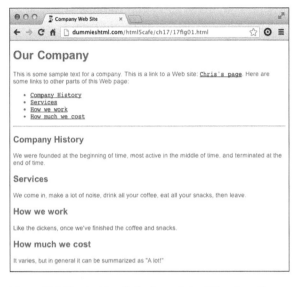

Figure 17-1: The font family for hyperlinks differs from the font family for the rest of the text.

Sizing text fonts with CSS

In addition to the font size names (xx-small, x-small, small, medium, large, x-large, or xx-large), you can also assign font sizes by using the following CSS units of measure: px (pixels), pt (points), % (percent), or em (the m-height for the font in use, whatever it may be). Pixels are a fixed-size unit that depends on the resolution of the user's monitor and doesn't scale. Designers are fond of using px for font sizes, because they allow a level of precision in translating from design files to Web pages. However, the use of px for specifying font sizes can have a negative impact on accessibility by the visually impaired, and on the scalability for smaller devices.

Points are a unit that is more commonly used for print than screen measurements. They have the same downside as pixels in that they are a fixed unit.

The em is the most widely used unit in sizing fonts in CSS nowadays, and this approach is considered a best practice for sizing fonts using style sheets. Choosing em units for font sizes makes it quick and easy for you to size type relative to your underlying font. For more information on using these units, which take the form font-size: 2em; (to double font size) or font-size: 0.8em; (to reduce a font to 80 percent of the base), see Chapter 11.

The percent unit operates very much like the em unit. The current font-size is equal to 100 percent. If you want to make the font size half as large you can set the font-size to 50 percent, if you want to make it 25 percent larger you can set it to 125 percent, and so on.

Sizing

The following properties allow you to control the dimensions of your text.

Font size

The style declaration to specify the size of text is

```
selector {font-size: value;}
```

The value of the declaration can be

 One of the standard font-property measurement values (listed in
   Chapter 11)

 One of these user-defined keywords:

   xx-small, x-small, small, medium, large, x-large, or xx-large

   The actual size of each font size keyword is determined by the browser,
   not by the style rule.

The following rules define

 A base font size of 85 percent for all text.

 A size in ems for all first-level headings.

```
body {color: #808000; font-family: Arial, sans-serif; font-size: 85%;}
h1 {font-family: "Trebuchet MS", Verdana, Geneva, Arial, Helvetica,
sans-serif; font-size: 2em; line-height: 2.5em; color: teal;}
```

The result appears in Figure 17-2.

Line height

The *line height* of a paragraph is the amount of space between each line
within the paragraph.

Line height is like line spacing in a word processor.

To alter the amount of space between lines of a paragraph, use the line-
height property:

```
selector {line-height: value;}
```

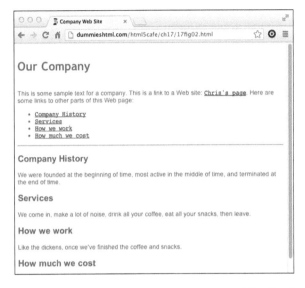

Figure 17-2: The body text is set to 85 percent, and first-level headings are set to 2em.

The value of the `line-height` property can be either

- One of the standard font property measurement values (listed above and in Chapter 11)
- A number that multiplies the element's font size, such as `1.5`

We assign a `quotation` class to the first paragraph throughout this chapter so you can see the changes. This allows us to apply these styles to the first paragraph by using

```
<p class="quotation">
```

in the HTML document.

The following rules style the first paragraph in italics, indent that paragraph, and increase the line height to increase readability (see Figure 17-3):

```
body {color: #808000; font-family: Arial, sans-serif; font-size: 85%;}
h1 {font-family: "trebuchet ms", verdana, geneva, arial, helvetica, sans-serif;
    font-size: 2em; line-height: 2.5em; color: teal;}
.quotation {font-style: italic; text-indent: 2em; line-height: 150%;}
```

Figure 17-3: Any element that belongs to the `quotation` class gets the same formatting.

Character spacing

You can increase or reduce the amount of spacing between letters or words by using these properties:

- `word-spacing`: The style declaration for `word-spacing` is

  `selector {word-spacing: value;}`

  Designers call the space between words *tracking*.

- `letter-spacing`: The style declaration for `letter-spacing` is

  `selector {letter-spacing: value;}`

  Designers call the space between letters *kerning*.

The value of either spacing property must be a length defined by a standard font property measurement value (listed in Chapter 11).

The following rule increases the letter spacing (kerning) of the first paragraph (see Figure 17-4):

```
.quotation {font-style: italic; text-indent: 10pt; line-
            height: 150%; letter-spacing: 0.2em;}
```

Figure 17-4: Kerning can be larger or smaller than the font's normal spacing.

Trying Out Text Treatments

CSS allows you to decorate your text by using boldface, italics, underline, overline, or strikethrough. CSS3 includes text effects such as inset text, drop shadows, and much more, which we talk about in Chapter 18.

Embolden with bold

Boldface font is one of the more common text embellishments a designer can use. To apply boldface in HTML, use the `<b>` tag or the `<strong>` tag. However, CSS provides you with more control over the font weight of the bolded text.

Syntax for applying bold

This style declaration uses the `font-weight` property:

```
selector {font-weight: value;}
```

The value of the `font-weight` property may be one of the following:

- `bold`: Renders the text in an average bold weight

- `bolder`: Relative value that renders a font weight bolder than the current weight (possibly assigned by a parent element)

- `lighter`: Relative value that renders a font weight lighter than the current weight (possibly assigned by a parent element)

✔ `normal`: Removes any bold formatting

✔ One of these integer values: `100` (lightest); `200, 300, 400` (normal); `500, 600, 700` (standard bold); `800, 900` (darkest)

Markup for applying bold

The following example bolds hyperlinks (see Figure 17-5), turns the underline off, and changes the color to green once a link is visited. We did this to Chris's page and the Company History items to show you what it looks like.

```
body {color: black; font-family: Arial, sans-serif; font-size: 85%;}
a {font-weight: bold; text-decoration: none;}
a:link {color: olive;}
a:visited {color: green;}
```

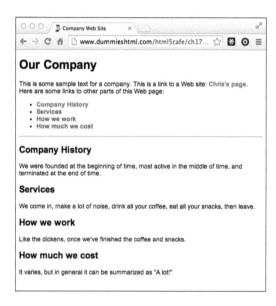

Figure 17-5: All hyperlinks are bolded.

Emphasizing with italic

Italics are commonly used to set off quotations or to emphasize text. To apply italics in HTML5, use the `<i>` or `<em>` tags. However, CSS provides you with more control over the font style of text through the `font-style` property.

Syntax for applying italic

This style declaration uses the `font-style` property:

```
selector {font-style: value;}
```

The value of the `font-style` property may be one of the following:

- ✔ `italic`: Renders the text in *italics* (a special font that usually slopes to the right)

- ✔ `oblique`: Renders the text as *oblique* (a different slanted version of a normal font; seldom if ever used for font definitions)

- ✔ `normal`: Removes any italic or oblique formatting

Markup for applying italic

The following example assigns an italic font style to the first-level heading:

```
body {color: #808000; font-family: Verdana, sans-serif; font-size: 85%;}
h1 {color: teal; font-family: "MS Trebuchet", Arial, Helvetica, sans-serif;
    text-transform: uppercase; font-style: italic; font-weight: 800;
    font-size: 2em; line-height: 30pt; text-align: center;}
```

Changing capitalization

You use the `text-transform` property to set capitalization in your document.

Syntax for changing capitalization

This style declaration uses the `text-transform` property:

```
selector {text-transform: value;}
```

The value of the `text-transform` property may be one of the following:

- ✔ `capitalize`: Capitalizes the first character in every word

- ✔ `uppercase`: Renders all letters of the text of the specified element in uppercase

- ✔ `lowercase`: Renders all letters of the text of the specified element in lowercase

- ✔ `none`: Keeps the value of the inherited element

Markup for changing capitalization

The following example renders the first-level heading in uppercase (shown in Figure 17-6):

```
body {color: black; font-family: Arial, sans-serif; font-size: 85%;}
    a {font-weight: bold;}
    a:link {color: olive; text-decoration: underline;}
    a:visited {color: green; text-decoration: none;}
    h1 {font-family: "Trebuchet MS", verdana, geneva, arial, helvetica, sans-
            serif; font-size: 2em; line-height: 2.5em; color: teal; text-
            transform: uppercase; text-align: center}
```

OUR COMPANY

This is some sample text for a company. This is a link to a Web site: <u>Chris's page</u>. Here are some links to other parts of this Web page:

- <u>Company History</u>
- <u>Services</u>
- <u>How we work</u>
- <u>How much we cost</u>

Figure 17-6: The first-level heading is rendered in all uppercase.

Getting fancy with the text-decoration property

The `text-decoration` property is a shorthand property for three new CSS3 text-decoration properties:

- `text-decoration-color`
- `text-decoration-line`
- `text-decoration-style`

Most often, however, the `text-decoration` property is simply used to add or remove underlines, overlines, or line-through to text.

Syntax for text decoration

This style declaration uses the `text-decoration` property:

```
selector {text-decoration: value;}
```

The value of the `text-decoration` property may be one of the following:

- `underline`: Underlines text
- `overline`: Renders the text with a line over it
- `line-through`: Renders the text with a line through it
- `none`: Removes any text decoration

There is one more possible value for the `text-decoration: blink`. Blinking text was probably the first form of animation on the web, and it was horribly over-used in the early days of web browsers. As a result, it got a very bad reputation and fell very much out of favor. In fact, blinking text became so unpopular that at least one HTML editor would reportedly delete your document if it detected blinking text!

The `blink` value of `text-decoration` isn't supported by every browser, and we hesitate to even mention it here. But, you may be the person who invents an ingenious use for blinking text and brings it back from the brink. Best of luck with that!

Keep in mind also that blinking and scrolling text can present issues for people with seizure disorders, vestibular disease, and other similar health concerns and should be avoided for those reasons too.

Markup for text decoration

The following example changes the link when the mouse hovers over it. In this case, it turns off any underlining for a link:

```
body {color: #808000; font-family: Verdana, sans-serif; font-size: 85%;}
a:link {color: olive; text-decoration: underline;}
a:visited {color: olive; text-decoration: underline;}
a:hover {color: olive; text-decoration: none;}
```

Checking Out the Catchall Font Property

You can summarize many font properties in one style declaration by using the shorthand `font` property. When it's used, only one style rule is needed to define a combination of font properties:

```
selector {font: style variant weight size/line-height font-family;}
```

The value of the `font` property is a list of any values that correspond to the various font properties:

- The following values must be defined in the following order although they aren't all required:

    - `font-size` (required)

    - `line-height` (optional)

      If line height is specified, it must be separated from the `font-size` value by a forward slash.

    - `font-family` (required)

      The `font-family` value list must be the last value in the font declaration.

Use commas to separate multiple font family names. For example, you can use the following style declaration to create a specific style for paragraph text that specifies `font-size`, `line-height`, and `font-family` in that (required) order:

```
p {font: 1.5em bold 150% Arial, Helvetica, sans-serif;}
```

✔ The following values are optional and may occur in any order within the declaration as long as they come before `font-size` and `font-family`. Individual values are separated by spaces:

- `font-style`
- `font-variant`
- `font-weight`

For example, you can use the following style declaration to create a specific style for a first-level heading that uses all of the required and optional values of the font shorthand property:

```
h1 {font: italic small-caps bold 2em/150% Arial, Helvetica, sans-serif;}
```

Experimenting with Web Fonts

CSS2 introduced the ability to download fonts to a user's web browser using the `@font-face` rule. However, `@font-face` got off to a rocky start, and was actually removed from the specification in CSS 2.1. It wasn't until CSS3 that it was added back in.

Today, `@font-face` is supported by almost every browser available and gives Web designers far more choices when choosing fonts than they ever had before.

Font file formats

Fonts come in various file formats. Font file formats are similar to image file formats in that different formats have different strengths and weaknesses. Also, different browsers feature support for different file formats.

Deciding which file format to use is often a matter of seeing what format the font you want to use comes in. The following are the most frequently used font file formats:

✔ **TrueType** has been around since the 1980s and is the standard format for the Microsoft system fonts.

✔ **OpenType** is based on TrueType and was developed by Microsoft and Adobe together. OpenType fonts support some advanced typographical features that aren't supported by TrueType. For Web Fonts, however, you're probably better off using TrueType fonts because of a bug in the way OpenType fonts are displayed in Windows.

✔ **Embedded OpenType (EOT)** is an Internet Explorer–only font file format. EOT fonts are the only way to use web fonts on older versions of Internet Explorer (before 9).

✔ **Web Open Font Format (WOFF)** isn't really a new font format, but a way to package TrueType and OpenType fonts for ease of use on the web.

Finding fonts

With web fonts, you can apply almost any font you can find to your web pages. However, having the ability doesn't mean that it's a good idea or that it's legal.

Many fonts are owned by companies that charge designers licensing fees to use their fonts. These companies, called *type foundries,* are concerned that the @font-face rule allows people to distribute their fonts without paying fees. To make sure that you're not using a font that you don't have the right to distribute, you should do one of the following:

✔ Purchase the fonts from a foundry site, such as www.fonts.com, and make sure that you read the licensing agreement.

✔ Pay for a service that allows you to select fonts from a database of commercial fonts to use on your site. An example of such a site is www.typekit.com.

✔ Use open source fonts. These are fonts that are made available with much less restrictive license agreements by their owners. The fonts in Google's Font Directory, which we look at in the next section, may be used for free on any website. Pretty awesome, huh?

Linking fonts

After you've found a font that you want to use, the next step is to link to it. This is where the @font-face rule comes in. The @font-face rule has the following structure:

```
@font-face {
    font-family: value;
    src: value;
    font-variant: value;
    font-weight: value;
    font-style: value;
}
```

Notice that font-face doesn't look like the other parts of CSS that you've seen so far. It starts with a @ symbol, for one. @font-face is what's called an *at-rule.* An at-rule's function is to give instructions to the CSS parser. In the case of @font-face, it gives instructions about what a particular font-family is and where it may be found.

The value of the font-family property is the name of the font. This must be a different value from any other font names used by your website, obviously. Other than that requirement, it can be pretty much anything you want.

Generally, however, the `font-family` is the name that the creator of the font has given the font.

The value of the `src` property is the location of the font file. It can be a URL or a reference to the font on the user's computer. You can specify multiple values for the `src` property, and the user's browser will try them in order and select one that it can use.

In the following example, the font named Baskerville will be used if the user has it on his computer. If that font isn't found, the font named Buenard-Regular.ttf will be used.

```
@font-face {
    font-family: MyBaskerville;
    src: local("Baskerville"),
    url("Buenard-Regular.ttf");
}
```

If you use a URL for the value of the `src` property, it may be an absolute or relative URL. If you use a relative URL, make sure that you upload the file to the same web server as your HTML and CSS documents.

Using Google Fonts

The Google Font Library is a repository of hundreds of freely available, and high-quality, fonts that anyone can use in any way at all — including on websites or in print.

The Google Fonts website, shown in Figure 17-7, lets you sort through the different available fonts, search for fonts, and preview what the fonts look like with sample text.

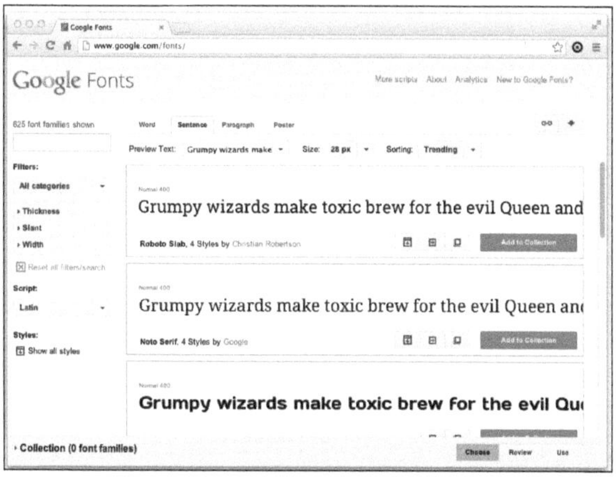

Figure 17-7: The grumpy wizards at Google have given the web a major gift.

To use a Google Font on your website, you can just follow these steps:

1. **Locate the font you want to use.**

   For this demonstration, we look at the sans-serif font family called Roboto. Figure 17-8 shows the preview of Roboto on Google Fonts.

   Figure 17-8: The Roboto font family, from Google Fonts.

2. **Click the Quick-use button in the lower right of the font preview box.**

   The Quick-use button is that one that looks like a box with an arrow pointing to the right.

3. **Choose the styles that you'll use.**

   A *style* is a variation on a font, such as a bolder version, or an italic version. Figure 17-9 shows the font style selection area on the Quick Use page.

   Figure 17-9: Select your styles.

4. **Choose the character sets that you want.**

   A *character set* is a collection of characters for a specific language or type of language. The default character set is usually Latin, which contains the characters that are used in the Western European languages, including English, French, Spanish, German, Italian, Portuguese, Icelandic, Dutch, Danish, Swedish, and Norwegian. Figure 17-10 shows the character set selection area.

Figure 17-10: Select your character set.

Each additional font style or character set that you select will increase the page load time, because each character set must be downloaded from Google before it can appear on your web page. So, if you expect to use only one character set, choose only that one. You can always come back and modify your selections later if you need to.

5. **Copy the standard `<link>` element from the Quick Use page and paste it into the `<head>` section of each HTML document that will make use of this font family.**

   Figure 17-11 shows the code section from the Quick Use page on Google Fonts. Listing 17-1 shows the link element pasted into the head of the HTML5 Cafe home page.

Figure 17-11: The generated font family link code from Google Fonts.

When you include this link code in your HTML document, you're actually including a style sheet from Google that contains the `@font-face` rule for the particular fonts you selected.

Listing 17-1: The Link Code Placed in the `<head>` Element

```
<!DOCTYPE html>
<html>
    <head>
        <meta charset="utf-8">
        <title>HTML5 Cafe: Home</title>
        <meta name="description" content="sample site for 9781118657201">
        <meta name="viewport" content="width=device-width">
        <link rel="stylesheet" href="css/normalize.css">
        <link rel="stylesheet" href="css/main.css">
        <link href='http://fonts.googleapis.com/css?family=Roboto' rel='stylesheet' type='text/css'>
    </head>
    <body>
        <div id="container">
            <nav id="topnav">
                <a href="index.html">HOME</a> | <a href="about.html">ABOUT US</a> | <a
href="menu.html">MENU</a> | <a href="contact.html">CONTACT US</a>
            </nav>
            <div id="content">
                <h1>Welcome to HTML5 Cafe!</h1>
                <p>Here you will find all sorts of delicious HTML5 and CSS3 treats. This is the
sample site for <a href="http://www.amazon.com/Beginning-HTML5-CSS3-Dummies-Computer/dp/
1118657209">Beginning HTML5 and CSS3 for Dummies</a>, by <a href="http://www.edtittel.com">Ed
Tittel</a> and <a href="http://www.chrisminnick.com">Chris Minnick</a>. To view all of the code
samples from the book, visit the <a href="menu.html">Menu</a>.
                </p>
                <figure id="home-image">
                    <img src="img/pitr_Coffee_cup_icon.png"
                    width="400" height="400" alt="delicious coffee">
                    <figcaption class="warning">
                        powered by coffee.
                    </figcaption>
                </figure>
            </div>
            <footer>
                copyright &copy; dummieshtml.com
            </footer>
        </div>
    </body>
</html>
```

6. **Use the new font family by adding the name of it to CSS font rules.**

   For example, to change the `<h1>` elements in HTML5 Cafe to the Roboto font family, type this CSS rule into the `main.css` file:

   ```
   h1 {font-family: 'Roboto', sans-serif;}
   ```

 Note that we use the generic `font-family` sans serif as a backup font in the previous CSS rule. This is to make sure that some sans-serif font will be used instead of Roboto if the browser happens to not support web fonts.

When you preview the HTML5 Cafe home page in a browser with the new font rule and the new linked `font-family`, it should resemble Figure 17-12.

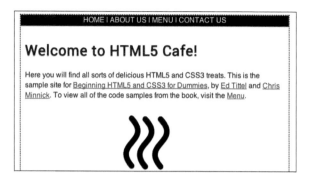

Figure 17-12: The HTML5 Cafe home page with the `<h1>` text in Roboto.

The difference between Roboto and the default sans-serif font that the site was using may be pretty subtle. For something dramatic and crazy, we've changed the header to a handwriting-style font family called Rock Salt in Figure 17-13.

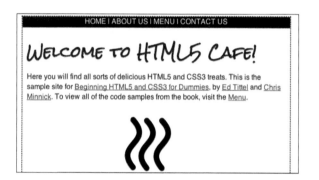

Figure 17-13: The HTML5 Cafe home page with the `<h1>` text in Rock Salt.

18

CSS Text and Shadow Effects

In This Chapter

▶ Creating shadows

▶ Creating inset text

▶ Creating 3D text

▶ Creating a letterpress effect

▶ Adding drop shadows

▶ Rotating text

*C*SS3 contains many new properties that web developers and design-ers can use to style, alter, transform, customize, tweak, and enhance text. The result of all these new properties is that the need to use images to achieve desired text effects is greatly reduced.

You get the following benefits out of being able to use styled text rather than images:

✓ Text takes up less storage space and therefore it downloads faster than images.

✓ Text can be read by screen readers and other types of alternative browsers for people with disabilities. Images cannot.

✓ Search engines can read and index text, which makes it easier for people to find your content. Text inside of images cannot be indexed.

CSS3 and the latest crop of web browsers are turning the web into a designer's paradise. If you know how to use the latest font-related CSS properties, the effects that you can achieve are impressive!

Most of the best CSS text effects rely on tricks of light and shadow. When you understand shadows, you can use them to create stunning effects not just with text but with any object on your web pages.

Creating Shadows

Shadows are a great tool for adding an illusion of depth to a web page. CSS3 has two properties for creating shadows:

- text-shadow: Adds a shadow to each letter in a text block
- box-shadow: Adds a shadow to any box element

By applying shadows in different ways, you can create effects such as drop shadows, letterpress text, and 3D text. We get to those later in this chapter, but first we show you the basics.

text-shadow

The simplest form of the text-shadow property looks like this:

```
h1 {text-shadow: 0.1em 0.1em #aaaaaa}
```

The syntax of this simple form of the text-shadow is:

```
text-shadow: offset-x offset-y color;
```

The offset-x and offset-y values tell how far horizontally (x-axis) and vertically (y-axis) to move the shadow relative to the text. You can specify the offset by using any of the standard measurement units in CSS. The color sets the color of the shadow and can be specified using any of the standard methods for naming colors in CSS.

The preceding example applies a gray (#aaaaaa) shadow 0.1em to the right and 0.1em down from the normal first level heading text. The result when applied to the HTML5 Cafe home page is shown in Figure 18-1.

HOME I ABOUT US I MENU I CONTACT US

Welcome to HTML5 Cafe!

Here you will find all sorts of delicious HTML5 and CSS3 treats. This is the sample site for Beginning HTML5 and CSS3 for Dummies, by Ed Tittel and Chris Minnick. To view all of the code samples from the book, visit the Menu.

Figure 18-1: A simple text shadow on the h1 element.

The text-shadow property has another, optional, parameter: the blur-radius. The blur-radius makes the shadow fuzzy and lighter. The larger the blur-radius value, the larger and lighter the blur will be. Like the offset, the blur-radius is a standard CSS length value.

To set the `blur-radius`, add a space and a length after the color.

```
text-shadow: 0.1em 0.1em #aaaaaa .2em;
```

When applied to the `<h1>` element, the result is shown in Figure 18-2.

HOME I ABOUT US I MENU I CONTACT US

Welcome to HTML5 Cafe!

Here you will find all sorts of delicious HTML5 and CSS3 treats. This is the sample site for Beginning HTML5 and CSS3 for Dummies, by Ed Tittel and Chris Minnick. To view all of the code samples from the book, visit the Menu.

Figure 18-2: A text shadow with a `blur radius` of 0.2em.

box-shadow

The `box-shadow` property creates one or more shadows for an element. Like the `text-shadow` property, the simplest use of a `box-shadow` requires only three values: `offset-x`, `offset-y`, and `color`.

```
.author img {
    margin-right: 10px;
    float: left;
    box-shadow: 4px 4px #777777;}
```

Figure 18-3 shows a `box-shadow` applied to Ed's picture on the About Us page of the HTML5 Cafe site.

Ed Tittel is a 30-plus-year computer industry veteran with an interesting background. A Princeton and multiple University of Texas graduate, Ed started his academic career with degrees in anthropology. Then, realizing the need for gainful employment, he moved into computer science, and has never looked back since starting his first programming job in 1981. These days, he makes his living blogging, writing articles (and the occasional book), and working as a consultant.

Figure 18-3: A simple shadow on Ed's picture.

To add a blur effect to the shadow, you can put the `blur-radius` after the `offset-y`:

```
.author img {
    margin-right: 10px;
    float: left;
    box-shadow: 4px 4px 6px #777777;}
```

The result is a more realistic and subtle shadow, as shown in Figure 18-4.

 Ed Tittel is a 30-plus-year computer industry veteran with an interesting background. A Princeton and multiple University of Texas graduate, Ed started his academic career with degrees in anthropology. Then, realizing the need for gainful employment, he moved into computer science, and has never looked back since starting his first programming job in 1981. These days, he makes his living blogging, writing articles (and the occasional book), and working as a consultant.

Figure 18-4: A shadow with a `blur-radius` applied.

Creating Inset Text

Inset text is text that appears to recede into the background. The key to inset text is to use a text shadow that's lighter than the text background color. This causes the text to look like it's inset and a shadow is being cast inside the letters. The more contrast between the shadow and the text and background, the more pronounced the effect will be.

For this example, we use the following HTML:

```
<h1 class="insetText">Welcome to HTML5 Caf&eacute;!</h1>
```

To create inset text, we recommend creating a class selector in your external style sheet. For example:

```
.insetText {text-shadow: 0px 1px 0px #ffffff;}
```

When applied to text, this rule creates a white shadow that is 1px lower than the text it's applied to. For the white shadow to be visible, the background must not be white. So, we set it to blue by creating and applying an additional class. Here's the new class:

```
bgGray {background-color:#999999;padding:4px;}
```

Now, take a look at the HTML with this class added. Notice that you can add multiple classes to the same element by separating them with spaces.

```
<h2 class="insetText bgGray">Welcome to HTML5 Caf&eacute;!</
          h2>
```

You can see the result in Figure 18-5.

Figure 18-5: The light shadow and darker background makes the text appear inset.

Creating 3D Text

Three-dimensional text is the opposite of inset text. In 3D text, the text appears to protrude from the page or even float above the page!

The key to 3D text is to use multiple text shadows together. We also introduce another new feature of CSS3 to help with this trick: opacity. Here's an example:

```
text-shadow: 0px 3px 0px #b2a98f,
             0px 7px 5px rgba(0,0,0,0.15),
             0px 12px 1px rgba(0,0,0,0.1),
             0px 17px 17px rgba(0,0,0,1);
```

We know this may look cryptic right now, but when you understand what we've done, it's actually pretty simple. Before we get to that, take a look at Figure 18-6, which shows the result of applying opacity to the HTML5 Cafe `<h1>` element.

Figure 18-6: A 3D effect applied to the `<h1>` on HTML5 Cafe.

Now, take a closer look at what's going on here.

First of all, this declaration has four shadows. Each shadow is separated by a comma, and the semicolon that ends the whole `text-shadow` declaration comes at the end. Each shadow has four properties. From the earlier "text-shadows" section, you know that these are `offset-x`, `offset-y`, `blur-radius`, and `color`.

But, look closely at the `color` property for each of the shadows. Here's something you haven't seen before: RGBA. The "A" in RGBA stands for *alpha*. When it comes to how transparency works in image editing software, *alpha compositing* is the process of combining an image with its background to give the illusion of transparency. In RGBA color, the *A* is a fourth value that ranges from 0 to 1. A value of 0 is completely transparent (just background, that is), and a value of 1 is completely opaque (just the image or the text shadow).

So, in the HTML5 Cafe header example, you're adjusting the transparency of blurred shadows that are offset different amounts from the text to give the appearance of hovering text. Pretty cool, huh?

Shadows and text effects can get pretty complicated, as you're starting to see. However, when you have the basic understanding of how they work, you don't need to always figure them out and write them by hand. Websites such as the 3D CSS Text Generator at `www.3dcsstext.com` can handle most of the hard work of creating the CSS markup for you.

Creating a Letterpress Effect

You can use transparency along with a new property called `background-clip` to do a much more realistic inset, or letterpress, effect than the simple one we created earlier in this chapter.

Here's the CSS:

```
h1 {
    background-color: #666666;
    -webkit-background-clip: text;
    -moz-background-clip: text;
    background-clip: text;
    color: transparent;
    text-shadow: 0px 3px 3px rgba(255,255,255,0.5);}
```

Notice that your old friends, the browser prefixes (also known as vendor prefixes), are back. The `background-clip` property isn't fully standardized just yet, so browsers have implemented their own versions of it.

As of this writing, `background-clip: text` is experimental. We include this technique here to demonstrate the amazing things that you can do with CSS, but make sure to test thoroughly on multiple browsers before you use this technique on a live website.

The `background-clip` property specifies whether the background extends under the border of the object. In this case, we're using a value of `text`. The most common use of this property is to add a background image to text, which can be used to create some really cool effects.

However, what you're doing here is adding a background on the inside of transparent text that has a shadow. So, what you get is just the shadow showing on the inside of text. The effect ends up looking like the image in Figure 18-7.

Figure 18-7: Using `background-clip` and transparency to create a realistic letterpress effect.

To better understand how this works, try removing the `background-clip` property to see just the shadow, as shown in Figure 18-8. (Remember that the so-called color of the text is set to `transparent`.)

Figure 18-8: Transparent text with a shadow without `background-clip:text`.

Without the `background-clip` property in place, it becomes apparent that its purpose is to just remove (or clip) everything outside of the borders of each letter.

Drop Shadows

Text isn't the only type of markup that you can apply shadows to. You can also create effects with box shadows. One very popular effect is called a *drop shadow*. Drop shadows give objects on a flat screen (or paper for that matter) more depth.

Figure 18-9 shows a picture with a drop shadow applied by using the `box-shadow` property.

Figure 18-9: A picture with a drop shadow applied using box-shadow.

This technique is simple, fast, and works in most browsers today. However, it has one big drawback: The drop shadow has to be a box.

In this example, it looks like a picture of the cat is hovering. But what if you want something a bit more sophisticated? What if you want the shadow to follow the shape of the cat?

Just a couple years ago, we would have said that you couldn't do it. You would need to add the shadow in an image editing program.

Happily, things change. Today, you can use the new CSS3 filter property to add a real drop shadow to a non-rectangular image — and the shadow even works in some percentage of your users' browsers.

Here's what the CSS looks like:

```
.shadowfilter {
    -webkit-filter: drop-shadow(9px 9px 9px rgba(0,0,0,0.5));
}
```

And here's how you can apply it to an image:

```
<img src="images/Gerald_G_Cartoon_Cat_Walking500px.fw.png" alt="cat"
        class="shadowfilter">
```

The result (at least when viewed in a WebKit browser (such as Google Chrome or Apple Safari) is shown in Figure 18-10. Get ready to impress even your hardest-to-impress web developer friends with this one.

Figure 18-10: A drop shadow applied using the
CSS drop-shadow filter.

Explaining how CSS filter effects work is beyond the scope of this book, but if you want to know more, check out the great tutorial at this site:

```
www.html5rocks.com/en/tutorials/filters/understanding-css
```

Text Rotation

You can use the CSS3 transform property to rotate objects and text to create interesting effects.

For something to be rotated, it must be a block-level element or have its display property set to block.

Here's the syntax for rotating an element with CSS transform:

```
selector {transform: rotate(value);}
```

The value inside the parentheses after `rotate` must be a positive or negative number of degrees that the element should be rotated. For example:

```
transform: rotate(-45deg);
```

Prefixes are currently necessary for transform to work in most browsers. So make sure to test any experimental CSS properties in multiple browsers — there's a chance that they may not work as you expect because of changes in the browser or the (still evolving) specification.

To apply rotation to the figure caption under the image on the HTML5 Cafe, use this style rule:

```
.warning {-webkit-transform: rotate(90deg);
    -moz-transform: rotate(90deg);
    transform: rotate(90deg);}
```

Because elements are rotated around their center point, it's often necessary to adjust their position to place them exactly where you want them to appear. For the following figure, we added relative positioning to the rotated warning class:

```
.warning {-webkit-transform: rotate(90deg);
        -moz-transform: rotate(90deg);
        transform: rotate(90deg);
        position: relative;
        top: -30px;
        right: -215px;}
```

The result is shown in Figure 18-11.

Figure 18-11: Rotated text.

19

Multimedia and Animation with CSS

In This Chapter

- Creating a print style sheet
- Using paged media styles
- Switching styles with @media
- Understanding keyframes
- Animating color

*O*ne of the best things about HTML5 and CSS3 is the increased ability of web designers to venture beyond the computer screen. With just HTML5 and CSS3, you can make your web pages available on different types of media, and you can enable multimedia capabilities. In the not-so-distant past, scripting, plug-ins, and additional software were required in order to do much of anything interesting on the web. Not so today!

In Chapter 17, we introduce you to the @font-face rule, which gives designers the ability to use any font they want in web designs. In Chapter 18, we introduce you to shadows and transform, which give designers the ability to handle complex effects without the use of a paint or photo manipulation tool. In this chapter, we take a look at two more CSS3 capabilities, media queries and animation, which are both rapidly changing the way we design and think of web pages.

Using CSS with Multimedia

CSS3 is useful for much more than styling text for desktop browsers.

People use web pages with their phones, tablets, projectors, TVs, and even watches and glasses. Some people even print out web pages for reading later.

With different style sheets, you can style the same content to work well on all these different devices. The key is to detect the type — or size — of device the user has and then serve them a custom style sheet for that particular device or media. Unfortunately, detecting what type of device a user is using is a best guess scenario. Viewport size is the only thing we can be sure of.

With the @media rule, you can specify how you want your web pages to look or behave on different media types.

Table 19-1 lists all the media types that CSS can recognize, as well as their uses.

Table 19-1	Recognized Media Types
Media Type	*Description*
All	Suitable for all devices
braille	For Braille tactile-feedback devices
embossed	For paged Braille printers
handheld	For hand-held devices (such as those with a small screen, monochrome monitor, and limited bandwidth)
print	For paged, opaque material and for documents viewed onscreen but in Print Preview mode
projection	For projected presentations, such as projectors or transparencies
screen	For color computer screens
speech	For speech synthesizers
tty	For media that use a fixed-pitch character grid, such as teletypes, terminals, or portable devices with limited display capabilities
tv	For television-type devices (such as those with low resolution, color capability, limited-scrollability screens, and some sound available)

CSS can make changes to customize how the same pages

✔ **Render onscreen**

✔ **Print**

A nifty color background might make your page a mess when it's printed on a black-and-white laser printer, but proper use of print-media styles can keep this sort of thing from happening!

✔ **Sound when read out loud**

Certain CSS properties apply only to specific types of media. For example, the page-break-before property, which specifies where a page break should occur, applies only to printed media. Other properties apply to multiple media. For example, width and font-family are important to all the visual media types (such as projection, screen, and print) but may require different values for each of these media types.

Visual media styles

Table 19-2 lists the CSS properties you're most likely to use in a typical web page. Our online content for this book includes brief descriptions of the most commonly used CSS properties and HTML tags and attributes.

Table 19-2	Visual Media Styles		
Property	**Values**	**Default Value**	**Description**
background-color	Any color, by name or hex code	Transparent	Background color of the associated element
background-image	URL	None	Image URL as background for element
Color	Any color, by name or hex code	Up to you.	Color of the foreground text
font-family	Any named font: cursive, fantasy, monospace, sans-serif, serif	Up to you. (Stick to common fonts.)	Font for rendering related element content
font-size	Number + unit, xx-small, x-small, small, smaller, medium, large, larger x, large xx, large %, Length (px, em, cm)	Medium	Size of the font for rendering related element content

(continued)

Table 19-2 *(continued)*

Property	Values	Default Value	Description
font-weight	Normal, bold, bolder, lighter, 100, 200, 300, 400, 500, 600, 700, 800, 900	normal 400 is the same as normal 700 is the same as bold	Weight (how bold or light) at which the font should appear
line-height	Normal number + unit % Length (px, em, cm)	Normal	Vertical spacing between lines of text
text-align	Left, right, center, justify	Up to you; normal text direction	Determines how text on the page gets aligned
text-decoration	None, underline, overline, line-through, blink	None	Special text effects
list-style-image	URL	None	URL for an image to display as a list bullet
list-style-position	Inside, outside	Outside	Wrap list text inside or outside bullet points
list-style-type	Disc, circle, square, decimal, decimal-leading-zero, lower-alpha, upper-alpha, none, armenian, georgian, lower-greek, lower-latin, lower-roman, upper-latin, upper-roman	Disc	Bullet type on lists

Property	Values	Default Value	Description
Display	Block, inline, none	Inline	Format of a defined section for a block element
Top	Number and unit auto	Auto	Absolute positioning: sets the top edge of an element above or below the top edge of the containing element
			Relative positioning: sets the top edge of an element above or below its normal position
Right	Percentage number + unit auto	Auto	Absolute positioning: sets the right edge of an element to the right or left of its containing element.
			Relative positioning: sets the right edge of an element to the right or left of its normal position
Bottom	Percentage number + unit auto	Auto	Absolute positioning: sets bottom edge of the element below bottom edge of its containing element
			Relative positioning: sets the bottom edge of the element below its normal position

(continued)

Table 19-2 *(continued)*

Property	Values	Default Value	Description
Left	Percentage number + unit auto	Auto	Absolute positioning: sets left edge of an element to the right or left edge of its containing element
			Relative positioning: sets the left edge of an element to the left or right of its current position.
Position	Static, absolute, relative, fixed	Static	Method by which an element box is laid out, relative to positioning context
Visibility	Collapse, visible, hidden, inherit	Inherit	Indicates whether an object will display on the page
z-index	Number auto	Auto	Stacking order for objects — 1 always puts the object at the very back
border-style	None, dotted, dashed, solid, double, groove, ridge, inset, outset	Not defined	Style displayed for object borders; can be broken out into border-top-style, border-right-style, border-bottom-style, and border-left-style

Property	Values	Default Value	Description
border-width	Thin, medium, thick, Number	Not defined	Width of border around an object; can be broken out into border-top-width, border-right-width, border-bottom-width, and border-left-width
border-color	Any color, by name or hex code transparent	Not defined	Color of object's border; can be broken out into border-top-color, border-right-color, border-bottom-color, and border-left-color
Border	Border-width + border-style + border-color	Not defined	Combined features for border around object; can be broken out into border-top, border-right, border-bottom, and border-left
Float	Left, right, none	None	Specifies whether object should float to one side or other for document
Height	Number + unit auto	Auto	Display height for object

(continued)

Table 19-2 *(continued)*

Property	Values	Default Value	Description
Width	Number + unit auto	Auto	Display width for object
Margin	Number + unit auto	Not defined	Display margins for object; can be broken out into `margin-top`, `margin-right`, `margin-bottom`, and `margin-left`
Padding	Number + unit auto	Not defined	Display blank space around object; can be broken out into `padding-top`, `padding-right`, `padding-bottom`, and `padding-left`
Cursor	`Auto`, `cross hair`, `default`, `pointer`, `move`, `text`, `help`, `URL`, `e-resize`, `n-resize`, `ne-resize`, `nw-resize`, `progress`, `s-resize`, `se-resize`, `sw-resize`, `w-resize`, `inherit`	Auto	Cursor appearance in browser window

All the properties listed in Table 19-2 are safe to use in any visual browser today. If you're unsure whether something will work in all browsers, the best way to find out is to test, of course. However, a lot of different browsers out are available, and it's often difficult and impractical to have different versions of a browser installed on the same computer. Professional web developers visit `http://caniuse.com` as a first step to find out what tricks might be necessary to get a property working with a certain browser.

Paged media styles

CSS can customize how a page looks when it's printed. We recommend these guidelines:

▸ **Replace sans-serif fonts with serif fonts.**

Serif fonts, which have small lines trailing from the edges of letters and symbols (called *serifs*) are easier to read than sans-serif fonts.

▸ **Insert advertisements that**

- Make sense when they aren't animated
- Are useful without clicking

In general, paged media styles help ensure that text looks as good when it's printed as it does in a web browser. Paged media styles also help you hide irrelevant content when pages are printed (banners, ads, and so forth), thus reducing wasted paper and user frustration. See Table 19-3 for an explanation of paged media properties in CSS.

Table 19-3	Paged Media Styles		
Property	**Values**	**Default Value**	**Description**
Orphans	Number	2	The minimum number of lines in a paragraph that must be left at the bottom of a page
page-break-after	Auto, always, avoid, left, right	Auto	The page-breaking behavior after an element
page-break-before	Auto, always, avoid, left, right	Auto	The page-breaking behavior before an element
page-break-inside	Auto, avoid	Auto	The page-breaking behavior inside an element
Widows	Number	2	The minimum number of lines in a paragraph that must be left at the top of a page

The example in Listing 19-1 uses these options for paged media styles:

- Make the output black text on a white background.
- Replace sans-serif fonts with serif fonts.

Listing 19-1:   Adding a Print Style Sheet

```
<!DOCTYPE html>
<html>
<head>
<title>This is my page</title>
<style type="text/css">
    body {background-color: black; color: white; font-family: sans-serif;}

    @media print {
     body {background-color: white; color: black; font-family: serif}
    }
</style>
</head>
<body>
    This page will look very different when sent to the printer.
</body>
</html>
```

If you're now wondering why none of the properties in Table 19-3 were set but other properties were, it's because (in this example) their defaults worked fine. Just because those page properties can be set doesn't mean that you can't set other properties also — it isn't an either/or situation.

Getting Animated

CSS animations provide a very simple way to animate transitions between styles. Unlike other ways of doing animation on the web, CSS animation requires no scripting and no plug-ins. It also generally performs better and uses fewer system resources (CPU cycles and memory) than other types of animation.

Before we get to the details, we step back and review some basic animation concepts.

Animation works by displaying a series of images to create the illusion of movement.

If you have two points, all you need to create an animation of something moving in a straight line between those points is a length of time that the movement should take. In this most basic example, the beginning and ending points are known and everything inbetween can be inferred or computed. The known points in the animation are called *keyframes*.

Speech styles

Speech synthesizers, which convert text into speech, aren't just for the visually impaired. They're also useful for web users who

↳ Have reading problems

↳ Need information while driving

The following example recommends voices to be played using male and female characters to make it clear which characters are speaking:

```
<style>
    @media speech {
        p.stanley {voice-family:
        male;}
        p.stella {voice-family:
        female;}
    }
</style>
```

Usually, you don't have to worry much about adding speech styles to your page. Today's speech synthesizers should work just fine if

↳ Your page is mostly text.

↳ You don't have a strong opinion about how it sounds, so any clearly male or female voice will do.

That said, you can find a complete listing of all speech style properties on this book's companion website.

Note: Most people who use these technologies have either set up their own custom styles or are used to the default styles, which are used to convey specific meanings to the listener. It can be disruptive to the user if they are unexpectedly different. Change voices with caution.

In traditional hand-drawn animation, keyframes are drawn by a senior artist, and the frames between keyframes are drawn by an assistant. These frames between the keyframes are called *inbetweens.*

In CSS animation, the CSS author creates keyframes, and the browser draws the inbetweens.

If you want the object to move in a way other than a straight line, you can specify additional keyframes between the beginning and ending points. Figure 19-1 shows an illustration of animation path involving start and end points and a keyframe between them. We've placed partially transparent frames between the keyframes to show some of the inbetweens.

CSS animations can be used to smoothly change the size of an element, change its color, rotate it, or move it from one location to another, for example.

For a list of all the animatable CSS properties, visit

```
https://developer.mozilla.org/en-US/docs/Web/CSS/CSS_
            animated_properties
```

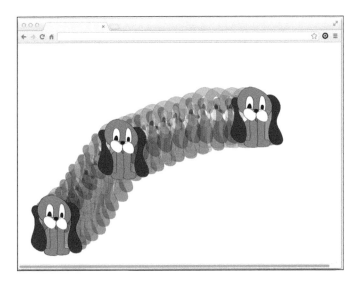

Figure 19-1: Keyframe animation.

Using the animation properties

The CSS animation properties configure how an animation will run. They don't actually animate anything — that's the job of the @keyframes rule.

The animation property is a shorthand for the following subproperties:

- animation-name: Used for assigning a name to an animation's keyframes.
- animation-duration: Specifies how long the animation should take to run.
- animation-timing-function: Used to specify acceleration curves that determine how the animation transitions through the keyframes. For example, an animation may start and end slowly and move faster in the middle.
- animation-delay: Configures the delay before the start of the animation.
- animation-iteration-count: Tells how many times to run the animation.
- animation-direction: Can be used to set an animation to run backwards when it reaches the end.

The following example configures an animation of the <figure> element on the home page of HTML5 Cafe:

```
#home-image {animation-duration: 4s;
             animation-name: slideup;}
```

At this point, there's no animation. But, you've set the stage by specifying that an animation named `slideup` should be applied and that it should take four seconds to run.

The animation named `slideup` doesn't exist yet. To create it, we need to use the `@keyframes` rule.

Creating animations with `@keyframes`

In the most basic use of `@keyframes`, you specify the beginning and end and then name the animation. After you've named an animation, it's available to be used by any element, through the `animation-name` property. Here's a simple animation that animates the top margin of an element from 200px to 0:

```
@keyframes slideup {
    from {margin-top: 200px;}
    to {margin-top: 0px;}
```

When defined and called as part of a style rule for an element, this new animation will transition from `margin-top: 200px` to `margin-top: 0px`. The result is that the `#home-image` will slide up into position after it's loaded.

Ah, but only if it were so simple! Once again, CSS animation is still not quite finished and approved, so vendor prefixes may be necessary. To avoid adding a whole lot of extra code here, we've left them out. However, be aware that you may need to add `-moz` or `-webkit` to the animation properties and the `@keyframe` rule in order for them to work in your browser.

Animating color

You can also use CSS animation to gradually change the color of an element from one color to another. When you do this, the color will start at the `from` value and transition through the RGB scale until it reaches the next keyframe.

For example, here's a color animation that goes from red to blue:

```
@keyframes redtoblue {
    from {color: #ff0000;}
    to {color: #0000ff;}
```

To apply this animation to an object, just add the `animation-name` and `animation-duration` (along with any of the other animation subproperties you want to specify) to a style rule, as follows:

```
h1 {animation-name:redtoblue;
    animation-duration: 8s;}
```

This animation takes exactly eight seconds to run. When it's done, the color of the `<h1>` element resets to the color it was before the transition. So, if you want the color to remain blue after the animation happens, add a color declaration to the style rule.

Figure 19-2 shows, as best as we can in print, the animation from red to blue.

Figure 19-2: Animating color from red to blue.

Part VI
The Part of Tens

In this part . . .

- Manufacturing magnificent mobile web designs with HTML5 and CSS3
- Minding your HTML (and CSS) *P*s and *Q*s
- Exterminating web bugs in HTML and CSS . . . with prejudice!
- Discovering some amazing and cool HTML tools and technologies
- Getting your hands on the best online markup references and resources

20

Ten Keys to Mobile Web Design

In This Chapter

▷ Understanding different mobile devices

▷ Optimizing for small screens

▷ Designing for distracted users

▷ Testing on different devices

*T*here's no doubt today that mobile devices have gone mainstream. Today's marketplace boasts a wide array of products, many competing manufacturers, and oodles of innovative features. However, before we wax too eloquent, we should clarify that we aren't talking about skimobiles, mobile homes, or even Mobile, Alabama. Rather, we're talking about the *mobile web,* which serves those portable multi-use phones and other devices (such as the iPad or a Wi-Fi–connected portable GPS) that are so easy to carry around and integrate into everyday life.

Mobile devices are unbeatable for quick access to directions and maps, checking out product reviews or comparisons, finding contact information, or simply surfing the Internet while on the go. Because of this, we think understanding mobile web design is important, too. That way, you can use your new skills and knowledge to account for the many unique challenges that mobile access can pose, and perhaps build a better website as a result.

Design for Different Mobile Devices

Unfortunately, the more you look around at the different types of mobile devices, the more it seems like there's no ready way to categorize them all or no single approach to implement web pages in their limited display space.

For example, you can find mobile devices categorized by one or more of the following characteristics:

- Input device (touchscreen, stylus, keyboard, or touchpad)
- Operating system (Symbian, Windows Mobile, Apple iOS, Android)

- Processor and memory
- Screen size
- Internet access
- Connectivity (Bluetooth, USB)
- Other cool features (camera, video, ringtones, games)

This list could go on and on. Basically, you get the idea that there are almost as many ways to profile mobile devices as there are mobile devices themselves.

On the most basic level, the safest and easiest way to classify mobile devices is into three groups:

- **Smartphone:** A smartphone is a phone that includes computer-like features, such as an operating system integrated into the phone, more powerful processor and memory, the capability to install and run custom applications, wireless access, color display, and advanced input capabilities. Because of these features, it also comes at a higher costs — it's more expensive to buy and costlier to use. The iPhone, shown in Figure 20-1, is one of the most popular smartphones.

Figure 20-1: An Apple iPhone.

- **Feature phone:** Feature phones usually incorporate less powerful processors and memory, have a basic and proprietary operating system, offer limited application possibilities (if any), and cost less than smartphones. (Feature phones often cost less than half of what smartphones do and, with more limited data handling capabilities, often cost about half as much for monthly service as well.) A typical example of a feature phone is the Nokia phone shown in Figure 20-2.

Figure 20-2: A standard Nokia feature phone.

✓ **Tablet:** A tablet is generally larger than a phone and doesn't have cell-phone capabilities. More powerful tablets are beginning to replace laptops and even desktop computers for some users.

Here's the bad news: Not only do phones differ in features and prices, but they also display websites differently. Feature phones have extremely limited CSS and JavaScript support — if they have any such support at all. However, before you throw your hands up in the air, we recommend learning more about mobile website design in the following sections. Feature phones aren't all bad, nor are smartphones all good. For both types of devices, some website compromises are necessary.

Design for People

When you start thinking about how to design mobile version(s) of your website so you can produce the best possible results for visitors using mobile devices, you need to ponder the unique challenges that the mobile web can pose for your site's design and implementation. You also need to have a clear picture of who will be using your mobile website.

Every single one of your mobile website's users will be human, and there's at least as much variation in people as there is in mobile devices. Unlike mobile devices, however, you can't — and shouldn't even try — to design with every possible user in mind.

Do your research and think about exactly who your target users are. Are they young or old? Male or female? Do they live in cities? Get as specific as you can when you define your users' profiles and think about the scenarios in which they will use your mobile website.

Creating a profile of your target user and usage scenarios is called *user-centric design.*

Design for Small Screens

If every mobile phone had the same screen size, we might not have needed to write about mobile web design for this book. Although you have many other considerations to think about when creating mobile websites or pages, limited display real estate is one of the most important to keep in mind.

Creating a single design with a fixed width doesn't work if you want to take best advantage of real estate available on each screen. Also, remember that many smartphones can be rotated, so the user may view your page in both landscape and portrait views.

Design for Low Bandwidth

Smaller screen size isn't the only thing that limits how well you can display images and multimedia on a cellphone; limited bandwidth is another important factor when designing and building a website for mobile access. Although a growing number of mobile users can take advantage of faster 3G and 4G mobile networks, many mobile device users are still hampered by connections best described as painfully slow.

The same challenges of limited bandwidth that throttled early web design and access for pioneering users in the early to mid-1990s now slow the mobile Internet. It lags far behind high-speed DSL and cable modem connections from a desktop or notebook computer.

As you design a mobile version of your site, follow these tips so that your site provides tolerable service for visitors with low-bandwidth connections:

- **Be ruthless with images and multimedia files.** Limit your mobile site to a precious few images to help tell your story and add visual interest. Keep things small and simple.

- **Replace banners and button images with text links.** Text links work on any device and consume only minimal storage space and bandwidth.

- **Be careful when including multimedia.** For example, don't put video or audio files on the front page of a mobile site. Instead, link to multimedia files so they're optional for mobile browsers. Also, include warnings about file size and the way the media displays on different devices.

Design for Touch

Most smartphones today are touch enabled. Compared with a mouse pointer, a person's finger is a pretty clumsy and imprecise instrument.

That means you need to do the following:

- **Make links easy to see and click.** Buttons and links should be big enough and have enough space between them to make it easy to tap them with a fat fingertip.

- **Limit the total number of links, especially on the low-end version of your site.** Help people move through your site by leading them from one short list of links to another until they reach the content that serves them best.

- **Organize link levels.** Don't include too many levels with your links. Consider adding breadcrumbs to help users find their way back through your site. *Breadcrumbs* are a list of links, usually at the top of a page, that help users identify where they are in the structure of the site. The links to each section and subsection are ahead of the current page in the site's structure, from the home page all the way down to the current page (which is accessible through the browser's address box).

✔ **Use a navigation menu, not a navigation bar.** Although most desktop websites include a navigation bar that links to all main sections in a site at the top of every page, that's generally not the best use for real estate on a small screen. Instead, consider including one link at the top of every page with a name like Menu, and then link it to a navigation bar. Figure 20-3 shows this technique as it's used on the mobile version of this book's companion website, www.dummieshtml.com.

Figure 20-3: The mobile version of www.dummies html.com with a collapsed menu link.

Including a list of links to all the main pages of your site on every page may not be worth the download time, but creating a small site map and including a link to that page from every other page on the site provides a similar option without lots of extra overhead. Use this strategy to include a list of links at the bottom of each page along with a Menu link up top that jumps visitors to the links at the bottom.

✔ **Consider back and forward buttons.** Back and forward buttons help users move through many pages of content or images.

Design for Distracted Surfers

One of the biggest differences between how people use mobile devices and how they use desktop computers is that when someone uses a mobile device, it's often not the primary thing that they're doing. For example, a user of your mobile website may be looking up your address while she's on the way to a meeting with you. Or, she might be grocery shopping and looking up product information on the web. She even might be socializing with friends and trying to settle an argument over how old Tina Yothers is. (CelebrityAgeMachine. com works well for settling these arguments, by the way.)

The bottom line is that mobile users tend to be distracted. Here are a few quick tips to make your mobile site easier for distracted visitors to use:

- Make key information, such as your address and phone number, easy to find right away.

- Make all links big and easy to click.

- Use text and contrasting background colors so the text is easy to read, even in low light (or on a display that's hard to read in strong sunlight).

Test on Many Mobile Devices

To appreciate the challenges of the mobile web, surf to your own website on a mobile phone. However, don't stop at one phone, especially if that phone is an iPhone or Android. The iPhone and Android may get all the headlines (and a majority of the traffic on the mobile web), but they're not the only phones likely to visit your site. Those same sites viewed on a BlackBerry or a Windows Phone may be completely unreadable.

Although you can test your mobile site by using online emulators, such as the high-end testing site at DeviceAnywhere (`www.deviceanywhere.com`), the best way is to hold a device in your hand so you can see how your site feels and looks on that phone.

Visit a mobile phone store and be really nice to the salespeople while you test your sites on their phones. Better yet, compare notes with friends and family. Ask people to visit your website on different phones and watch what they do, how they find their way around (or where they get lost), and how hard it is for them to get to the information they need when they interact with your site.

Design for Simplicity

Even on the best mobile devices, typing and clicking links can be a challenge. Always make links big and easy to click for mobile visitors and don't overload any page with too many options.

The best approach is to lead users through a series of simple choices, limiting options to no more than five to seven big links at any stage. Directing visitors to increasingly specific sets of links is best until users can choose the information they want or need.

When possible, avoid drop-down lists or anything else that uses AJAX or JavaScript around links. At the very least, provide alternatives when avoiding JavaScript is unrealistic. Because many mobile devices don't support these types of web technologies, it makes these links impossible to use.

Some information, such as contact information, should never be more than one click away. In nearly all cases, including your phone number on the main page of your mobile site is good practice — after all, you know your visitor has a phone handy!

Set Up Mobile Web Addresses

So that everyone with a mobile phone can easily get to the URL of your mobile site (by typing as little as possible), set up multiple mobile addresses and direct them all to the mobile version of your site.

Until a clear winner appears in the mobile URL game, use all the most common addresses to increase the odds that your visitors find you on their first try.

The following are typical mobile URLs in common use on the mobile web:

- m.*yourdomain*.com: Recommended for ease of typing.
- wap.*yourdomain*.com: This is a common address for sites created using the WML (Wireless Markup Language).
- *yourdomain*.com/mobile: Common alternative because of easy server setup.
- *yourdomain*.com/i: For versions built specifically for the iPhone.
- *yourdomain*.mobi: Requires registering a .mobi version of your domain name, which many sites don't seem to bother with.

Whatever you do, drop the www. — no one should ever have to type those three letters and that dot again on the modern web.

Your mobile site may not actually be a separate site. One popular alternative to creating separate sites for mobile and desktop users is to utilize media queries (as discussed in Chapter 19), to switch between different style sheets depending on the size of the user's browser window. Web designers call this technique for creating mobile websites *responsive design*.

Include a Link to the Desktop Site

Always include a link to the full, desktop version of your site on your mobile site. This link helps people who may be familiar with your desktop site and prefer to use it even on their smartphone where it may not work as well.

In addition, it's always possible that someone with a tablet device that receives the mobile site may find it easier to use the full version of the site rather than the mobile version.

Making it as easy as possible for the mobile user to use your website is the key to mobile web design.

21

Ten HTML Do's and Don'ts

In This Chapter

▷ Concentrating on content

▷ Going easy on the graphics, bells, whistles, and roaring dinosaurs

▷ Creating well-formulated HTML and then testing, testing, testing

▷ Keeping it interesting after the building is over

By itself, HTML is neither particularly complex nor extremely difficult. *HTML ain't rocket science,* as some high-tech wags (including a few rocket scientists) have put it. Nevertheless, important do's and don'ts can make or break the web pages you build with HTML and CSS. Consider these humble suggestions as guidelines for making the most of your markup without losing touch with your users (or watching your page blow up on its launch pad).

If points we make throughout this book seem to crop up here, too — especially regarding proper and improper use of HTML — it's no accident. Heed ye well the prescriptions and avoid ye the maledictions. But hey, they're your pages. You can do what you want. Your users will decide the ultimate outcome. (We'd *never* say, "We told you so." Would we?)

Don't Lose Sight of Your Content

Any website lives or dies by its content. That a site is meaningful, that it delivers information directly, easily, and efficiently, and that a user can reasonably expect to find something new and interesting there with each new visit — all are pluses. But all those things (and more) rest on solid, useful content that gives visitors a reason to come (and return) to your site.

So we return to the crucial question of payload: page content. Why? Well, as Darrell Royal (legendary football coach of the University of Texas Longhorns in the '60s and '70s) is rumored to have said to his players, "Dance with who brung ya." In normal English (as opposed to Texan), this means that you should stick with the people who've supported you all along, and give your loyalty to those who've given it to you.

We're not sure what this means for football, but for web pages it means keeping faith with your users and keeping content paramount. If you don't have strong, solid, informative content, users quickly get that empty feeling that hits when pages are content free. When that happens, they'll be off to richer hunting grounds online, looking for content wherever it can be found.

To satisfy user hunger, put your strongest content on your site's major pages. Save the frills and supplementary materials for secondary pages. The short statement of this principle for any kind of markup is "Tags are important, but what's between the tags — the content — is what really counts."

Do Structure Your Documents and Your Site

For users, a clear roadmap of your content is as important for a single home page as it is for an online encyclopedia. When longer or more complex documents grow into a full-fledged website, a roadmap becomes more important still. This map ideally takes the form of (you guessed it) a flow chart of page organization and links. If you like pictures with a purpose, the chart could appear in graphic form in an explicitly labeled site map.

We're strong advocates of top-down page design: Don't start writing content or placing tags until you understand what you want to say and how you want to organize your material. Start building your HTML document or documents using paper and pencil (or your modeling tool of choice). Sketch out relationships within the content and among your pages. Know what and where you're building before rolling out the heavy equipment.

Good content flows from good organization. It helps you stay on track during page design, testing, delivery, and maintenance. Organization helps users find their way through your site. Need we say more? Well, yes: Don't forget that *organization changes over time.* Revisit and critique your organization and structure on a regular basis — and don't be afraid to change either one to keep up with changes in your website's content or focus.

Do Make the Most from the Least

Markup, scripting, and style sheets make much possible, but not all possibilities deserve implementation — websites can't live by snazzy graphics, special effects, and blinking marquees alone. Let your design and content drive the markup, graphics, and interaction. With good design and content, your site will do its job without befuddling your visitors.

Gratuitous links to useless information are nobody's friend; if you're tempted to link to a webcam that shows a dripping faucet — resist, resist, resist!

Structure and images exist to *highlight* content. The more bells, whistles, and dinosaur yowls dominate a page, the more they distract visitors from content. Use structure and graphics sparingly, wisely, and carefully. Anything more impedes content delivery. Go easy on animations, links, and layout tags, or risk having your message (even your page) devoured by a hungry T. Rex.

Do Build Attractive Pages

When users visit web pages with a consistent framework that focuses on content, they're likely to feel welcome. The important thing is to *supplement* content with graphics and links — don't overwhelm users with a surfeit of pictures and links. Making web pages pretty and easy to navigate adds to a site's basic appeal and makes your cyber-campers even happier.

If you need inspiration, cruise the web and look for layouts and graphics that work for you. If you take the time to analyze what you like, you can work from other people's design principles without having to steal details from their layouts or looks (which isn't a good idea anyway).

When designing web documents, start with a basic, standard page layout. Pick a small, interesting set of graphical symbols or icons and adopt a consistent navigation style. Use graphics sparingly (yes, you've heard this before); make them as small as possible — limit size, number of colors, shading, and so on, while retaining visual appeal. After you build simple, consistent navigation tools, label them clearly and use them consistently. Your pages can be appealing *and* informative given enough time and effort.

Don't Lose Track of Those Tags

If you start with solid markup and good content — and then plow through what you've built to make sure everything works the way it should (and communicates what it ought) — you're on your way to a great website. But after construction is over, testing begins. And only when testing produces positive results should you open your virtual doors to the public.

Although you're building documents, it's easy to forget to use closing tags, even when they're required (for example, the `</a>` that closes the opening anchor tag `<a>`). When you're testing web pages, some browsers can compensate for such errors, leaving you with a false sense of security.

The web is no place to depend on the kindness of strangers. Scrutinize your tags to head off possible problems from browsers that might not be quite so understanding (or lax, as the case may be). Validation (using `http://validator.w3.org`) is always a good idea, too.

As for claims that some HTML authoring tool vendors make ("You don't have to know any HTML!"), all we can say is, *"Uh-huh, suuurre...."* HTML is a big part of what makes web pages work; if you understand it, you can troubleshoot with minimal fuss. Also, only you can ensure that your pages' inner workings are correct and complete, whether you build them yourself or a program builds them for you.

We could go on and on about this, but we'll exercise some mercy and confine our remarks to the most pertinent items:

- **Keep track of tags while you write or edit HTML by hand.** If you open a tag — be it an anchor, a text area, or whatever — create the closing tag for it right then and there, even if you have content to add. Most HTML editors do this for you.

- **Use a syntax checker to validate your work during the testing process.** Syntax checkers are automatic tools that find missing tags or errors. Use these syntax checkers whether you build pages by hand or with software. The free W3C validator lives at `http://validator.w3.org`.

- **Test pages with as many browsers as you can.** This not only alerts you to missing tags but can also reveal potential design flaws or browser issues (covered in the later section, "Do Avoid Browser Dependencies"). This exercise also emphasizes the need for alternate text. That's why we check our pages with Lynx (a character-only browser). Ask friends, colleagues, and co-workers to check out your work, and tell them to use as many browsers as they can, too. Please!

- **Always follow HTML document syntax and layout rules.** Just because browsers don't require elements such as `html`, `head`, and `body` doesn't mean you can omit them. It means browsers don't care whether or not you use them. But browsers are not your audience. Your users (and future browsers) may indeed care.

Although HTML isn't exactly a programming language, it makes sense to treat it like one. Following formats and syntax helps you avoid trouble, and carefully testing and rechecking your work ensures a high degree of quality and compliance with standards, as well as a relatively trouble-free website.

Do Avoid Browser Dependencies

When building web pages, the temptation to view the web only in terms of your favorite browser is hard to avoid. That's why you must recall that users view the web in general (and your pages in particular) from many perspectives — and through many different browsers.

During the design and writing phases, you'll probably hop between HTML and a browser view of your work. At that point, you should switch among browsers and test your pages using different ones (including at least one text-only browser like Lynx). This helps you visualize your pages better and helps keep you focused on content. Using a text-only browser is also a great way to ensure that visually impaired visitors can still relate to your site.

Check out the Spoon Browser Sandbox page at www.spoon.net/browsers. It lets you emulate numerous browsers on a Windows PC, including multiple versions of IE, Firefox, Chrome, Safari, and Opera. Additionally, you can use free public Telnet servers with Lynx (a character-mode browser) installed. Also, visit http://brainstormsandraves.com/articles/browsers/ lynx for a good discussion of using Lynx when testing web pages. (You can also find pointers to Lynx downloads for Windows, DOS, Mac OS, and other platforms there.) There's even a free Firefox plug-in for Lynx previews inside a pop-up window. (Search for "Firefox addon/1944" in your favorite search engine to get the latest version).

During testing and maintenance, browse your pages from many points of view. Work from multiple platforms; try both graphical and character-mode browsers on each page. Testing takes time but repays that effort with pages that are easy for everyone to read and follow. It also helps viewers who come at your materials from many platforms and helps your pages achieve true independence from any single viewpoint. Why limit your options?

If several pages on your site use the same basic HTML, create a template for those pages (include both an HTML skeleton and one or more external CSS style sheets). Test that template with as many browsers as you can. When you're sure the template is browser-independent, use it to create other pages. This helps every page look good, regardless of the browser that visitors use, and moves you closer to real HTML enlightenment.

Don't Make It Hard to Navigate Your Wild and Woolly Web

Users who view the splendor of your site don't want to be told *you can't get there from here.* Aids to navigation are vital amenities on a quality website. A *navigation bar* requires a consistent placement and use of controls to help users get from A to B. To help users minimize (or even avoid) scrolling, use links judiciously and be careful to observe what constitutes a complete screen (or screenful) of text. Text anchors make it easy to move to previous and next screens, as well as to the top, index, and bottom of any document. Just that easy, just that simple — or so it appears to the user.

We believe in *low-scroll* pages: Users should have to scroll *no more than one* screenful from a point of focus or entry to find a navigation aid that lets them jump (not scroll) to their next point of interest. If users must scroll, vertical scrolling is okay, but horizontal scrolling is an absolute no-no!

We don't believe navigation bars are mandatory or that names for controls should always be the same. But we do believe that the more control you give users over their browsing, the better they like it. The longer a document gets, the more important controls become; they work best if they occur about every 30 lines (or with a set of always-visible page controls).

Don't Think Revolution, Think Evolution

The tendency to sit on one's fundament, if not rest on one's laurels, after launching a website is nearly irresistible. It's okay to sit down, but it isn't okay to leave things alone for too long or to let them go stale from lack of attention and refreshment. If you stay interested in what's on your site after it's ready for prime time, your content probably won't go past its expiration date. Do what you can (and what you must) to stay on top of things, and you'll stay engaged — as should your site visitors!

Over time, web pages change and grow. Keep a fresh eye on your work and keep recruiting fresh eyes from the ranks of those who haven't seen your work before to avoid what we call *organic acceptance.* (You might know this term better as *complacency* or even *indifference.*)

This concept is best explained by the analogy of your face in the mirror: You see it every day; you know it too well, so you aren't as sensitive as someone else to how your face changes over time. Then you see yourself on video, or in a photograph, or through the eyes of an old friend. At that point, changes obvious to the world reveal themselves to you as you exclaim, "I've gone completely gray!" or "My spare tire could mount on a semi!"

Changes to web pages are usually evolutionary, not revolutionary. They proceed in small daily steps; big leaps are rare. Nevertheless, you must stay sensitive to the underlying infrastructure and readability of your content as pages evolve. Maybe the lack of onscreen links to each section of your Product Catalog didn't matter when you had only three products — but now that you offer 25, they're a must. You've heard that form follows function; in web terms, the structure of your site needs to follow changes in its content. If you regularly evaluate your site's effectiveness at communicating, you know when it's time to make changes, large or small.

This is why user feedback is crucial. If you don't get feedback through forms or other means, solicit some from your users. If you're not sure how you're doing, consider this: If you don't ask for feedback, how can you tell?

Don't Get Stuck in the Two-Dimensional-Text Trap

Because of centuries of printed material and the linear nature of books, our mindsets also need adjustment. The text trap is of our own making, and comes from a lifetime of experience in reading printed materials. But the nonlinear potentials of *hypermedia* give new meaning to the term *document,* especially on the web. (Hypermedia is digital content that includes text, images, video, sound, and so forth, along with hyperlinks, and it provides many ways to escape the text trap.) It can be tempting to pack pages full of capabilities until they resemble a Pony Express dynamite shipment that gallops off in several directions at once. Be safe: Judge hypermedia by whether it

- ✔ Adds interest
- ✔ Expands on your content
- ✔ Makes a serious — and relevant — impact on users

Within these constraints, such material can vastly improve any user's experience of your site.

Stepping intelligently outside old-fashioned linear thinking about text can improve your users' experience with your site and make your information more accessible. That's why we encourage careful use of document indexes, cross-references, links to related documents, and other tools to help users navigate your site.

Keep thinking about the impact of links as you look at other people's web materials; it's the quickest way to escape the linear-text trap. If you're seeking a model for website behavior, don't use your new trifold four-color brochure, however eye-popping it may be. Instead, think about how customer-service talks to new customers on the phone: "How can I help you today?"

Don't Let Inertia Overcome You

When dealing with web materials post-publication, it's only human to goof off after finishing a big job. Site maintenance isn't as heroic or inspiring as creation, but it involves most of the activity required to keep things functioning — that is, ensure links still work, images still appear, interactive materials work as they should, and so forth. Sites that aren't maintained often become ghost sites; users stop visiting when developers stop working on them. Never fear — a little work and attention to detail keep pages working and current. If you start with something valuable and keep adding value, a site's value appreciates over time — just like any other property. Start with something valuable and leave it alone, and it loses function and value.

Consider your site from the viewpoint of a master aircraft mechanic: Correct maintenance is a real, vital, and on-going accomplishment, without which you risk a crash. A website, as a vehicle for important information, deserves regular attention; maintaining a website requires discipline and respect.

Keeping up with change translates into creating (and adhering to) a regular maintenance schedule. Make it somebody's job to spend time on a site regularly; check to make sure the job's getting done. If people get tagged to handle regular site updates, changes, and improvements, they flog other participants to give them tasks when scheduled site maintenance rolls around. Pretty soon, everybody's involved in keeping things working — just as they should be. This keeps visitors coming back for more!

22

Ten Ways to Kill Web Bugs Dead

In This Chapter

▷ Avoiding gaffes in markup and spelling

▷ Keeping links hot and fresh

▷ Gathering beta testers to check, double-check, and triple-check your site

▷ Applying user feedback to your site

*A*fter you put the finishing touches on a set of pages but before you go public on the web for the entire world to see, it's time to put them through their paces. Testing remains the best way to ensure site quality and effectiveness.

Thorough testing *must* include content review, analysis of HTML and CSS syntax and semantics, link checks, and various checks to make darn sure that what's built is what you really want. Read this chapter for gems of testing wisdom (learned from a lifetime of web adventures) as we seek to rid your web pages of bugs, errors, and lurking infelicities. Out! Out! Darned Spot!

Make a List and Check It — Twice

A sense of urgency that things must work well and look good on a website never fails to goad you to keep your site humming along. That said, if you work from a visual diagram of how your site is (or should be) organized, you'll be well equipped to check structure, organization, and navigation. Likewise, put your pages through their paces regularly (or at least each time they change) with a spell checker, and you'll be able to avoid unwanted *tpyos*.

Your design should include a roadmap (often called a *site map*) that tells you what's where in every individual HTML document and style sheet in your site. The site map also clues you into the relationships among your site's pages. Keep this map up to date as you move from design to implementation. (In our experience, things always change as you go down this path.) As you continually update your site map, be sure to include all intra- and inter-document links.

A site map provides the foundation for a test plan. Yep, that's right — effective testing isn't random. Use your site map to

- ✏ Investigate and check every page and every link systematically.

- ✏ Make sure everything works as you think it should — and that what you built has some relationship (however surprising) to your design.

- ✏ Define the list of things to check as you go through the testing process.

- ✏ Check everything at least twice (red suit and reindeer harness optional).

Master Text Mechanics

By the time any collection of web pages comes together, you're looking at thousands of words, if not more. Yet many web pages are published without a spell check, which is why we suggest — no, *demand* — that you include a spell check as a step when testing and checking your materials. (Okay, we can't force you, but you know it's for your own good.) Many HTML tools, such as Aptana, Kompozer, and Dreamweaver, include built-in spell checkers, the first spell-check tools you should use. These HTML editors also know how to ignore markup and just check your text.

Even if you use HTML tools only occasionally and hack out most of your markup by hand, do a spell check before posting your documents to the web. (For a handy illustration of why this step matters, keep a log of spelling and grammatical errors you find during your web travels. Be sure to include a note on how those gaffes reflect on the people who created the pages involved. Get the message?)

You can use your favorite word processor to spell check your pages. Before you check them, add HTML and CSS markup to your custom dictionary, and pretty soon the spell checker runs more smoothly — getting stuck only on URLs and odd strings that occasionally occur in web documents.

If you prefer a different approach, try any of the many HTML-based spell-checking services now available on the web. We like the free Lite Edition of the CSE HTML Validator (www.freehtmlvalidator.com).

If the CSE HTML Validator Lite spell checker doesn't float your boat, visit a search engine and search for *web page spell check.* Doing so lets you produce a list of spell-checking tools made for web pages.

One way or another, persist until you root out all typos and misspellings. Your users may not thank you for your impeccable use of language, but if they don't trip over errors while exploring your work, they'll think more highly of your pages (and their creator), even if they don't know why.

Don't forget to put your eyeballs on the copy and thoroughly proofread the text, too. No spell checker in the world will recognize "It's time two go too the store" as badly mangled text, although you should catch that right away. Better yet, hire a professional editor or proofreader to help out during testing.

Lack of Live Links — a Lousy Legacy

New content and active connections to current, relevant resources are the hallmarks of a well-tended website. You can't achieve these goals without regular (sometimes, constant) effort, so plan for ongoing activity. The rewards can be huge — starting with a genuine sense of users' excitement at what new marvels and treasures reveal themselves on their next visit to your site. Such anticipation is impossible to fake.

We performed an unscientific, random-sample test to double-check our own suspicions; users told us that positive impressions of a particular site are proportional to the number of working links they find there. The moral of this survey: *Always check your links.* This is as true after you publish your pages as it is before they're made public. Nothing irritates users more than a link that produces the dreaded 404 File Not Found error instead of the good stuff they seek! Remember — link checks are as indispensable to page maintenance as they are to testing.

If you're long on 21st-century street smarts, hire a robot to do this job for you: They work long hours (no coffee breaks), don't charge much, and check every last link in your site (and beyond, if you let them). The best thing about robots is that you schedule them to work at your pleasure: They always show up on time, always do a good job, and never complain (though we haven't found one that brings homemade cookies or remembers birthdays). All you do is search online for phrases like *link checker.* There are lots to choose from! To begin with, you might use these:

- ✔ **W3C Link Checker** (`http://validator.w3.org/checklink`): It's easy to use and less work to set up, too.

- ✔ **Online Link Checker** (`www.2bone.com/links/linkchecker.shtml`): This is another good option that is free.

- ✔ **REL Link Checker Light** (`www.relsoftware.com/rlc/downloads`): This is a free version of REL Software's commercial Web Link Validator, and it's good enough for smaller hobby, personal, or modest business sites.

- ✔ **Xenu Link Sleuth** (`http://home.snafu.de/tilman/xenulink.html`): This is another free package you can try.

If a URL points to one page that simply points to another (a pointer), you can't leave that link alone. Sure, it works, but for how long? And how annoying! Therefore, if your link-checking expedition shows a pointer that merely points to another pointer (yikes), do your users a favor by updating the URL to point *directly* to the real location. You save users time, reduce Internet traffic, and earn good cyberkarma.

When Old Links Must Linger

If you must leave a URL active after it becomes outdated to give your users time to bookmark your new location, instruct browsers to jump straight from the old page to the new by including the following HTML command inside the old doc's <head>:

```
<meta http-equiv="refresh" content="0"; url="newurlhere">
```

This nifty line of code tells a browser that it should refresh the page. The delay before switching to the new page is specified by the value of the content attribute, and the destination URL is determined by the value of the url attribute. If you build such a page, also include a plain-vanilla link in its <body> section, so users with older browsers can follow that link manually instead of automatically. You might also want to add text that tells visitors to update their bookmarks with the new URL. Getting there may not be half the fun, but it's the whole objective.

Make Your Content Mirror Your World

When it comes to content, the best way to keep things fresh is to keep up with the world in which your site resides. When things change, disappear, or pop up in that world, similar events should occur on your website. Because something new is always happening, be sure to provide visitors a reason to keep coming back. What's more, if you can accurately and honestly reflect (and reflect upon) what's happening in your world of interest, you'll grab loyalty, respect, and continued patronage.

Look for Trouble in All the Right Places

There's an ongoing need for quality control in any kind of public content, but that need is particularly acute on the web, where the whole world can stop by (and where success often follows the numbers of those who drop in *and return*). You must check your work while you're building the site and then continue to check your work over time. This practice forces you to revisit your material with new and shifting perspectives and to evaluate what's new and what's changed in the world around you. That's why testing and checking are never really over; they just come and go — preferably, on a regular schedule!

You and a limited group of handpicked users should thoroughly test your site before you share it with the rest of the world — and more than once. This process is called *beta testing,* and it's a bona fide, five-star *must* for a well-built website, especially if it's for business use. When the time comes to beta-test your site, bring in as rowdy and ornery a crowd as you can find. If you have picky customers (or colleagues who are pushy, opinionated, or argumentative), you might have found them a higher calling: Such people make ideal beta testers — that is, if you can get them to cooperate.

Don't wait until the very last minute to test your website. Sometimes the glitches found during the beta-test phase can take weeks to fix. Take heed: Test early and test often; you'll thank us in the end.

Beta testers will use your pages in ways you never imagined possible. They interpret your content to mean things you never intended in a million years. They drive you crazy and crawl all over your cherished beliefs and principles. These colleagues also find gotchas, big and small, that you never knew existed. They catch typos that spell checkers couldn't. They tell you things you left out and things that you should have omitted. They give you a fresh perspective on your web pages, and they help you see them from extreme points of view. And they do all this before your users do! Trust us, that's a blessing — even if it's in disguise.

The results of all this suffering, believe it or not, are positive. Your pages will be clearer, more direct, and more correct than they would have been had you tested them by yourself. (If you don't believe us, of course, you *could* try skipping this step. And when real users start banging on your site, forgive us if we don't watch.)

Cover All the Bases with Peer Reviews

If you're creating a simple home page or a collection of facts and figures about your private obsession, this tip may not apply to you. Feel free to read it anyway — it just might come in handy down the road.

If your pages express views and content that represent an organization, chances are *about 100 percent* that you should run your pages through peer-and-management review before publishing them to the world. In fact, we recommend that you build reviews into each step along the way as you build your site — starting by getting knowledgeable feedback on such basic aspects as the overall design, writing copy for each page, and the final assembly of your pages into a functioning site. These reviews help you avoid potential stumbling blocks, such as unintentional off-color humor or unintended political statements. If you have any doubts about copyright matters, references, logo usage, or other important details, bring the legal department in. (If you don't have one, you may want to consider a little consulting help for this purpose. Paying to avoid legal trouble beforehand is always cheaper than paying to get out of such trouble after the fact.)

Building a sign-off process into reviews so you can prove that responsible parties reviewed and approved your materials is a good idea. We hope you don't have to be that formal about publishing your web pages, but it's far, far better to be safe than sorry. (This process might best be called *covering your bases,* or perhaps it's really covering something else? You decide.)

Use the Best Tools of the Testing Trade

When you grind through your completed web pages, checking your links and your HTML, remember that automated help is available. If you visit the W3C validator at `http://validator.w3.org`, you'll be well on your way to finding computerized assistance to make your HTML pure as air, clean as the driven snow, and standards-compliant as, ah, *really well-written HTML.* (Do we know how to mix a metaphor, or what?)

Likewise, using link checkers covered earlier in the chapter is smart; run them regularly to check links on your pages. These faithful servants tell you if something isn't current, and they tell you where to find links that need fixing.

Schedule Site Reviews

Every time you change or update your site, you should test its functionality, run a spell check, perform a beta test, and otherwise jump through important hoops to put your best foot forward online. But sometimes you'll make just a small change — a new phone number or address, a single product listing, a change of name or title — and you won't go through the whole formal testing process.

That's perfectly understandable — but one thing inevitably leads to another, and so on. Plus, if you solicit feedback, chances are good that you'll learn something that points out a problem you'd never noticed or considered before. Schedule periodic site reviews, even if you've made no big changes or updates since the last review. Information grows stale, things change, and tiny errors have a way of creeping in as one small change succeeds another.

If there's any code on your site (JavaScript, Active Server Pages, Java Server Pages, or whatever), you'll want to give it a thorough workout and inspection, too. A pool-shooting buddy of ours who works in quality control for a major technology company was recently assigned to review a website built to provide real-time security and error information to developers who use its products. He told us that it was obvious the developers didn't try everything, in every possible combination, at the same time. When he did so, he broke things they didn't know could be broken. Better to do this yourself (or hire somebody to do it for you) and fix it in advance rather than pay the price of public humiliation.

Just as you take your car in for an oil change or replace your air-conditioning filter, plan to check your website regularly. Most big organizations we talk to do this every three months or so; some do it more often. Although you might think you have no bugs to catch, errors to fix, or outdated information to refresh, you'll often be surprised by what a review turns up. Make this part of your routine, and your surprises will be less painful — and require less work to remedy!

Foster User Feedback

Who better to tell you what works and what doesn't than those who use (and hopefully, depend on) your site? Who better to say what's not needed and what's missing? But if you want user feedback to foster site growth and evolution, you must not only ask for it, you have to encourage it to flow freely and honestly in your direction. Then you need to act on that feedback to keep those wellsprings working.

Even after you publish your site, testing never ends. (Are you having flashbacks to high school or college yet? We sure are.) You may not think of user feedback as a form (or consequence) of testing, but it represents the best reality check your web pages are ever likely to get, which is why doing everything you can — including offering prizes or other tangibles — to get users to fill out HTML forms on your website is a good idea.

This reality check is also why reading *all* feedback you get is a must. Go out and solicit as much feedback as you can handle. Carefully consider all feedback that you read and implement the ideas that can improve your web offerings. Oh, and it's a really good idea to respond to feedback with personal e-mail to make sure your users know you're reading what they're saying. If you don't have time to do that, make some.

The most finicky and picky of users can be an incredible asset: Who better to pick over your newest pages and to point out the small, subtle flaws they so revel in finding? Your users can develop a real stake in boosting your site's success, too. Working with users gets them more involved and helps guide the content of your web pages. Who could ask for more? Put it this way: You may yet find out, and it could be very helpful.

If You Give to Them, They'll Give to You!

Sometimes, simply asking for feedback or providing surveys for users to fill out doesn't produce the results you want — either in quality or in volume. Remember the days when you'd occasionally get a dollar bill in the mail to encourage you to fill out a form? It's hard to deliver cold, hard cash via the Internet, but a little creativity on your part should make it easy for you to offer your users something of value in exchange for their time and input. It could be an extra month on a subscription, discounts on products or services, or some kind of freebie by mail. (Maybe you can finally unload those stuffed Gila monsters you bought for that trade show last year.)

There's another way you can give back to your users that might not cost you too much. An offer to send participants the results of your survey, or to otherwise share what you learn, may be all the incentive participants need to take the time to give you feedback or answer questions. Just remember that you're asking your users to give of their time and energy, so it's only polite to offer something in return.

23

Ten Cool HTML Tools and Technologies

In This Chapter

▸ Identifying your HTML toolbox needs

▸ Discovering a favorite HTML editor

▸ Adding a graphics application to your toolbox

▸ Authoring systems for the web

▸ Understanding essential utilities for web publishing

*H*TML documents are made of plain text, which means you can build one using a no-frills text editor such as Notepad (PC) or TextEdit (Mac). Once upon a time, that was all web authors used. But as the web has evolved, so have the tools used to create web pages. Nowadays, web authoring is complex enough that a simple text editor doesn't cut it unless

✔ You don't care (much) about graphics and HTML validation.

✔ You're on a quick in-and-out mission to make small changes to an existing HTML document.

After you gain more experience with HTML, you'll build your own HTML toolbox. This chapter is designed to help you stock that toolbox. In fact, some of these tools may already be on your system, quietly waiting to help you create amazing web pages.

When you go shopping for items for your HTML toolbox, look for good buys. Students and educators often qualify for big discounts on major-brand software — if you're in that category, use a search engine to look for *"educational software discount."* But careful shopping can save anybody money on just about any software purchase. Try comparison-shopping at sites such as CNET Shopper (http://shopper.cnet.com) or PC Magazine (www.pcmag.com/shop).

WYSIWYG HTML Editors

WYSIWYG (what you see is what you get; pronounced *wiz-eee-wig*) editors do everything but your laundry. Lots of WYSIWYG editors offer code views the way helper editors do (see the following section), plus a lot more.

A WYSIWYG editor creates markup for you while you create and lay out web page content on your monitor, often by dragging and dropping visual elements or working through GUI menus and options. As you work, the WYSIWYG editor shields your eyes from bare markup. These tools are like word processors or page-layout programs; they do lots of work for you.

WYSIWYG editors make your work easier and save hours of endless coding — you have a life, right? — but you should use WYSIWYG editors only during the design stage. For example, you can use a WYSIWYG editor to create a complex table in under a minute during initial design work. Later, when the site is live, you would then use an HTML helper editor to refine and tweak your HTML markup directly.

Dreamweaver

Dreamweaver is among the best of WYSIWYG web development tools for Mac and PC systems. Many (if not most) web developers use Dreamweaver. Dreamweaver is an all-in-one product that supports

- Website creation
- Maintenance
- Content management

The current version, Adobe Dreamweaver CC, belongs to a suite of products — Adobe Creative Cloud, usually abbreviated CC — that work together to provide a full spectrum of Internet solutions. Adobe CC comes in a big bundle that includes such components as InDesign, Photoshop, Illustrator, Acrobat Professional, Dreamweaver, After Effects, Premiere Pro, Soundbooth, Encore, and more. For $50 a month, you can buy the Adobe Creative Cloud Collection and get all these components. For $20 a month, you can get just Dreamweaver CC without the extras.

Dreamweaver features an easy-to-follow GUI so you can style web pages using CSS without even knowing what a style rule is. Many of the benefits of Dreamweaver stem from its sleek user interface and its respect for clean HTML. You can find more information on Dreamweaver by visiting the Adobe website at www.adobe.com/products/dreamweaver.

Other WYSIWYG editors

The following editors have many fans, and both produce great web pages:

- **KompoZer** is a web page editor that offers text and WYSIWYG editors, along with color coding, automatic code completion, HTML validation, nice site management chops, and more good stuff. Plus, it's free. Check it out at `http://kompozer.net`.

- **Microsoft Expression Web 4** is a Windows-based web package that offers a code editor (text) and a visual editor (WYSIWYG), along with scripting tools, great graphics support, search engine optimization (SEO) tools, and more. It retails for $150 or so, but if you shop around, you can find it for under $100; there's a free version, too. Check it out at `http://www.microsoft.com/en-us/download/details.aspx?id=36179`.

This is just a small sample. For even more WYSIWYG options, try searching for *"WYSIWYG HTML editor"* on the web.

Helper HTML Editors

An HTML helper works the way it sounds. It helps you create HTML, but it doesn't do all the markup work for you. HTML is displayed raw — tags and all. You can reach right into the code and tweak it (provided you have this book). This is often called a *code view* or *markup view*.

Good helpers save time and lighten your load. Functions like these make HTML development easier and more fun:

- Tags are a different color than content.
- The spell checker knows tags aren't misspelled words.

Use a helper editor when you're building complex tables or multilevel lists. The more complex your markup, the more help a helper editor can provide!

Aptana Studio

Aptana Studio is a full-blown development tool that supports JavaScript, Personal Home Page (PHP), CSS, and HTML. Aptana also provides a very full-featured HTML editor that's well suited for beginners and professionals. Aptana requires some HTML knowledge to use but assists you at every step.

We like the Aptana interface and its many facilities. You can

- Automatically sync directories with your FTP server.
- Incorporate all kinds of cool plug-ins. (Aptana is based on Eclipse, a well-known and widely used integrated development environment, or IDE.)

Aptana makes it easy to work with other languages, such as Ruby on Rails, jQuery, Python, and more, using widely available plug-ins.

✔ Create, edit, and validate CSS, JavaScript, HTML, and PHP.

✔ Use automatic code completion and text-coloring capabilities to separate HTML, CSS, JavaScript, and so forth.

✔ Take advantage of a huge collection of documentation and tutorials and active community support and interaction.

Aptana is an open source project, which means it's free. You can download Aptana from www.aptana.com. If you're not inclined to tackle a do-it-yourself type of web development environment, check out our other contenders in the following section.

Other helper editors

You can find lots of great HTML helper editors. Here's our slate of alternatives:

✔ **Komodo Edit** is a classy, highly functional software package that gets high ratings from everyday users and experts. It's not WYSIWIG, but it gets the job done. Komodo includes lots of great features and functions, including built-in validators for CSS, HTML, and accessibility features; color coding and tag completion for HTML and XML; multi-file search and replace; and support for web-related languages, such as Perl, Python, Tcl, PHP, JavaScript; and much more.

Komodo Edit is a free, scaled-down version of the $295 Komodo IDE product from ActiveState.com. Unless you also develop software, Komodo Edit should meet your needs well and completely.

Download the free version from www.activestate.com/komodo-edit/downloads. It supports Windows, Mac OS X, and Linux.

✔ **HTML-Kit** is a compact Windows tool with

 • Menu-driven support for both HTML and Cascading Style Sheets (CSS) markup

 • A nice preview window for a browser's-eye view of your markup

If you want to download HTML-Kit, go to www.chami.com/html-kit. You can download a free version or register your copy for $65 and obtain a bunch of extra tools, including a spiffy table designer, a log analyzer, and a nifty graphical HTML/XML editor that lets you view and navigate all those documents through their syntactical structure.

✔ **Open Source Notepad**++ offers useful and functional support for HTML and CSS, among lots of other languages and markup. Find it at http://notepad-plus-plus.org.

Inexpensive Graphics Editors

Graphics applications are beasts. They can do marvelous things, but figuring out how to use them can be overwhelming at first. Even scaled-down toolsets (such as Photoshop Elements) take time and genuine effort to understand and use well.

If you aren't artistically inclined, consider paying someone else to do your graphics work. Graphics applications can be pricey and complicated. But you should have some kind of high-function (if not high-end) graphics program to tweak images should you need to. Our highest rating goes to Adobe Photoshop, but considering its cost and the average newbie HTML hacker's budget, we discuss a lower-cost alternative first.

At around $120 (with discounts as low as $60), Adobe Photoshop Elements is an affordable PC- and Mac-based starter version of the full-blown Photoshop (the gold standard for graphics). You can do almost anything with Photoshop Elements you might need for beginner- or intermediate-level graphics editing.

This product is for you if you want to add images to your site, but you don't want to work with graphics all the time or use fancy special effects. To find out more about Photoshop Elements, visit www.adobe.com/products/photoshop-elements.html.

If you're really on a tight budget, check out these graphic editors:

- **Paint Shop Pro Photo X5:** This PC-only graphics editor is a good buy because it does nearly everything that Photoshop does and costs less than Photoshop Elements. You need to shop around to find the lowest price, though. (Corel charges $80 or $90 for this package.)

- **GIMP:** If you're really on a shoestring budget, check out the free GNU Image Manipulation Program, better known as GIMP. It's an open source package whose functionality rivals that of Photoshop without the expensive price tag. GIMP supports a user-customizable interface, offers all kinds of sophisticated image and photo enhancements, and includes digital retouching, broad device support, and tons of graphics file formats. It works with Linux, Windows, Mac OS X, Sun OpenSolaris, and the FreeBSD operating systems. Check it out at www.gimp.org and then download it!

Professional Graphics Editors

If you work with photographs or other high-resolution, high-quality images or artwork, you may need one of these web graphics tools.

Adobe Photoshop

If it weren't so darned expensive, we'd grant top honors to Photoshop CC. Alas, $20 a month is too high for many novices' budgets. Wondering whether to upgrade from Photoshop Elements? Adobe mentions these capabilities among its top reasons to upgrade:

- **Improved file browser:** Shows and tells you more about more kinds of graphics files and gives you more powerful search tools.
- **Shadow/Highlight correction:** Powerful built-in tools add or manipulate shadows and highlights in images.
- **More powerful color controls:** Color palettes and color-matching tools with detailed controls that Elements lacks.
- **Text on a path:** Full-blown Photoshop lets you define any kind of path graphically and then instructs your text to follow that path. This capability supports fancy layouts that Elements can't match.

If you need to use sophisticated visual effects, edits, or tweaks on high-resolution photorealistic images, full-blown Photoshop is your best bet. For basic websites, however, Photoshop is overkill — it can do just about anything to photos or images of all kinds, which of course is why it's the most popular professional graphics editing tool.

Like its little brother Photoshop Elements, full-blown Photoshop works with both Mac and PC operating systems. The current version is Adobe Photoshop CC. It's included in all of the Adobe product suites.

Photoshop CC add-ons and plug-ins provide specialized functions — such as complex textures or special graphics effects. This extensibility is nice because graphics professionals who need such capabilities can buy them (most cost $100 and up, with $300 being a pretty typical price) and add them without muss or fuss. But those who don't need them don't have to pay extra for the base-level software.

Adobe Fireworks

Fireworks is a graphics program designed specifically for web use, so it offers lots of nice features and functions for that purpose. The current version is Adobe Fireworks CC. Fireworks has one killer feature — it lets you save portable network graphics (PNG) files with layers defined that work more or less the same way that Photoshop Document (PSD) files do.

Fireworks is tightly integrated with other Adobe products and therefore is of potentially great interest if you're using (or considering) Dreamweaver. Simply put, this combination of Adobe products makes it very easy to add graphical spice to web pages.

For more information about Fireworks and related Adobe products, check out www.adobe.com/products/fireworks.

W3C Link Checker

A broken link on your site can be embarrassing. To spare your users the dreaded 404 Object Not Found error message, use a link checker to make sure your links are correctly formatted before and after you publish on the web. Many HTML editors and web servers include built-in local link checkers, and they may even scour the web to check external links.

Other websites may change or disappear after you publish your pages. Regularly check your links to make sure they still work. The worst broken link is one that points to a page on your *own* site, which is no longer there.

The W3C link-checking tool is free, easy to use, and works surprisingly quickly (thanks to HP donating the servers to support the W3C). Here's how it works: You drop a URL in for a document you want to check, and the tool comes back to you with information about the links it finds on that page. It even does recursive checking if you click the Check Linked Documents check box on the submission page. Try this champion link checker for yourself at http://validator.w3.org/checklink.

You can also download a version of this tool that you can run on your own machine from http://validator.w3.org/docs/checklink.html. You have a couple of download options:

- Grab a compiled version for your computer and operating system and run it as-is.
- Grab the source code and tweak it for your needs and situation.

Other Link Checkers

The following programs are pretty good link checkers. They just require a little elbow grease to learn and use. Better yet, their price is right: free!

- **Xenu's Link Sleuth:** This free link-check takes some effort to learn to use, and likewise to learn how to interpret its reports. But that effort is justified, and the program is fast, accurate, and compact. Stick with this tool, and it will repay your investment in time and effort with excellent link checking capabilities. Download it from http://home.snafu.de/tilman/xenulink.html.

✓ **LinkChecker:** LinkChecker offers free, complex, and sophisticated link-checking services, including color-coded output, support for lots of protocols and services, all kinds of URL filters and link-checking controls, cookie checks, HTML and CSS syntax checks, and lots more.

To find out more, take a look at `http://wummel.github.io/link checker/`.

HTML Validators

Validation compares a document to a set of document rules — a Document Type Definition (DTD), an XML Schema, or whatever other rules explicitly describe its syntax and structure. Simply put, validation checks the actual markup and content against the rules that govern it and flags any deviations it finds.

Typically, a document author follows this process:

1. **Create an HTML document in an HTML editor.**

   For example, imagine this step results in a file called `mypage.htm`.

2. **Submit mypage.htm to an HTML or XHTML validation site for inspection and validation.**

   If any problems or syntax errors are detected, the validator reports such errors in an annotated version of the original HTML document.

3. **If the validator reports errors, the author corrects those errors and resubmits the document for validation.**

Sometimes, breaking HTML rules is the only way for your page to look right in older web browsers. But document rules exist for a reason: Nonstandard or incorrect HTML markup often produces odd or unpredictable results.

Browsers usually forgive markup errors. Most browsers identify HTML pages without an `html` element. But someday, markup languages may be so complex and precise that browsers won't be able to guess whether you're publishing in HTML or another markup language. Get the markup right from the beginning and save yourself a bunch of trouble later.

HTML validation is built into many HTML editors, including Dreamweaver and all the other WYSIWIG and HTML Helper tools we mention at the outset of this chapter. You can find validators at

✓ **W3C validator:** The W3C has a free, web-based validation system available at `http://validator.w3.org`. It provides copious output about what errors or inconsistencies it finds in your documents until you fix them all. It also includes an option for viewing annotated source code so you can see exactly where it's finding items it doesn't like. This is a great tool, and it is well worth using. This tool is a vital element in building a solid, well-crafted website of any kind, and it helps you fix errors and address browser issues with panache.

✒ **Built-in validators:** Many tools in this chapter offer HTML validation. These include HTML-Kit, Aptana Studio, Dreamweaver, and Expression Web. Use 'em if you got 'em; get 'em if you don't!

FTP Clients

After you create your website on your computer, you must share it with the world. So you need a tool to transfer your web pages to your web server. One convenient way to accomplish this task is through FTP (File Transfer Protocol). Many HTML editors include FTP support, but you can also use a separate FTP client to upload and download files to your web server. FTP has been around since the early days of the Internet (way before the web arrived).

After you select a server host and you know how to access a web server (your service provider should supply you with this information), you must upload your pages to that server. That means you need FTP or some reasonable facsimile thereof.

All FTP programs are similar and easy to operate. We recommend these:

✒ **FileZilla** is a fast, capable, free, open source FTP program with an intuitive drag-and-drop user interface. It's available online at `http://filezilla-project.org`.

✒ **Cyberduck** (open source for the Mac) is available at `http://cyberduck.io`

✒ **Cute FTP Lite** (shareware, costs $60, but offers great functionality and ease of use) is available at `www.cuteftp.com`.

✒ **Fetch** for the Mac is located at `http://fetchsoftworks.com`.

Miscellaneous Helpful Web Tools

Miscellaneous tools can help you manage and control your website. Here, we present you with a collection of items that you can try out to see whether they deliver functionality that justifies downloading, learning, and using them (we think they're nifty, but, ultimately, that's up to you to decide):

✒ **HTML-Kit** supports plug-ins to add functions, such as link checks and spell checks. Most of these plug-ins are free or inexpensive. Check out `www.chami.com/html-kit/plugins`.

- **Easy HTML Construction Kit** offers a collection of useful conversion, reformatting, and template management tools for a paltry $25 at www.hermetic.ch/html.htm.

- **Firebug** is a Firefox plug-in you can use to help you debug programs and web pages. It lets you click sections of a page and then examine their individual properties and behaviors. Find it at http://getfirebug.com.

- **Browser Sandbox** comes from spoon.net; it provides a tool that lets you run multiple versions of IE, Firefox, Safari, Chrome, and Opera inside the following browsers: IE (6, 7, 8), Firefox (2, 3, 3.5), Safari (3, 4), Chrome (all versions), and Opera (9, 10). Browse to http://spoon.net/browsers.

- **Dropbox** makes it easy to synchronize files and directories across multiple computers anywhere on the Internet. It supports Windows, Mac, Linux, and various smartphone operating systems. Look it up at www.dropbox.com.

- **Google Analytics** provides a plethora of statistics about visitors to your website, including user origin, operating system (OS), web browser, and oodles more. Want to understand your audience? Get Google Analytics free at www.google.com/analytics.

- **Crazy Egg** and **Clickdensity** offer heat maps that illustrate exactly how people are using (and moving through) your website. No matter what or how you think your users might be using your site, these tools tell you what's really happening. Find them at www.crazyegg.com and www.clickdensity.com.

- **iPhone Tester** and **iPad Peek** provide helpful tools to see how your website looks on an iPhone and iPad without having to buy or otherwise obtain one. Check them out at www.iphonetester.com and www.ipadpeek.com.

Part VII
Appendixes

the

appendixes

Visit www.dummies.com for more great *For Dummies* content online. Also, there's a website just for this book online at www.dummieshtml.com.

In this part . . .

- ✔ A listing of our Twitter supporters
- ✔ A quick tour of the Dummies HTML website

Appendix A

Twitterati

*T*hanks to all our Twitter followers: filipbrocke, Deidreggtc, InstituteOfFun, TheFatPanther, Georgettatzer, BeccaD4wn, TheRealJ_Hen, kriszankumar, JCMorgan3, TheBimber, SeatingSupply, JBColeLtd, Stereo_89, cxrana, brandeerenee, MICHELEANNICCH3, marksuth, BozzPulsa, 1ashishsharma, rgregorylee, amalausline, SwaggerByHUGS, norsk_kriger, CraigFairlie, jhbucf94, rakbar, Yathu7, RankBetter, apuraelpasomula, AshleyJStokes, krkarki1, m_belarrem, realft1, SStg950, customicons, _hutch__, uxidea, wxmanmac, LosDragonflyos, hereiamraja, S_Beya, ed2go, yshakh, tjtigers18, SALTandMARROW, louie_fahd, helloaisha, MichaelGpics, JonahLupton, insanen, spoutFIRE, lagantzufgy8, danielclayton, NikkiGuest, CarnegieKaty, NC10WebTeam, netgenie4, J2L2C, componentmedia, arfanmahmood, Acrovin, Amin_Rafiq, codexstudios_, jinovince, ike185, munirlodin, DesignDisease, Avi_bisram, ningraj69, CM_Masen, EuropeLinkLtd, PaulDavidJones, jmoralesamo, ReyFirlit, ogvweb, k2Designing, Dom_TC, elijah2fernande, lenabucatariu, WebbyTreats, ianpanrita, jezmow, ace_cinta, Jmdesignpt, woodenecho, JohanThePro, Knipuit, govault, conneqtive, onvert, rezaghassemipro, HuchotaRangi, jjangel8, Idanah, MarvinRosenthal, chrisminnick, 42function, MIST_images, AMcGlamry, atstudiosuk, CBGCMUM, publicSusmit, JimAtkWebDesign, solstudioim, caproductdesign, pojekLLC, Geraldzzki, Mario70me, Afnadesign, harimur, Bluegala, karteldk, Ulmanion, bettingjobs_ kh, kobe_ru, epic_ouch, DesignDigger, bluekdev, Yuko_Kawashima, kingof bitching, vremarketing, itlac, olallis, sara_samy0123, 1realitycreator, MommyCita72, mhctoledo, alltechdesigns, ekrem_koc, RHAWK78, saorabhkr, designtampa, quintenheyninck, goldsource, dragongala, BoomThemes, HomeLeads1, ArizonaCascade, CarrauScott, cLuTcHSoLuTiOnZ, LongHornDeliver, wpzoom, milkywayNo7, Bloggerine, tuberide_70, DeebiesOnline, KlygoWebDesign, akwitter, sriaditya2, Teapot_Nick, ttabito, pb127, Metrodesk, PRoberts633, ignacionimo, FurkanDinler, ProfessorOge, geekocitycomp, ZombieCafe, aCcO_bOLeRo, landlbrowne, TEENYMEDUSA, Goognostic, webmynesystem, DANNYCHARRON, dom_chester, FreeWebsiteForU, katja_bak, SEO_ Expertindia, softepi, StiMis075, agwebdeveloper, FreelanceMingle, Author, konyakov, RFerrero, rissyroos, infinitydesignd, furor_s, moongoon, isa_ corolla, NSD_HomeMaker, Fafimeku, ealaycock, ameerrokhri, dianagraphics, nikkifoxxdesign, sxsw11tweets1, asaraach, ele_cee, likerye, grgretz, janblogt, maria_jahan11, bizvertsgraphic, orangepleasure, LookAndFeelArt, llanero6, FAME900, CandidKilsborne, DealsFromNYC, webpappa, effective_web, zavoinu, gudanglontar, molokodesigns, RealDarrenpb, E2_Solutions, RynoTheGreat, rdownsdesign, Jmdtechnologies, Frumatictr, aggregatedesign, Dezmembrariro, Sozohosting, studentlife1, LouveniaShearon, hlinke, _loulaj, CatLadyGeek, cochdraig, Anetta_K, meghanDD7, shailaja10, cstoughton9, ScrantonWebDev, Distimpareason, IndianHinduName, dongalbraith, elenaandreeva, marcelfelixcom, BlandBrands, cocojaylee, TheVaasaCentaur, chieund37, looveeru, reTWEET_you, TheSchool, doomtop, Uxrevisions, shetech, invioeguru, JumpBiest, kashmircreative, jobaerulkaes, pilotjobupdate, flashnewsonline, mascotads, LuckychairNews, nizhaloviyam, stephenho1mes, pixelsharing, BeautyBleak, BoricuaSpliff, yuji_ko_info, kareemoff, MiaGemsJewelry, dericious, PolarCentric, webwales, wendas_tweets, Certo, hoylandweb, imaria, Mlpup, Ricksta82, saub09, viktor_kkk, jkatke, noufanweb, Cleverfidel, SMHMAG, mstlaurent, karezzy, wmarshid, deadmeta4, Nimadera, kburton23, robertosolanom, nationalnet, rashanoureldin, anthonycmain, ivokhin, anthonyroose, condomiami, apsace, KennthPang, CarHeDa, LorenzoVl, paulcredmond, theinklog, webvana, web_mint, w3Servcies, DomDanson, marcvangijn, jmanzitti, RichardConroy, danaeaguilar, Lamc82, phlipper, creative_cakery, Robert_Cummings, janinegrand, swkolupailo, scott2211, tweetHOOPLA, freundedwerbung, jeclark, susannahpryal, alexconner, shaun_capehart, cehwitham, mslaurenlou, PoorKidOnCrack, favz, bryandowning, danieladr, berit_jensen, Ingenious_mind, brianarn, urbandave, steddie1, wedeacon, Ade_101, RedHottopDesign, romymk, ronaldberner, eddo32, djbolton, lookwebdesign, andersandersson, Pumpki, taur_in, melissapillon, pgaboury, just_tuts, afreehour, stefan_persson, hamptonsmedia, leahjs_, phatchopolis, timferrell, prosurf_pl, adietz, RorschachDesign, pyhrus, gorazdmurnik, kennydelaney, POwall, sambang, LawrenceTaur, kevinpfab, mrkiji, heitortsergent, hoshman6000, MisaAmiya, jaymanpandya, mannersandpoise, myCodeHeroes, mikelitchfield, adorephoto, andymeek, Mcroyle, SixFourWeb, klawrenc, dhulk, nixonmedia, ColorStormCo, 360construct, Alicia_Staples, jonathanbaltz, KimKritzinger, kevinoh, mmarnall, _norrsken_, Brain_Pulse, KSSpengler, big_matt_b, bregtcolpaert, alistaircalder, jeffkan, danfauver, thek1w1, pacotix, Jay_Searra, mrstolt, Xand49, neur0tica, thaiszorghi, woodleader, gibbon77, Sophie_Will_, thezenmonkey, nicolasrauber, domlussier, tomhermans, sg4380, atomrow, MattTyas, disseny_web, Atzimba, jmz360, george_elias, schofeld, jchawner, krukinternet, suzannehullah, jaytem, kylebellamy, MatthewCooney, geoffcampbell1, crumenos, perfectc_nl, reiot, buraksarica, toejklemme, ChristinaBruun, arthurbrownjr, simplybcreative, cab3llc, SayHidk, neilnand, the18, urosgruber, Elisje, marvos, WVMagicDesign, ValentinoVelez, Blueys, aariste, JJ_Web, Moja_Baba, mikeheaver, MichaelHermus, dawny_cupcake, Shane_Howell, virtualizacia, bbisser, HappinessBook, galovesongs, iamrewind, emilyrumbelow, attawayUCM, alexswerdlow, ShunaP, eduardofaria, delphikit, vi_rox, SkyZee, adhipg, christodhunter, dcsignpatrol, nickjvm, sillybear, persocon, JustinRhodes, IcarusWingz, axing, ns_museum, aminabbasian, stephenwalcher, celinemontheard, marklkelly, lollyjayne9, peachleen, aleksandar_k, OrionCards, prokka, phelo, Fubart, fievelwill, chillman2, sonicdivx, Didifournier, zimmic, thejaycarlson, blindacre, JamesEggers, marzhal, CynthiaSavard, mantebridts, coldwellbanker, metslifer, jkintscher, MathRivest, usingJquery, kaybrex, macx, Jaeesen, PatrykNr2010, MelGibbNZ, omersilent, SUEL_Design, shawnhud, apaatsio, twit_asim, piuleony_, crashmaster007, Tara_Nielsen_, magalocr, viktoralarsson, Grayski, sealpond_se, amberweinberg, iamrobertv, t_films, donroyco, creativeye, JimmyJamesDc, GrayJunior, srikanthpanaman, forensick, imrelentless, spaceghost65, StevenHook, seanodotcom, andreaDuquette, vivek2562, marcogallen, Dharmangp, twelveofour, mitsubstanz, inxilpro, KristerKari, JeroenEijkhof, chris_gg, torrentroot, darkforce_er, goncaloborrega, GillBoron, hameedraha, blaneywebdesign, atatz, siderakis, jabridesign, stewartritchie, reggielamson, albertlo, eirikhm, AhtiK, vherrin, chrisajohnso, metalchic, MMudassir, neilthurlwell, amyberger, TechAsNeeded, naamyo, edmeehan, alphahost, stefstivala, mmahgoub, juneja_23ravi, InDieta, javierland, grfxdznr, dswtech, iAndroid_SA, actionmoviefrea, OgleMedia, smashingmag, ayoungh, gustotech, sansansihoke, infocuswebsolu, normalnorman, EdGraphicsLLC, anaura, justinmcgarry, worpeddesign, jnelson74, MrJonMay, BKB_mschroeder, Vtomatis, almakov, msux, 1111theatre, timjgleeson, snow_burger, ryan_yates, moshner, mattrogowski, iconfinder, whitbreaddesign, leanderdirkse, MJKilgore, shahrilabdullah, coaststudios, sunilsk, AaronKalair, garethspictures, abulafio, dalesimpson, chucke, moo_marketing, bretbouchard, brendadhk, juarezpaf, LisaWeik, davidvivero, Brer, Yuibox, Kathryn_Wells, FrankS, tudorizer, tumbledesign, ibrahimali, JeffAwesome, ronwikso, systematiqa, BrianBBrian, japellerano, robbygoodwin, jamescchristie, piksal, josephj60, riscaa, anthonypants, chucken, mgjesdal, Fontlicious, spyn, cameronbaney, 10For2, mike_o_sullivan, chrislevy, javaph, brad_slavin, Larsenal, davidnilsson, scans007, maguay, andrewinebarger, mixrecords, jessamazing, AddictToSystems, iThorning, mcgrafics, anderschdk, JaswinderVirdee, jayjdk, Velehto, jbayone, ot, charlesboyung, SonicInteractiv, tyson, ImpressiveWebs, hagel, eckermanj, petechappell, micahbrich, doodlemoonch, maartenmachiels, yngveh, userintuitive, 3ch0, web2000, jhontr, brianmark, afxjzs, jeffersonnoble, gmcbride, tombrokeoff, JimFl, bloodycheese, katevanderploeg, CrapSandviche, Buffalo_Gruden, The_Slade, TexasMonique, cinderstudios, poneal, thereal geddylee, 38thirty, andrewingram, yummygum, ljohndotnet, kworry, Danger_ Mouse, UncleBumpy, rafaeluzzi, kielabokkie, johncloys, hunefalk, illustrationdan, rmanzanet, cmaddison, fabbrikk, NateReid, felipus, Maximegalon, edhassinger, SelAromDotNet, DouglasRogers, robrubinoff, gregrwilkinson, adambrehm, AnthonyLatona, ciberch, cs188, ekochman, alec_, IoNPulse, davidmcooper, FWatervoort, AlwaysTyred

Appendix B

About the Dummies HTML Website

The Dummies HTML website (www.dummieshtml.com) contains every example from this book, as well as blog posts from Ed and Chris, links to great HTML and CSS resources, and the occasional correction to the occasional error that may have slipped through the cracks during our extensive editing and fact-checking process.

The site itself can also serve as an example of good web design and construction practices. In this appendix, we cover some of the thinking, tools, and techniques that went into the building of www.dummieshtml.com.

About WordPress

As with the previous edition of the Dummies HTML website, we chose to use WordPress as our content management system.

WordPress is free software for creating websites and blogs. WordPress makes it easy for anyone to set up and manage a website that contains all of the features you'd expect a blog to have, including the following:

- Unlimited pages and blog posts
- Reader comment functionality
- A media library for storing your images, videos, and sound files
- Customizable menus

WordPress is also highly customizable, and thousands of people have built themes for customizing how a site looks and plug-ins for changing how it works.

The dashboard

Figure B-1 shows the WordPress dashboard. Each WordPress site has its own dashboard, where you can access the various functions of the site and create new content.

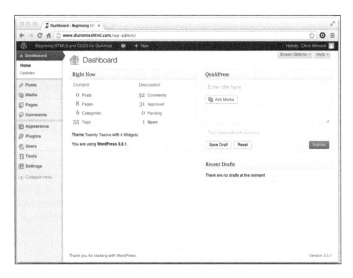

Figure B-1: The WordPress Dashboard.

Appearance and themes

From the Dashboard, you can access the Appearance and Themes administration items. Figure B-2 shows the Manage Themes screen for the Dummies HTML site.

Figure B-2: The WordPress Manage Themes screen.

We chose a theme called Twenty Twelve for our site. However, hundreds of other themes are available, and you can find and install many of them by going to the Install Themes screen, shown in Figure B-3.

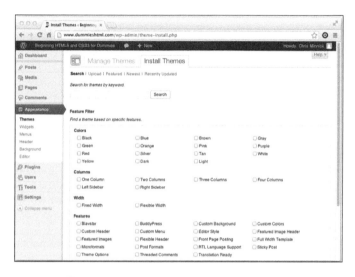

Figure B-3: The WordPress Install Themes screen.

Pages and posts

After you've installed WordPress and selected a theme, you'll spend most of your time creating either posts or pages.

Posts are individual content items, such as blog posts or articles, that can be tagged, categorized, displayed in lists, and commented on by readers. You can access the blog posts on the Dummies HTML site by clicking the Blog link in the menu that runs horizontally across the top of each page.

Pages make up the structure of a WordPress site. Your site's home page, the About the Author (or About the Company) page, and content you wouldn't typically categorize or list goes on pages. On the Dummies HTML site, the Welcome, Downloads, Errata, Store, About Us, Links, and Contact Us pages are all pages.

Widgets

If you look at any page of the Dummies HTML WordPress site, you see a column to the right of the main content that remains the same as you go from page to page. This is called a *sidebar.* The items within the sidebar are *widgets.*

Currently, the site has three sidebar widgets:

- **Search:** Use this text box to locate specific content on the site.
- **Connect With Us:** Click the icons in this widget to follow us on Twitter, like us on Facebook, or subscribe to our RSS feed.
- **Recent Comments:** See what questions and comments people are leaving on our posts and pages here!

Responsive Design

The Dummies HTML website uses a responsive design to ensure that it will work and look good on any size of desktop or mobile device. However, you don't need to open the site on a mobile device to see how this responsive design works. To test it, just resize your browser window gradually from wide to thin and watch as the content and menu items reflow to fit the current screen size. When the browser width is reduced to the width of a smartphone, the menu is reduced to a single collapsible link to save space.

Figure B-4 shows the progression of the site design from its maximum width to its minimum width.

HTML5 Cafe

The HTML5 Cafe website that we built to demonstrate features of HTML5 and CSS3 discussed throughout this book can be accessed at `www.dummies html.com/html5cafe` or by clicking the HTML5 Cafe link in the menu of the Dummies HTML website.

HTML5 Cafe is made up of four main web pages, two style sheets, and three images.

The home page

The HTML5 Cafe home page, shown in Figure B-5, establishes the purpose of the site, displays a simple coffee cup graphic, and contains the caption (and Chris's personal 5:30 a.m. writing mantra) "powered by coffee."

If you view the source of the home page, you see some code that should be familiar to anyone who has read the chapters of this book.

A quick shortcut to view the source markup of a web page in most browsers is to press CTRL + U (on Windows) or CMD + OPTION + U (on the Mac).

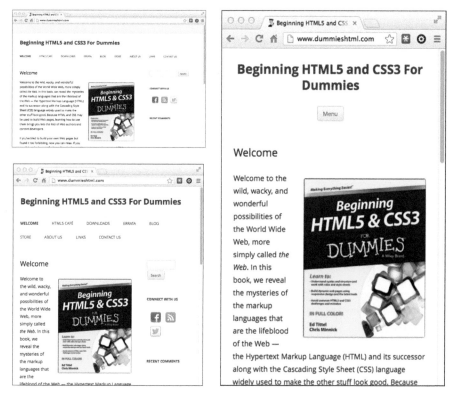

Figure B-4: Responsive web designs adapt to the browser width.

Figure B-5: The HTML5 Cafe home page.

About Us

The About Us page of HTML5 Cafe, shown in Figure B-6 displays bios for Ed and Chris, the authors of the book you now hold in your hands. As with every About Us page we've ever seen, the photos on this page were designed to make us look much better and friendlier than we are in real life. We almost look like guys you might want to reach out to and say "hi" or perhaps find out what we've been up to. Just in case you decide that you do want to do that, we've linked our names to our respective blogs.

Figure B-6: The HTML5 Cafe About Us page.

The Menu

The Menu page, shown in Figure B-7, is where we've stashed all of the examples from each chapter of the book. The chapter links here are linked to .zip files containing working HTML5 and CSS3 code that you can try out on your own computer. If you don't feel like retyping all of the book's examples, simply download the examples from each chapter as you work your way through the book.

Contact Us

The Contact Us page is a very common web convention for providing a page of information about how to get in touch with the creator of the site, or locate the company, or get directions or operating hours.

On our Contact Us page, we provide a simple contact form for demonstration purposes. If you want to contact us (the authors), one way would be to use this form to send us a message.

Figure B-7: The HTML5 Cafe Menu.

HTML5 Boilerplate

We built the CSS and HTML for HTML5 Cafe by using HTML5 Boilerplate. HTML5 Boilerplate is a free and open source template for creating HTML5 websites.

What's great about HTML5 Boilerplate is that its authors have collected the best of the known and agreed-upon best practices and necessary tricks that web authors have discovered for writing HTML5 web pages into one neat package. To use HTML5 Boilerplate and take advantage of countless hours of professional web developers' energy and know-how, all you need to do is go to `www.html5boilerplate.com` and download the latest version.

HTML5 Boilerplate downloads as a single `.zip` file. After unzipping it, you find a number of files and directories. The most important of these is `index.html`. Start with a copy of HTML5 Boilerplate's `index.html` for each file in your website, and you'll be well on your way to moving from beginning HTML5 and CSS3 to advanced HTML5 and CSS3.

Index

• Symbols •

! important attribute, 210
// (slashes), 130
@font-face rule, 273–274, 277
@import statements, 214
@keyframes rule, 302–303
{ } (curly braces), 14
< > (angle brackets), 14

• A •

<a> element, 125
absolute hyperlinks, 142
absolute positioning, 227–228
action attribute, 101–102
adjacent-sibling selectors, 202
Advanced Video Coding (AVC), 156
alt attribute, 29
alternative text ("alt text")
  image maps, using with, 151
  keyword stuffing, 146
  overview of, 143
  search engine indexing, 144
American Standard Code for Information
    Interchange (ASCII), 30
anchors, 125–126
angle brackets (< >), 14
animation, CSS
  @keyframes rule, 303
  advantages of, 301
  changing colors gradually, 303–304
  online resources, 301
  overview, 301–302
  vendor prefixes, 303
animation properties, 302
Aptana Studio
  advantages of, 38
  download information, 10
  Dummies Book Theme, downloading, 39
  features of, 335–336
  local pages, editing, 47–48
  web pages, editing, 48
area element, 151

<article> element, 35
ASCII (American Standard Code for
    Information Interchange), 30
<aside> element, 35
@font-face rule, 273–274, 277
@import statements, 214
@keyframes rule, 302–303
at-rule, 274
attribute selector, 203
attributes. See also individual attributes by
    name
  defined, 18
  elements, adding to, 20
  forms-related, table of, 118–120
  naming stand-alone values, 110
  overview of, 29
  rules for placing, 29–30
audio codecs, 156
audio support. See web page media
<audio> element, 158
auto property, 239–241
autoplay attribute, 158, 160
AVC (Advanced Video Coding), 156

• B •

background property, 255, 259
background-color property, 255
backgrounds
  colors, changing, 258–259
  matching multiple elements, 259
  online resources for, 260
bandwidth limitations, 311
beta-testing, 329. See also website testing
block-level elements, 64, 126, 220–221
<blockquote> element, 68–69
blur-radius value, 282–284
body
  defined, 53
  importance of, 54
<body> element, 14, 44
border properties, 234
border property, 192, 245
border-color property, 245

borders
  border-width properties, setting, 243–244
  defined, 234
  shorthand for styles, using, 244–245
border-style property, 244–245
border-width property, 244–245
box-shadow property, 283–284
broken link diagnosis, 129
browser prefixes
  animation, using with, 303
  overview, 198–199
  shadow effects, using with, 286
  text transformations, using with, 289
Browser Sandbox, 321, 342
browsers. *See* web browsers
button generator, 247–248

● *C* ●

<caption> element, 26, 82, 85
cascading
  deciding principles, 205–206
  defined, 174
Cascading Style Sheets 3 (CSS3)
  border enhancements, 247–249
  browser prefixes, 198–199
  browser support for, 21, 172
  color keywords, adding, 251–253
  effects, adding to buttons and boxes, 247–249
  filter properties, 288
  font choices, expanding, 262, 271–272
  importing fonts with @font-face, 281–284
  modules, 186–189
  multiple backgrounds, applying, 259
  multiple media types, 291
  online resources for, 166, 186, 189, 260
  opacity control, adding, 285
  shadow control, adding, 281–284
  text rotation support, 289
Cascading Style Sheets (CSS). *See also* online resources; *specific CSS features*; syntax, CSS; web page creation
  absolute versus relative value measurements, 184–185
  advantages of, 171–174
  background color, changing, 258–259
  color, controlling with, 26–27, 35, 66, 251–255
  color-coding key, 26–27
  default style sheet, 175–176
  deprecated <hr> attributes, replacing with, 72

device versus display pixels, 182–183
differing syntax and markup order, 26
environments affected by, 182
graphics, avoiding for speed, 141
heading appearance, controlling with, 67
HTML, relationship to, 1, 10, 20–24, 171
image borders and alignment, controlling, 149
Level 3 modules, descriptions, and standards, 186–189
overview, 20–22, 171–173
property controls, list of, 180–181
responsive design, 184, 352
style options, list of, 174
table appearance, controlling, 94
table border properties, controlling, 84–85
table width and height, controlling, 87
text color, changing, 256
versions of, 20–21
viewport overview, 183–184
case-sensitivity, 129
character codes
  ISO Latin-1 character set, 31
  UTF-8 versus UTF-16 Unicodes, 31–32
character entities
  codes for, 19
  defined, 18, 30
  displaying hidden tag characters, 32
  encoding non-ASCII text, 30–31
  online resources for codes, 19
check boxes, 106–107
checkbox attribute, 106
checked attribute, 106
child selector, 203
circle attribute, 151
class selectors, 200–202
Clickdensity, 342
codecs, 156
<col> element, 85
<colgroup> element, 82, 85
color
  animating gradual changes, 303–304
  backgrounds, changing, 258–259
  coding markups with, 26–27
  controlling with CSS, 26–27
  current state, indicating with, 256–258
  forms, enhancing with, 117
  graphics, providing without, 146–148
  hexadecimal notation, adjusting with, 212, 253–254
  JPEG format, advantages of, 140–141
  keywords for, 251–253

online resources, 252–253, 255
PNG format, advantages of, 140–141
RGB values, adjusting with, 253–254
style sheets, advantages of, 171, 174, 180–181
text, enhancing with, 36
color property, 192, 255, 283, 285
cols attribute, 111
colspan attribute, 93
comma-separated values (CSV), 116
compatibility issues, 28, 55
content
  defined, 234
  driving markup with, 318–319
  placement of important material, 318
  proofreading thoroughly, 326–327
  refreshing regularly, 317–318, 328
  space usage, 236–237
controls attribute, 158, 160
coords attribute, 151
copyright value, 200–201
Crazy Egg, 342
CSE HTML Validator Lite, 326
CSS (Cascading Style Sheets). *See also* online
  resources; *specific CSS features*; syntax,
  CSS; web page creation
  absolute versus relative value
    measurements, 184–185
  advantages of, 171–174
  background color, changing, 258–259
  color, controlling with, 26–27, 35, 66, 251–255
  color-coding key, 26–27
  default style sheet, 175–176
  deprecated <hr> attributes, replacing
    with, 72
  device versus display pixels, 182–183
  differing syntax and markup order, 26
  environments affected by, 182
  graphics, avoiding for speed, 141
  heading appearance, controlling with, 67
  HTML, relationship to, 1, 10, 20–24, 171
  image borders and alignment,
    controlling, 149
  Level 3 modules, descriptions, and
    standards, 186–189
  overview, 20–22, 171–173
  property controls, list of, 180–181
  responsive design, 184, 352
  style options, list of, 174
  table appearance, controlling, 94
  table border properties, controlling, 84–85
  table width and height, controlling, 87

text color, changing, 256
versions of, 20–21
viewport overview, 183–184
"CSS Structure and Rules" (Web Design
  Group), 205
CSS3 (Cascading Style Sheets 3)
  border enhancements, 247–249
  browser prefixes, 198–199
  browser support for, 21, 172
  color keywords, adding, 251–253
  effects, adding to buttons and boxes,
    247–249
  filter properties, 288
  font choices, expanding, 262, 271–272
  importing fonts with @font-face, 281–284
  modules, 186–189
  multiple backgrounds, applying, 259
  multiple media types, 291
  online resources for, 166, 186, 189, 260
  opacity control, adding, 285
  shadow control, adding, 281–284
  text rotation support, 289
CSS3 Button Generator, 24 7–248
CSV (comma-separated values), 116
curly braces ({ }), 14
Cute FTP Lite, 341
Cyberduck, 341

date formats, 166
date strings, 166–168
<datetime> attribute, 166–168
<dd> element, 77
debugging tools, 219
declarations, 173, 191–192, 194–195
delisted, 59
deprecated attributes and elements
  defined, 172
  examples of, 72
descendant selector, 203–204
DevTools (Chrome), 219
Dictionary of HTML META Tags, 60
<div> element, 101
<dl> element, 77
DOCTYPE declaration, 54–56
document testing. *See* website testing
document tree, 257
Document Type Declaration (DTD), 54–56
domains, 17
Dreamweaver, 38, 334

drop shadows, 287–289
Dropbox, 342
drop-down lists, 109–111
`<dt>` element, 77
DTD (Document Type Declaration), 54–56
Dummies HTML website, 349

● *E* ●

Easy HTML Construction Kit, 342
element type selectors, 199
elements. *See also individual elements by name*; markups; tags
  anchors, 125–126
  angle brackets, 14
  block-level, 64, 126, 221
  curly braces, 14
  defined, 19
  deprecated, 72, 172
  empty, 143
  examples of, 22–23
  flow content, 220
  HTML documents, assembling for, 19–20
  inline, 126, 220–221
  media, 158–162
  nested markups, 28
  normal flow versus out of flow, 222
  online resources, 221
  phrasing content, 220
  placing in documents, 54
em values
  adjusting for relative value measurements, 186
  defined, 185
e-mail addresses
  in hidden fields, 108
  online security resources, 137
  security issues, 137
Embedded OpenType (EOT) font format, 273
empty elements (singleton tags), 143
entities. *See also* character codes
  defined, 18, 30
  displaying hidden tag characters, 32
  encoding non-ASCII text, 30–31
  online resources for codes, 19
EOT (Embedded OpenType) font format, 273
eXtensible Markup Language (XML), 18
external style sheets, CSS
  @import statements, accessing with, 214
  advantages of, 212

  defined, 171
  filename protocols, 212
  `<link>` elements, accessing with, 213
  required elements for, 213

● *F* ●

feedback
  inviting user comments, 331
  rewarding user participation, 332
Fetch, 341
`<figcaption>` element, 26, 234
`<figure>` element, 235–236
file attribute, 108
file download links, 135
File Transfer Protocol (FTP), 16
filenames, 17, 44–45, 129
FileZilla FTP client, 49–50, 341
Firebug, 342
FLAC audio format, 155
flat file, 116
float properties, 228–229
flow content, 220
flowcharts, 318
`<font>` element, 172
@font-face rule, 273–274, 277
font-family property, 194, 262–263, 274–275
fonts
  blinking, managing, 271–272
  bold, applying, 268–269
  capitalization, changing, 270–271
  family declarations, recommended, 263
  finding, 274
  font-family property, 262–263
  formats, choosing, 273–274
  Google Font Library, 275–279
  italic, applying, 269–270
  legal issues, 274
  line height, adjusting, 265–266
  line-through, managing, 271
  linking, 274–275
  online, accessing, 264–265, 277
  online resources for, 274
  overlines, managing, 271
  quotation class, assigning, 266
  scrolling, managing, 271–272
  shorthand properties, 262, 271–273
  sizing, 264–268
  spacing, adjusting, 267

text rotation, 289–290
underlines, managing, 271
font-style property, 269–270
<footer> element, 35
footers
 adding back buttons, 93
 footnote suggestions, 92
 setup options, 94–95
form frameworks, 120–121
form handlers, 101
form markup elements, 97
form validation. *See* validation
<form> element, 26, 101
forms. *See* web page forms
FTP, 116
FTP clients, 49–50, 341

• *G* •

gateways, 11
Generate it! Layout Generator, 230–232
get method, 101
GIF (Graphics Interchange Format), 140
GIMP, 337
Google Analytics, 342
Google Font Library, 275–279
graphics. *See also* web page images
 avoiding unnecessary images, 141
 limiting use of, 318–319
 online resources for, 141
graphics editors
 affordable, 337
 professional, 337–339
Graphics Interchange Format (GIF), 140
"Graphics on the Web" (W3C), 141

<h1> element
 creating heading levels, 66–68
 marking headings with, 44
H.264 video format, 156–157
HD video support, 156
<head> element, 14, 34, 56–57
<header> element, 35
headers
 defined, 53
 importance of, 54
 overview, 57

headings
 appearance, controlling with CSS, 67
 formatting with element levels, 66–67
 organizing web pages with, 66
height attribute, 29, 160
helper HTML editors
 overview, 335
 suggested, 335–336
hex code, 253
hex triplet, 253
hexadecimal notation, 212, 253
hidden attribute, 108
hidden input fields, 108
high attribute, 163
horizontal rules, 71–72
hostname, 130
<hr> element, 71–72
href attribute, 125–127, 136, 151
HTML (HyperText Markup Language). *See also* online resources; *specific features by name*; tools, HTML; validation
 browser viewing variations, 15, 38
 character entities, 30–32
 color-coding for clarity, 26–27
 CSS, relationship to, 1, 10, 20–24, 171
 differences in versions, 3, 17–18
 elements, adjusting with attributes, 29–30
 example of, 22–23
 filename protocols, 44–45
 framesets, 56
 main components of, 18
 marking elements with single tags, 28
 marking elements with tag pairs, 27
 overview, 10, 18–19
 syntax and rules, 25–26
 templates, 19
HTML editors, 10, 27, 38, 335–336
<html> element, 54
HTML5 (HyperText Markup Language 5)
 advantages over previous versions, 18
 audio markup, writing, 158–159
 browser media support, 157
 compatibility issues, 28
 date and time tracking, 166–168
 media enhancements, 137, 153
 online resources for, 1, 4–5
 video markup, writing, 159–162
"HTML5 Block Level Elements: Complete List", 64
HTML5 Boilerplate site, 23, 54, 176–178, 355

HTML5 Cafe, 34, 352–353
HTML-Kit, 38, 336, 341
HTTP (HyperText Transfer Protocol), 16, 130
http-equiv attribute, 59–60
HTTPS (Secure HTTP), 17
hyperlinks
  absolute versus relative, 127, 142
  addresses, forming properly, 130
  anchoring to images, 127
  broken, checking for, 134
  broken, diagnosing, 129
  checking continuously, 327–328
  copy-and-paste issues, 129–130
  creating, requirements for, 125
  creating simple, 128
  current state, indicating with color, 256–258
  destination options, 127
  direct pointers, checking for, 328
  e-mail access, supplying, 136–137
  external style sheets, accessing with, 213
  file utilities, 135–136
  HTML5 media advantages, 137
  image maps, creating, 150–151
  images as triggers, 149–150
  improving website experience with, 323
  inserting into HTML, 36
  interdocument access, 134
  intradocument access, 132–133
  limiting use of, 318–319
  location of URL, 126
  for mobile devices, 311
  mobile site, connecting to desktop
    version, 315
  navigating Internet with, 10–11
  online fonts, accessing, 274–275, 277
  online resources, 132, 134, 151–152, 330,
    339–340
  opening new windows, 130–131
  overview, 125
  refreshing outdated URLs, 328
  specifying site links, 128
  user feedback, rewarding, 332
  websites, accessing other, 134
hypermedia, 323
HyperText Transfer Protocol (HTTP), 16, 130

image maps
  creating linkable, 150–151
  online resources, 151–152
images. *See* graphics; web page images
<img> element, 28, 143
@import statements, 214
! important attribute, 210
inbetweens, 301. *See also* animation, CSS
inheritance rules, 204–205
inline elements, 220–221
inline styles
  ! important attribute actions, 210
  advantages of, 209
  defined, 207
  disadvantages of, 208–209
  location of, 171
  user style sheet interactions, 210
input controls, 102–103
input fields
  check boxes versus radio buttons, 106–107
  drop-down lists, 109–111
  explanatory labels, adding, 103
  file uploads, 108–109
  hidden, 108
  passwords, 105–106
  reset buttons, 112–114
  submit buttons, 112–114
  text, 103–105
  text boxes, 111
  types of, 103
<input> element, 102–104
interactive applications, 153
internal style sheets, CSS
  advantages of, 210
  defined, 207
  location of, 210
  scope of values, adjusting, 210–212
Internet Protocol (IP), 16
Internet protocols
  defined, 16–17
  specifications, 17
Internet Service Provider (ISP), 49
iPad Peek, 342
iPhone Tester, 342
ISP (Internet Service Provider), 49

icons, explained, 4
id attribute, 132
ID selectors, 199–200

JavaScript
  controlling pop-up windows, 132
  online resources for, 114

suggested reading, 168
updating HTML5 controls, 168
JPEG (Joint Photographic Experts Group), 140
jQuery Validation Plugins site, 120

● *K* ●

keyframes, 300–301. *See also* animation, CSS
@keyframes rule, 302–303
keyword stuffing, 146
Komodo Edit, 336
KompoZer, 335

● *L* ●

layout management, CSS. *See also* fonts;
    mobile devices, designing for; web page
    text formatting
  absolute positioning, 227–228
  border declarations, adding, 237–238
  border styles, setting, 244–245
  border widths, specifying, 243–244
  box model overview, 233–234
  buttons, creating, 247–248
  debugging with Chrome DevTools, 219
  float properties, 228–229
  ID versus figure selectors, 237
  layout generators, 230–232
  margin widths, specifying, 239–241
  normal flow versus out of flow, 222
  offsets, specifying, 226
  online resources, 230, 247–248
  out of flow advantages, 223–224
  padding declarations, adding, 237–238
  padding widths, specifying, 241–243
  positioning elements with CSS, 217–218
  positioning options, 225–226
  relative positioning, 226–227
  shorthand properties, 238, 241–245
  text alignment, 246
  text indenting, 247
letterpress effect, 286–287
letter-spacing declaration, 267
<li> element, 26, 28
line height, 265
line-height property, 265–266
link checkers, 327, 339–340
LinkChecker, 340

links
  absolute versus relative, 127, 142
  addresses, forming properly, 130
  anchoring to images, 127
  broken, checking for, 134
  broken, diagnosing, 129
  checking continuously, 327–328
  copy-and-paste issues, 129–130
  creating, requirements for, 125
  creating simple, 128
  current state, indicating with color, 256–258
  destination options, 127
  direct pointers, checking for, 328
  e-mail access, supplying, 136–137
  external style sheets, accessing
      with, 213
  file utilities, 135–136
  HTML5 media advantages, 137
  image maps, creating, 150–151
  images as triggers, 149–150
  improving website experience with, 323
  inserting into HTML, 36
  interdocument access, 134
  intradocument access, 132–133
  limiting use of, 318–319
  location of URL, 126
  for mobile devices, 311
  mobile site, connecting to desktop
      version, 315
  navigating Internet with, 10–11
  online fonts, accessing, 274–275, 277
  online resources, 132, 134, 151–152, 330,
      339–340
  opening new windows, 130–131
  overview, 125
  refreshing outdated URLs, 328
  specifying site, 128
  user feedback, rewarding, 332
  websites, accessing other, 134
LinkScan/QuickCheck, 339
lists
  appearance, controlling with CSS, 78
  definition, online resources for, 79
  formatting, 73–75
  nesting within other lists, 79–80
local pages, 15
long tail support, 154
loop attribute, 158
lossy, 155
low attribute, 163

● *M* ●

`margin` properties, 234
margins
  auto calculations, 241
  collapse, 239–240
  definition of, 234
  shorthand property rules, 241–243
  specifying properties for, 240–241
markups. *See also* elements; tags
  angle brackets, 14
  Aptana Studio, advantages of, 38
  color-coding, 26
  for CSS, creating, 21–22
  curly braces, 14
  defined, 14
  example of, 22–23
  for HTML, creating, 18–20
  nested, 28
  single tags, 28
  syntax and rules, 25–26
  word processors, avoiding, 11, 38
`max` attribute, 163
`maxlength` attribute, 104
media elements, 158–162
media support. *See* web page media
`mediagroup` attribute, 160
`<meta>` element
  Dictionary of HTML META Tags, 60
  overview, 57–58
  redirecting pages with, 58–60
metadata
  overview of, 57–58
  redirecting pages with, 58–60
`<meter>` element, 163–165
`method` attribute, 101
Microsoft Expression Web 4, 335
MIME (Multi-part Internet Mail
    Extensions), 120
`min` attribute, 163, 165
mobile devices, designing for
  classifying device types, 307–310
  limited bandwidth, working with, 311
  linking to desktop site, 315
  pages, keeping simple, 314
  responsive design, value of, 184, 352
  testing on multiple platforms, 313
  touch-screen limitations, 311–312
  user needs, considering, 310, 313
  web addresses, keeping simple, 314–315

MP3 audio format, 155
MPEG (Motion Picture Experts Group), 156
MPEG-4 video format, 156
multimedia, advantages of using, 323
`multiple` attribute, 110
multiple media displays, CSS. *See also* mobile
    devices, designing for
  adapting from screen to print, 299–300
  CSS media types, 292
  customizing for specific media, 292–293
  device detection, 291–292
  paged media styles, 299
  visual media styles, 293–298
`muted` attribute, 161

● *N* ●

`name` attribute, 103, 106
`<nav>` element, 35
navigation tools
  inserting into HTML, 36
  providing for websites, 321–322
nested markups, 28
nesting elements, 204–205
nesting lists
  common uses for, 79
  formatting rules, 80

● *O* ●

offsets, 226
`offset-x` property, 283, 285
`offset-y` property, 283, 285
Ogg Theora video format
  overview, 156
  WHATWG recommendations for, 157
Ogg Vorbis audio format
  overview, 155
  WHATWG recommendations for, 156
`<ol>` element
  creating numbered lists with, 73–75
  using with `<li>` elements, 26, 28
Online Link Checker, 327
online resources
  browser compatibility, checking, 298–299,
    321, 342
  codes for entities, 19
  color codes, finding, 253–255
  CSS animation properties, 301

CSS articles and markups, 4–5, 182
CSS button generator, 247–248
CSS filter tutorial, 289
CSS style sheets, 176–178
CSS syntax rules, 205
CSS3 changes, 166, 186, 189, 260
CSS3 standards, 189
debugging web pages, 342
definition list discussions, 79
deprecated attributes and elements, 172
Dictionary of HTML META Tags, 60
disabling style sheets, 193
Dummies HTML website, 349
elements usage details, 221
embedded content discussions, 157
form framework sites, 120–121
forms, help for on Webmonkey, 101
FTP programs, 341
Generate it! Layout Generator, 230–232
graphics editors, 151, 337–339
graphics formats, 141
HTML helper editors, 335–336
HTML tools, 341–342
HTML WYSIWYG editors, 334–335
"HTML5 Block Level Elements: Complete List", 64
HTML5 Boilerplate site, 23, 176–178, 355
HTML5 Cafe, 34, 39, 86, 92, 152
HTML5 pointers, 1, 4–5
image map editor, 151
image map tutorials, 152
iPhone display testing, 342
JavaScript information, 114,132
link checkers, 327, 339–340
media format conversion tools, 162
<meta> element help, 58
meter displays, 164
multiple background techniques, 260
optimizing images, 142
PHP scripts, 115–116
progress bar displays, 166
sample form markup, 104
sample table layout, 92–93
software shopping, 333
spell checkers, 326
SQL injection attacks, avoiding, 137
synchronizing files, 342
syntax validator, 320
table markup validator, 83
template management, 342

W3C validator, 330
website analysis, 342
website link checker, 134
WYSIWYG editors, 334–335
Open Source Notepad++, 336
OpenType font format, 273
optimum attribute, 163
<option> element, 109
Opus audio format, 155

• *P* •

<p> element, 14, 44
padding
defined, 234
shorthand properties rules, 241–243
specifying properties for, 241
padding properties, 234
paragraph formatting. *See also* web page text formatting
block quotes, 68–69
controlling with CSS, 66
<p> element, creating with, 65–66
white space, keeping intact, 69–71
password attribute, 105
passwords, input field, 105–106
paths, 17
peer review, 329–330
PHP scripts, 115–116
phrasing content, 220
picas, 184
pixels
defined, 182, 185
device versus CSS display, 183
PNG (Portable Network Graphic), 141
points, 185
poly attribute, 151
Portable Network Graphic (PNG), 141
post method, 101–102
poster attribute, 161
<pre> element, 70–71
prefixes. *See* browser prefixes; vendor prefixes
preformatted text element (<pre>), 70–71
preload attribute, 158, 160, 161
professional graphics editors, 337–339
protocol identifiers, 130
protocols, Internet, 16–17
pseudo-classes

indicating link status with, 256–258
overview, 204
rules for usage, 257

● *R* ●

`radio` attribute, 106
radio buttons, 106–107
`rect` attribute, 151
redirecting pages, using metadata in headers,
   58–60
REL Link Checker, 327
`<rel>` attribute, 213
relative hyperlinks, 142
relative positioning, 226–227
relative value measurements, 185–186
reset buttons, 112–114
responsive design, 184, 352
RGB values, 253–254
`rows` attribute, 111

● *S* ●

secure HTPP (HTPPS), 17
security
  e-mail issues, 108, 137
  SQL injection attacks, 137
`<select>` element, 109
`selected` attribute, 111
selectors, CSS
  adjacent-sibling type, 202
  attribute type, 203
  child type, 203
  choosing elements with, 173
  class type, 200–202
  declarations, 194–195
  defined, 191
  descendant type, 203–204
  element type, 199
  ID type, 199–200
  pseudo-class type, 204
  universal type, 195–199
  validation tools, 195
shadows
  box, 283–284
  drop, 287–289
  inset text, 284–285
  letterpress effect, 286–287
  online resources for, 289

text, 282–283
  3-D text, 285–286
`shape` attribute, 151
shorthand properties
  backgrounds, 259
  borders, 244–245
  fonts, 262, 271–273
  margins and padding, 241–243
  overview, 238
Simple Mail Transfer Protocol (SMTP), 16
singleton tags (empty elements), 143
site maintenance, 317–318, 322, 323–324
`size` attribute, 104
slashes (//), 130
SMTP (Simple Mail Transfer Protocol), 16
`<source>` element, 137, 158
specifications, 17
spellchecking, 326–327
Spoon Browser Sandbox, 321
SQL injection attacks, 137
`src` attribute, 29, 143
streaming media, 153
style sheets. *See also* online resources;
    specific CSS features; syntax, CSS; web
    page creation
  absolute versus relative value
    measurements, 184–185
  advantages of, 171–174
  background color, changing, 258–259
  color, controlling with, 26–27, 35, 66, 251–
    255
  color-coding key, 26–27
  default style sheet, 175–176
  deprecated `<hr>` attributes, replacing with,
    72
  device versus display pixels, 182–183
  differing syntax and markup order, 26
  environments affected by, 182
  graphics, avoiding for speed, 141
  heading appearance, controlling with, 67
  HTML, relationship to, 1, 10, 20–24, 171
  image borders and alignment,
    controlling, 149
  Level 3 modules, descriptions, and
    standards, 186–189
  overview, 20–22, 171–173
  property controls, list of, 180–181
  responsive design, 184, 352
  style options, list of, 174
  table appearance, controlling, 94

table border properties, controlling, 84–85

table width and height, controlling, 87

text color, changing, 256

versions of, 20–21

viewport overview, 183–184

<style> element, 210

submit buttons, 112–114

syntax, CSS. *See also* selectors, CSS

browser prefixes, 198–199

cascading, 205–206

declarations, 191–192

font-family property, 194

inheritance rules, 204–205

online resources, 195, 205

overview, 191–193

style rules, 191

user overrides of styles, 193

• T •

<table> element

including captions within, 26

using with <tr> and <td> elements, 82

tables. *See* web page tables

tab-separated values (TSV), 116

tags. *See also* elements; markups

angle brackets, 14

closing immediately, 320

curly braces, 14

defining content elements with pairs, 27

marking empty elements with single, 28

nesting lists, caution with, 80

validation of, 319

target attribute, 131

<tbody> element, 82

TCP (Transmission Control Protocol), 16

<td> element, 82, 85

templates

building HTML documents with, 19

testing on multiple browsers, 320

testing. *See* website testing

text, CSS. *See also* fonts; shadows; web page text formatting

advantages of using, 281

importance of typography, 261

for mobile devices, 311

rotation, 289–290

sizing, 264–268

text blocks

defined, 63

formatting paragraphs, 65–66

HTML5 block-level elements, 64

inline elements versus, 64, 220

online resources for, 64

text boxes, 111

text editors, disadvantages of, 333

text-align property, 246

<textarea> element, 111

text-indent property, 247

text-shadow property, 282–283

text-transform property, 270

<tfoot> element, 83

<tfooter> element, 83

<th> element, 85, 93

<thead> element, 82, 85

Theora video format. *See* Ogg Theora video format

time formats, 166

time strings, 166–168

<time> element, 166–168

title attribute, 29, 145

<title> element, 43, 61

tools, HTML

deals on, 333

FTP clients, 341

graphics editors, 337–33

helper HTML editors, 335–336

link checkers, 339–340

miscellaneous, 341–342

text editors, disadvantages of, 333

validators, 340–341

WYSIWYG editors, 334–335

touch-screen limitations, 311–312

<tr> element, 82, 85

transform property, 289–290

Transmission Control Protocol (TCP), 16

TrueType font format, 273

TSV (tab-separated values), 116

type attribute, 103, 106, 137

type foundries, 274. *See also* fonts

• U •

<ul> element

creating bulleted lists, 75–76

using with <li> elements, 26, 28

Unicode Character Code Charts, 19
universal selectors, 195–199
URI (Uniform Resource Identifier), 158
URL (Uniform Resource Locator)
  checking broken link filenames, 129
  components of, 16–17
  copy-and-paste issues, 129–130
  creating links with, 125
  file download links, 135–136
  forming properly, 130
  forms, using with, 101–103
  htm versus html extensions, 129
  for mobile devices, 314–315
  processing data with, 115
  refreshing outdated links, 328
usemap attribute, 150–151
user agents, 25
user style sheets, 205

• V •

validation
  checking forms, 113–115, 117, 120
  online resources for, 120, 340
  overview, 340
  suggested software for, 335, 340–341
Validatious website, 120
validators, HTML, 340–341
value attribute, 106, 163–165
vendor prefixes
  animation, 303
  overview, 198–199
  shadow effects, 286
  text transformations, 289
video format conversion, 162
video support. See web page media
<video> element, 137, 158
viewport
  overview, 183–184
  responsive design, 184, 352
visually impaired access, 15, 29, 126, 143,
    151–152
VP8/9 audio-video format, 156–157

• W •

W3C (World Wide Web Consortium)
  general discussion, 17
  "Graphics on the Web," 141
  website address, 126
W3C Link Checker, 327, 339

W3C validation service, 83, 195, 330
WAV (Waveform Audio File Format), 156
Web Accessibility Initiative (WAI), 146
web addresses
  checking broken link filenames, 129
  components of, 16–17
  copy-and-paste issues, 129–130
  creating links with, 125
  file download links, 135–136
  forming properly, 130
  forms, using with, 101–103
  htm versus html extensions, 129
  for mobile devices, 314–315
  processing data with, 115
  refreshing outdated links, 328
web browsers
  alternative text, displaying, 143–145
  anchor elements, displaying, 126
  headings, displaying on graphical browsers,
      67–68
  headings, displaying on text-only browsers,
      68
  HTML, considering when writing, 15
  HTML viewing variations, 15, 38
  local pages, viewing, 15, 46–47
  online resources for, 298–299, 321
  popular choices for, 15
  relationship to HTML and CSS, 11–13, 14–15
  source markups, checking with, 89
  testing on, 15, 38, 298–299, 320
Web Design Group, 205
Web Graphics Tutorial (Quackit), 141
Web HyperText Application Technology
    Working Group (WHATWG), 17–18
Web Open Font Format (WOFF), 274
web page content
  versus presentation, 14
  keeping current, 328
web page creation
  Aptana Studio, 10, 39–40
  basic steps, 39, 54
  <body> elements, setting up, 61–62
  DOCTYPE declaration, writing, 55–56
  ease of, 2
  editing, 48
  headers, defining, 56–57
  <html> elements, adding, 56
  HTML5 Boilerplate site, 23, 54, 176–178, 355
  informative titles, writing, 61
  local pages, editing, 47–48
  local pages, viewing, 46–47

markup, adding to text files, 41–44
metadata, inserting into headers, 57–58
multimedia, using wisely, 318–319, 323
naming and saving files, 44–45
navigation, adding, 321–322
organizing with flow charts, 318
planning simple designs, 40–41
posting pages online, 49–50
required markup elements, 54
text, displaying in browsers, 62
with text editors, 10
user feedback, getting, 322
web page forms
    `action` attributes, using, 101
    attributes related to, 118–120
    browse buttons, adding, 109
    check boxes, creating, 106–107
    data collection examples, 99–100
    default choices, adding, 111
    drop-down lists, creating, 109–111
    file upload fields, creating, 108–109
    hidden fields, creating, 108
    information options, types of, 100
    `<input>` elements, 102–103
    `method` attributes, using, 101
    multiple options, adding, 110
    naming input controls, 102–103
    obtaining scripts from ISPs, 116
    online resources for, 101
    password fields, creating, 105–106
    processing data from, 115–116
    radio buttons, creating, 106–107
    reset buttons, creating, 112–114
    scroll bars, adding, 110
    search examples, 98–99
    submit buttons, creating, 112–114
    text fields, creating, 103–105
    upload risks, managing, 109
    user-friendly, designing, 117–118
    validating data entries, 113–115
web page images
    alignment controls, 149
    alternative text, adding, 143–146
    borders, 149
    cross-platform formats, 140–141
    enhancing download speed, 146–147
    formats, 141
    keyword stuffing, 144
    local storing, 142
    mobile devices, limiting for, 311
    navigating links, creating, 149–150

online resources for, 141–142
overview, 140
relative versus absolute links, 142
scaling, 146–148
search engine indexing, 144
title text, adding, 145–146
web page media
    alternative file formats, providing, 162
    audio formats supported, 155–156
    audio markup, writing, 158–159
    browser support, 157
    desirable format features, 154–155
    format conversion, 162
    HD video support, 156
    HTML5, advantages of, 153
    long tail support, providing, 154
    meter bars, displaying, 163–165
    MP3 compression trade-offs, 155
    online resources for, 157, 162, 164, 166
    progress bar displays, creating, 165–166
    video formats supported, 156–157
    video markup, writing, 159–162
    video playback displays, creating, 160
web page organization
    bulleted lists, formatting, 75–76
    color, inserting, 36
    CSS markups, 35–36
    definition lists, formatting, 77–79
    document heads, defining text with, 34
    hidden comments, 32–33
    hierarchy, creating with lists, 35
    images, inserting, 36
    links, inserting, 36
    numbered lists, formatting, 73–75
    required markup elements, 54
    specified structure, 33
    tables, 35
    text containers, 34–35
web page tables
    appearance, controlling with CSS, 94
    appropriate versus inappropriate uses,
        81–82
    back buttons, adding to footers, 93
    basic elements of, 87
    border attributes, applying, 84–85
    captions, 93
    elements of, 82–83
    footer setup options, 94–95
    footer usage options, 92
    header elements, 85
    online resources for, 83, 88–89, 92–93

web page tables *(continued)*
overview, 81
sample layouts, 89–91, 94
spanning rows and columns, 87–88
syntax and markup order, 83–84
width, calculating, 88
web page text formatting. *See also* layout
management, CSS
block quotes, 68–69
headings, organizing with, 66–68
HTML5 block-level elements, 64
paragraph formatting, 65–66
text blocks, rules for, 63
white space, keeping intact, 69–71
WebM video format, 156–157
website maintenance, 317–318, 322, 323–324
website testing
beta-testing benefits, 329
checking links continuously, 327–328, 330
online resources for, 320–321, 326–327
overview, 325
peer review, 329–330
planning for, 326
proofreading thoroughly, 327
scheduling routine procedures, 328–331
site maps, usefulness of, 325
spell-checkers, using, 326
tag usage, tracking, 320
user feedback, 322, 331
WHATWG (Web HyperText Application
Technology Working Group), 17–18

width attribute, 29, 161
WMV (Windows Media Video), 156
WOFF (Web Open Font Format), 274
word processors
avoiding for writing HTML, 11, 38
versus HTML editors, 37
WordPress
advantages of, 349
creating pages and posts, 351
dashboard overview, 349
sidebar widgets, adding, 351–352
themes, 350–351
word-spacing declaration, 267
World Wide Web Consortium. *See* W3C
World Wide Web (WWW)
gateways, 11
Internet protocols, 16–17
Internet Service Providers, 49
navigating with hyperlinks, 10–11
Wufoo, 120
WYSIWYG editors
overview, 334
suggested choices for, 334–335

Xenu Link Sleuth, 327
XML (eXtensible Markup Language), 18

About the Authors

Ed Tittel is a freelance writer, a consultant, and an occasional expert legal witness on web technologies who works at home near beautiful Austin, Texas. Ed has written for the computer trade press since 1986 and has worked on more than 140 books. Ed has worked on many other titles for Wiley, too, including numerous *For Dummies* books on subjects that range from Carrier Ethernet to XML. His full-length titles cover NetWare, Windows Server, and XML; Ed's custom topics include Unified Threat Management, XBRL, Data Center Networking, and lots more.

Ed blogs, provides expert insight and Q&A, and writes for numerous TechTarget websites, including SearchNetworking.com, SearchSecurity.com, and SearchWindows.com. He also writes for Tom's IT Pro, the CIO Magazine website, and EmergingEdTech.com. When he's not busy working, Ed likes to travel, shoot pool and spend time with his family. He also loves to spend time in the kitchen cookin' like crazy, or sous-cheffin' for his equally cuisine-happy and lovely wife, Dina. Contact Ed via e-mail at ed@edtittel.com.

Chris Minnick is the CEO of Minnick Web Services, LLC, a company that specializes in developing websites and mobile apps for media companies. He also teaches a very popular online course called "Creating Mobile Apps with HTML5" for Ed2Go; is the author of several books, including *WebKit For Dummies;* and writes articles on web development and mobile apps for websites and print magazines. Chris's weekly newsletter goes to thousands of readers, including some of the most influential people in media and the webChris has been involved with numerous mobile and web startups and is active as a mentor and hackathon judge in his adopted hometown of Sacramento, California. In addition to running the most fun business in the world and enjoying the heck out of his writing, Chris is also a winemaker, a musician, a swimmer, and an enthusiastic (if unsophisticated) cook and eater. Contact Chris via email at chris@minnick.com.

Authors' Acknowledgments

Ed Tittel: Wow! It's hard to believe this will be essentially the 14th edition overall for *HTML For Dummies*. Of all the books I've worked on, this one has covered more time and versions than any of the others By itself, it accounts for around ten percent of my overall book output. So thanks again readers, for keeping this book going strong. We'd also like to thank those same readers and the Wiley editors for providing welcome feedback to drive continuing improvement of this book. Don't stop now — keep telling us what you want. Especially, tell us what you liked and didn't like about this full-color bookLet me also thank some people from previous editions, including Jeff Noble, whose recent elevation to the directorial ranks at CA necessitated his withdrawal from this edition, plus Steve James, J. Michael Stewart, Natanya

Anderson, Dori Smith, Tom Negrino, Mary Burmeister, Brock Kyle, Chelsea Valentine, Dawn Davidson, and Kim Lindros. And, of course, I'm indebted to my co-author and friend, Chris Minnick, for adding so much real-world insight, experience, and a more mobile-friendly outlook to our coverage. I am grateful for your ideas, your hard work, and your experience in reaching budding web experts. Thanks, too, to Mary Kyle Inks, who expertly project managed this effort. At Wiley, I must thank Bob Woerner and Nicole Sholly for their outstanding efforts, and Virginia Sanders, Claudia Snell, and Patrick Redmond for their efforts on copy editing, technical editing, design, layout, content, and coverage. A special shout-out to the friendly folks in Composition Services for artful page layouts, and for keeping all the color-coded elements straight. And finally, many, many thanks to my agent at Waterside Productions, Carole Jelen, who not only brought me this book to start with, but who's helped make it such a star over the past 18 years it's been in print.

Thanks to my lovely wife, Dina Kutueva-Tittel, and our ever-inquisitive son, Gregory, for putting up with my sometimes whacky and intense schedule. Thanks again to my Dad, Al Tittel, for all he's done for my family and me, and for dropping in two or more times a year, Texas heat notwithstanding. I hope you're around to see our 15th edition come to print! Finally, profound thanks and remembrances to Cecilia Katherine Kociolek Tittel (4/3/1919–9/11/2009). Thanks, Mom, for encouraging my love of words and writing: I still miss you every day.

Chris Minnick: Thanks to Ed Tittel for giving me the opportunity to work on this book. You've been a mentor and friend to me for many years. Your skills, professionalism, and generosity continue to inspire me and it's such a pleasure to work with you. Thanks to everyone else who worked on this book and whom Ed has already thanked, but especially to our project manager Mary Kyle, our editor Nicole Sholly, and my agent Carole Jelen.

Thank you so much to my lovely and awesome wife, Margaret, who has always been there for me in good times and less good times, understands my silly work schedule, and always has such great ideas, advice, and perspectives. Thanks to my family, without whom I wouldn't be the guy I am today (or perhaps even be alive): my mom Patricia Minnick, my dad Patrick Minnick, my brother David, my sister Kathy, and my sister Beth.

Thanks to my team at Minnick Web Services, including our facilitator, Eva Holland, for her coordination and help with the class and client wrangling. Thanks especially to my long-time colleague and friend, Priscila Hoffman, for standing by me and MWS for so long and for answering the door when the U.S. Marshals visited. Thanks to Steven Konopacki and Conrad Vachon for teaching me to write and teach and to say mysterious and unexpected things that make people wonder and remember. Finally, thanks to my good friends Jeff Schwarzschild for reminding me that there's always something to be enthusiastic about, and Sam Hubbard for reminding me to figure out where I'm going to put down that heavy object *before* I start moving it!

Publisher's Acknowledgments

Executive Editor: Bob Woerner

Senior Project Editor: Nicole Sholly

Copy Editor: Virginia Sanders

Technical Editor: Claudia Snell

Editorial Assistant: Anne Sullivan

Senior Editorial Assistant: Cherie Case

Project Coordinator: Patrick Redmond

Cover Image: © iStockphoto.com/ OlgaYakovenko